Writing the Rapture

Writing the Rapture

Prophecy Fiction in Evangelical America

CRAWFORD GRIBBEN

OXFORD
UNIVERSITY PRESS

2009

OXFORD
UNIVERSITY PRESS

Oxford University Press, Inc., publishes works that further
Oxford University's objective of excellence
in research, scholarship, and education.

Oxford   New York
Auckland   Cape Town   Dar es Salaam   Hong Kong   Karachi
Kuala Lumpur   Madrid   Melbourne   Mexico City   Nairobi
New Delhi   Shanghai   Taipei   Toronto

With offices in
Argentina   Austria   Brazil   Chile   Czech Republic   France   Greece
Guatemala   Hungary   Italy   Japan   Poland   Portugal   Singapore
South Korea   Switzerland   Thailand   Turkey   Ukraine   Vietnam

Copyright © 2009 by Oxford University Press, Inc.

Published by Oxford University Press, Inc.
198 Madison Avenue, New York, New York 10016

www.oup.com

Oxford is a registered trademark of Oxford University Press

Library of Congress Cataloging-in-Publication Data
Gribben, Crawford.
Writing the rapture : prophecy fiction in evangelical America / Crawford Gribben.
p. cm.
Includes bibliographical references and index.
ISBN 978-0-19-532660-4
1. Christian fiction, American—History and criticism.   2. End of the world in literature.
3. Rapture (Christian eschatology)   I. Title.
PS374.C48G75 2009
813'.54—dc22   2008021139

9 8 7 6 5 4 3 2 1

Printed in the United States of America
on acid-free paper

For Mum and Dad

The script has already been written.

—Grace Halsell, *Prophecy and Politics:*
Militant Evangelists on the Road
to Nuclear War (1986)

The world today is like a stage being set for a great drama. The major actors are already in the wings waiting for their moment in history. The main stage props are already in place. The prophetic play is about to begin.

—John F. Walvoord, *Armageddon, Oil, and the*
Middle East Crisis: What the Bible Says about
the Future of the Middle East and the
End of Western Civilization (1991)

This script has already been written.

—Tim LaHaye and Jerry B. Jenkins,
Desecration (2001)

Preface

Some things we must assign to fate.
—James BeauSeigneur, *In His Image* (1997)

Evangelical prophecy belief has been part of my life for as far back
as I can remember. I grew up in an Irish family whose roots in the
Plymouth Brethren movement stretched back over one hundred
years. It was a family in which the material culture of the theology
of the "rapture" provided the basic props of communal life. One of
the objects I continue to treasure most is my grandfather's *Scofield
Reference Bible* (1909; second edition 1917). This was the textbook of
the movement: Scofield's eschatology was central to what it meant to
be Brethren, and his "dispensationalism" was a core component of
preaching in the congregations we knew best. The "official" theology
was not always uncritically accepted, and the timing of the rapture
was a popular subject for debate in family gatherings. But dispensationalism underpinned many of the hymns we sung and many of the
books we read.

I don't remember when I first encountered evangelical prophecy
fiction. I might have found an old Sydney Watson novel at my grand-
parents' farm, or I might have brought one home from the shelf of
stray volumes that sat in the men's room at church. I (and other family
members) have very vivid memories of watching Don Thompson's *Thief
in the Night* (1972) when I was somewhere in my mid-teens. But when-
ever my exposure to the genre began, prophecy fiction—and Watson's

series in particular—was an important part of the popular culture of the Brethren movement into which I was born.

Perhaps it was significant, then, that prophecy fiction also defined my growing distance from this variety of evangelical faith. I discovered *Left Behind* sometime in the winter of 1995, some months after my doctoral studies began. One of my housemates had brought the novel back from his summer travels in the United States. But I was being introduced to *Left Behind* at precisely the moment I was leaving the Brethren movement. At the time, it seemed easy to identify the novels with all I found most objectionable about the dispensational faith. But my appreciation for these novels began to grow. Over the next twelve years, I watched their influence extend far beyond the subculture of our marginal Protestant movement. Rapture novels are now among the best-selling titles in the world, and their authors are now among the most successful in American literary history. Their narratives have evolved to offer a complex analysis of the dangers and opportunities of modernity, together with a hesitating apologia for isolation from it. The perspective of the Left Behind novels is, in some important senses, one I no longer share, but, over the last twelve years, I have grown in affection for evangelical prophecy fiction and the dispensational movement from which it first emerged and now find myself to be a generally reluctant but sometimes sympathetic fellow traveler. Much of the following narrative has a personal importance, but there are other cogent reasons to "take seriously the artefacts . . . that many nonevangelicals laughingly dismiss as kitsch."*

Even books on eschatological themes should include a retrospective glance. I began to work on this book as a research fellow at Trinity College Dublin, continued working on it after my appointment to the University of Manchester, and completed it after my return to Trinity in September 2007. I would like to thank the many colleagues in both institutions that helped me to reflect on this tradition. In Dublin, Darryl Jones, Amanda Piesse, and Mark Sweetnam convinced me that there was a story here worth telling, and Ian Campbell Ross graciously extended the boundaries of the Centre for Irish-Scottish Studies' "National Literatures" project to encourage my early interests in developing this book. In Manchester, I gained a great deal in discussions with Philip Alexander, George Brooke, Jeremy Gregory, Todd Klutz, Peter Knight, Murray Pittock, Geoff Ryman, and other colleagues in literary and theological studies, with members of the Erhardt Seminar, and with my postgraduate students Jennie Chapman, Joseph Purcell, and Sarah Wareham. I would like to thank Jerome de Groot, Liam Harte, David Matthews, and Brian Ward for a particularly helpful conversation at a critical stage in the project's development. I have appreciated the assistance of colleagues all the more

* Heather Hendershot, *Shaking the World for Jesus: Media and Conservative Evangelical Culture* (Chicago: University of Chicago Press, 2004), p. 2.

as their various perspectives on prophecy fiction are often quite different from my own. Outside these institutions, I have enjoyed cooperating on a variety of projects with Kenneth Newport and John Wallis of the Centre for Millennialism Studies at Liverpool Hope University, and with Douglas Shantz of the University of Calgary, who invited me to address the subject of evangelical prophecy fiction in the Iwaasa Lectures on Urban Theology in October 2006. My colleagues in the Brethren Archivists and Historians Network, Neil Dickson, Tordur Joannson, Michael Schneider, Timothy C. F. Stunt, and Paul Wilkinson, have generously shared their knowledge of the prophecy fiction tradition, and Ian Clary, Michael Haykin, and Randall Pederson chased down some hard-to-find references. I have been conscious that I have been reading these novels on the "wrong" side of the Atlantic and far from an established network of dispensational institutions. Douglas Cowan and Thomas Ice have been reliable guides to this often unfamiliar terrain. I am grateful to acknowledge the advice of Joe Walker, a Los Angeles historian, who provided vital information on the Oilar family, and Greg Wills, professor of church history at Southern Baptist Theological Seminary. I am also very grateful for the many friends and colleagues who provided valuable feedback on my earlier work on these themes.

I would like to thank those who have made this publication possible. Both Jerry B. Jenkins and James BeauSeigneur consented to answer my questions about their work. I would also like to thank the staff of the Andover-Harvard Theological Library, Harvard Divinity School; Bonn University Library, especially Gabrielle Dressel; the Gamble Library, Union Theological College, Belfast, especially Stephen Gregory; the W. S. Hoole Special Collections Library, University of Alabama; the John Rylands University Library, Manchester, especially Graham Johnson, archivist of the Christian Brethren Archive; the Mugar Library, Boston University; the Pre-Trib Research Center, Liberty University, Lynchburg; the Speer Library, Princeton Theological Seminary; Trinity College Library, Dublin; and the library of Westminster College, Cambridge. Oxford University Press granted permission to reuse material that originally appeared in an essay in *Literature and Theology* (2004), which was developed in my short account of *Rapture Fiction and the Evangelical Crisis* (2006), and Baylor University Press consented to my revisiting themes that appeared in my essay in *Expecting the End: Millennialism in Social and Historical Context* (2006). Cynthia Read, my editor at Oxford University Press, and Daniel Gonzalez, her editorial assistant, have championed this project from its earliest stages and have overseen its improvement through helpful comments provided by Amy Johnson Frykholm and another, anonymous, reader. Of course, I alone should be held responsible for any remaining errors of fact or interpretation. Others have provided me with space and time in which to read, think, and write. As always, I owe most thanks to my family, especially Pauline, Daniel, and Mum and Dad. Soli Deo Gloria.

Contents

Writing the Rapture

Introduction

The conclusion is by no means foreordained.
—James BeauSeigneur, *In His Image* (1997)

Writing the Rapture describes the tradition that has produced the best-selling fiction series in the most powerful nation in the history of the world.[1] This recent series—known by the title of its debut, *Left Behind* (1995)—has emerged from a mode of evangelical literature and film that is increasingly identified as "prophecy fiction."[2] Prophecy fiction has produced some of the most controversial texts in contemporary American culture. Its novels and films focus on events that many evangelicals expect to occur at the end of the age, but while these types of fiction "claim to be about the future," they are "very much about the present."[3] Their faith-based and conservative critique of American modernity develops with their description of the social conditions of the Antichrist's rule. During that period, these novels imagine, the resources of history's most advanced regime will be directed toward the final eradication of Christians and Jews. But throughout the genre, that regime has become a palimpsest that has been routinely identified with the social trends of the present that authors find most objectionable.[4] Prophecy fiction conveys its critique of modernity by exploiting the anxieties of its audience, elaborating an antimodernism that has governed the tradition since it emerged at the turn of the twentieth century while simultaneously embracing aspects of that modernity when they can be used for evangelical ends. Throughout its history, prophecy fiction has sought to provide a comprehensive mythology for modern American life. Its function is to explain the future, to make the unknown familiar, to reassure its readers that both the deterioration of culture and the marginalization of evangelicals are part of a divinely ordained agenda. But its function is not only to defend the cultural withdrawal of its readers. Prophecy fiction novels encourage believers to actively resist American modernity while encouraging calculated interventions within it. They domesticate geopolitics, justifying the most hawkish themes in the foreign policies of successive presidential administrations and make a complex world knowable, however frightening they suggest its immediate future might be. They tend to argue for American isolation, and they evidence a profound skepticism of international bodies.[5] They are often deeply concerned by conflict in the Middle East, but argue that the first person to negotiate a lasting peace between Israel and her neighbors must be recognized as history's most dangerous world leader. In religion, politics, and social mores, at national and international levels, prophecy fiction elevates "disagreement . . . above agreement" and "division above unity."[6] Left Behind, the genre's best-known product, epitomizes the wider trend. Prophecy fiction is an assault on liberal America. The best-selling fiction series in the world's most powerful nation is profoundly critical of some of its most cherished ideals.

I

The religious culture that has produced prophecy fiction has often positioned itself critically against the environments that have shaped it. Since its origins in the eighteenth century, and even in the nineteenth century, when the movement's theology was "the prevailing mode of Christian thinking in the English-speaking world," evangelicalism has been reconstructed by the social contexts in which it has emerged.[7] As a radically populist movement, the movement has never been short of cultural barometers, though many of its foremost spokespersons have been reluctant to admit them.[8] It is an illuminating paradox: evangelical apologists make regular claims to transcend cultural change in media that often demonstrate subservience to it. While its theologically orientated advocates have regularly identified evangelicalism with ahistorical Christian orthodoxy, at the popular level the movement seems "bound up with the enterprise of modernity" and continually recontoured by the process of social and political change.[9]

This tension has been signaled in the debate about the movement's origins. Historians have attempted to define evangelicalism in categories drawn variously from theological and sociological disciplines.[10] Their conclusions suggest that evangelicalism may not be best thought of as a coherent whole, but rather as a series of related subcultures, each with its own nuances and concerns. Scholars have reached greater unanimity in their analyses of the relationships between these varieties of evangelicalism and their various host cultures. Their verdicts have pointed consistently to the evolution of evangelical belief in the movement from Enlightenment and Romanticism toward modernity and postmodernity. Evangelicalism—whatever it is understood to be—has always been culturally constructed.[11]

The most distinguished historians of evangelicalism agree that the movement emerged as a distinct religious culture in England and New England in the early part of the eighteenth century. While clearly contiguous with earlier patterns of popular Protestant piety, evangelicalism gave a new emphasis to religious activism and presupposed a new kind of confidence in the interpretation of religious experience.[12] These epistemological innovations were welded onto an existing eschatological structure. Evangelicals have always been interested in eschatology—especially in America, where powerful strains of evangelical millennialism are neither alien to traditional expressions of faith nor unique to any particular moment of religious history. In America, one commentator has recently suggested, "the largest component of the religious spectrum . . . remains what it has been since colonial times: a fundamentalist evangelicalism with powerful millenarian strands."[13] (Harvey Cox has noted that "Americans have always had a stronger than average dose of millennialism in their veins."[14]) Early evangelicals were therefore slow to develop distinctive eschatological schemes.[15] Nevertheless, as the eighteenth century rolled into the nineteenth, the huge variety of eschatological opinions that had circulated among transatlantic Puritans gradually gave way to a basic duality: premillennialism, which taught that the second coming of Jesus Christ should be expected before the millennium and that little could be expected of human societies in the interim; and postmillennialism, which taught that the second coming should be expected after the millennium and that human societies could and should be transformed for the better.[16] These perspectives were appropriated both by political radicals and conservatives: in the mid-nineteenth century, for example, postmillennial and premillennial theories were used to support the slaveholding economies of the South and to call for their reform. But as the nineteenth century progressed, and as evangelicals on both sides of the Atlantic continued to view their societies through the lens of social crisis, a new variety of premillennialism grew dramatically in influence.

This "dispensational premillennialism" had been formulated in the 1820s and 1830s among a small but elite circle that had been initially associated with Trinity College Dublin and the University of Oxford.[17] This innovative theological system was a paradigm of cultural and ecclesiastical despair. Its adherents believed that powerful forces of decay would grow in influence as the end of the age approached.

They believed that current events were confirming this reading of prophecy and that the "rapture"—the sudden disappearance of true believers—was the next event on Scripture's prophetic calendar. This dispensationalism appealed to those evangelicals dissatisfied with the theological prevarications of the mainstream churches, as well as those whose disappointment with the possibilities of mission work among Irish Roman Catholics was both a cause and consequence of their increasing pessimism as to the short-term prospects of the truth. Extrapolating a basic ecclesiology from their eschatological convictions, many of these evangelicals began to meet informally for the private study of Scripture and the celebration of the Lord's Supper. These "meetings" fed their adherents into such radically anticlerical and primitivist movements as the Plymouth Brethren, within which the momentum for further ecclesiastical experiment was supplied by leaders such as John Nelson Darby (1800–82). Darby, a graduate of Trinity College Dublin and a former priest of the Church of Ireland, promoted his variety of dispensationalism both within and outside the Brethren movement.[18] He was a remarkably successful advocate of the new ideas. His influence on the eschatological thought of evangelicals was "both profound and pivotal, more so perhaps than any other Christian leader for the last 200 years."[19] But his legacy was to be most enduring in North America, where he traveled widely, and where, by the end of the nineteenth century, his dispensationalism had gained an almost creedal status through the influence of popular prophetic publications and the Bible Conference movement.[20] On both sides of the Atlantic, dispensationalism explained from the Bible what its adherents believed they were witnessing—the terminal decline of Christendom. The system's adherents insisted that the world could only grow worse as the second coming approached and that evangelicals should concentrate their efforts on evangelism rather than social reform. Dispensationalists believed that there was no hope for Western civilization: it was a futile effort, as D. L. Moody famously put it, to polish the brass on a sinking ship.[21]

Moody's maxim indicates the kind of influence that the new eschatology came to exercise in North America. The dispensationalism he popularized provided a critical element of the doctrinal platform of the movement that would do so much to shape the evangelical future. This "fundamentalism," first thus identified by its enemies in the 1920s, proposed a reified evangelicalism and promoted a theological platform that reaffirmed central components of traditional Protestantism in the face of the liberal skepticism that was being encouraged by the conclusions of evolutionary geology and late nineteenth-century biblical criticism.[22]

Fundamentalists and dispensationalists shared a common commitment to an emphatically literal prophetic creed. And their approach appeared to pay dividends. At the beginning of the twentieth century, their expectations of decay in mainstream denominations appeared to be confirmed. Responding to the new challenges, conservative evangelical leaders identified a series of key doctrines within which no liberal dalliance would be tolerated and disseminated their refusal to compromise through pan-denominational prophecy conferences and the pamphlet series that supplied the movement with its new name—*The Fundamentals: A Testimony to the Truth* (1910–15). Simultaneously, Oxford University Press was marketing the *Scofield Reference Bible* (1909; second edition 1917), an annotated edition of the Authorized (King James) Version that provided readers with a subtle modification of Darby's dispensational system in marginal notes by the Reverend C. I. Scofield.[23] The world's leading university press had lent its cultural authority to the central manifesto of the fundamentalist movement in return for the vast revenues that more than fifty million sales of successive editions of the *Scofield Reference Bible* have continued to accrue.[24] The *Scofield Reference Bible*'s identification with Oxford University Press took the dispensational movement back to one of the universities from which it had emerged, and the reputation of those leading academics mentioned in its foreword propelled its distinctive worldview out of the populist ferment of evangelical dissent.

The new movement of fundamentalists had some eminently respectable leaders, including J. Gresham Machen (1881–1937), a professor at Princeton Theological Seminary, but Machen's untimely death and a series of theological and sociological divisions robbed the unstable movement of its best leaders and much of its intellectual capital.[25] In contrast to earlier movements of conservative evangelicals, many fundamentalists came to adopt an anti-intellectual habit of mind, and, for large sections of their movement, the defense of dispensational premillennialism became as important as the defense of the virgin birth. In the aftermath of the Scopes trial in June 1925, as conservative Protestants were being identified as "gaping primates of the upland valleys," their marginalization was written into "the social contract of American secular modernity," and fundamentalists retreated toward the cultural margins to rebuild their infrastructure as their best leaders reexamined the terms of their doctrinal base.[26] Despite their preference for isolation, fundamentalists were strongly influenced by the political traumas of the 1940s and 1950s.[27] But as the decades passed, some eminent fundamentalist leaders, with expanding social and political ambitions, moved away from dispensationalism and adopted less apocalyptic readings of Revelation alongside a wider vision for cultural reform. These believers, sporting a "progressive fundamentalism with a social message," were identified as "new evangelicals" or as "neo-evangelicals."[28] Other fundamentalists, by contrast, retained their separatist impulse and concentrated on communicating the truth of dispensationalism as they developed a range of popular cultural media that provided for its survival. By that stage, prophecy novels had become a prominent feature of the movement's popular culture. The genesis of evangelical prophecy fiction, at the beginning of the twentieth century, paralleled the development of *The Fundamentals* and the consolidation of dispensational orthodoxy. Evangelical prophecy fiction was born into a stable and widely popularized dispensational faith, but, throughout its history, it has reflected the changing identities of the movements that have embraced it.

Given these origins, it is hardly surprising that the fundamentalist emphasis on literal interpretation should have made such a big impact on prophecy fiction. The form, if not the content, of prophecy fiction necessarily calls attention to problems of interpretation. This emphasis on literal interpretation drives prophecy novels, as it does dispensationalism more generally, toward a precritical approach to Scripture. But the hermeneutic has become unsettled. In the middle of the twentieth century, a number of leading dispensationalists retreated from strict futurism (which argued that all prophecy concerned the very end of the age) toward a more strategic and apologetically useful variant of historicism (which argued that some prophecies could be fulfilled in the period before the end of the age and therefore combined apocalyptic rhetoric with a more urgent and contemporary social commentary). Until 1948, leading dispensationalists had uniformly insisted that the rapture would be the next event on the prophetic calendar.[29] But for many of these writers, the establishment of the state of Israel offered a "proof of prophecy" that would be of foundational importance in their attempt to prove the reliability of their interpretive system. Prophecy scholars, working from the basis of their literal hermeneutic, had long anticipated that Jews would be regathered to the Promised Land, though they had not generally conceived that any such regathering in the period before the rapture could be considered a fulfillment of prophecy.[30] But by the middle of the twentieth century, many dispensationalists found the establishment of Israel too good an opportunity to miss. Scholars reconsidered the relationship between Israel and the rapture and began to rewrite the central textbooks of their movement. In 1967, the correction was written into a revised edition of the *Scofield Reference Bible*. Three years later, it was widely popularized when Hal Lindsey published the most influential dispensational textbook of them all, *The Late Great Planet Earth* (1970), a powerful monument to cold war fear which led in 1977 to a movie version with narration by Orson Welles.[31] Lindsey's book sold 7.5 million copies during the 1970s, and the *New York Times Book Review* identified it as the best-selling American nonfiction book of the decade.[32] By 1991, it had sold in excess of twenty-eight million copies, and Lindsey had become "the most widely read interpreter of prophecy in history."[33] Simultaneously alarmist and entertaining, Lindsey's "war of the worlds" offered an apocalyptic identification of America's enemies in the nuclear standoff of the late cold war. But while it chronicled the means of future global holocaust, *The Late Great Planet Earth* blurred the line between fact and fiction by highlighting its rhetorical status, offering chapter titles such as "Russia Is a

Gog." Simultaneously, Lindsey reversed decades of dispensational conservatism by hinting at date-setting speculations.[34] Nevertheless, as playfully ironic rhetoric combined with lurid imagery and massive sales, *The Late Great Planet Earth* blurred the boundaries between prophetic entertainment and biblical interpretation and, in large sections of North American fundamentalism, defined the mood of the 1970s and 1980s.

But the claim that 1948 was a fulfillment of prophecy profoundly undermined the coherence of dispensational ideas. By introducing the idea that prophecy could be recognizably fulfilled in the period before the rapture, writers opened up the future.[35] Popular-level dispensationalism increasingly gave way to what its critics have described as "dispen-sensationalism," and, as a result, popular dispensational writers turned increasingly to the production of edifying entertainment.[36] But the new paradigm was far from future-proof, and Lindsey's legacy would present grave difficulties for future expositors after the implosion of the Soviet Union and the apparent collapse of the Eastern Bloc frustrated the apocalyptic crescendo that Lindsey and others had predicted. Advocates of dispensational premillennialism are currently recontouring their expectations in the light of this significant geopolitical change. Advocates of the new "progressive dispensationalism" have, however, yet to produce any revision of this narrative in the mode of prophecy fiction.[37] In the process, it has become evident that their rewriting of the rapture is part of a long tradition of the revision of eschatological expectations within the dispensational tradition. Dispensationalism is an evolving system of faith within the constantly evolving fundamentalist and neo-evangelical cultures.

Of course, as this reminder of theological and sociological instability suggests, there is not and never has been a neat division between fundamentalists and neo-evangelicals. Neo-evangelicals have never been precluded from maintaining dispensational beliefs, nor have fundamentalists been precluded from rejecting them. (One fundamentalist leader did claim, however, that there existed a necessary link between fundamentalism and premillennialism: "There is no greater bulwark against modern liberalism than the doctrine of the premillennial return of Christ . . . Modernists are never premillenarians."[38]) Nevertheless, both movements have attempted to delineate their boundaries, and the relationship between the two movements has not always been easy. Evangelicalism, embracing both fundamentalism and neo-evangelicalism, is not a homogenous movement. "What the media and academics see . . . as a monolithic force is, in fact, a diverse and somewhat uneasy coalition of churches and individuals," one observer has commented.[39] Those evangelicals who embrace dispensationalism have therefore varied enormously in character and creed. In popular parlance, and in this book, the term "evangelical" is used to describe a broad range of interlocking but often competing movements, ideas, and ministries, from culturally engaged neo-evangelicals to world-denying fundamentalists. This broad category represents a changing constituency that may network with Billy Graham, Wheaton College, and *Christianity Today*—or that may denounce them in apocalyptic terms.

However the boundaries are delineated, nevertheless, it is clear that dispensationalism best survived among fundamentalists, and that those believers who moved between the alternate strands of popular Protestantism—individuals like Billy Graham, who left his fundamentalist background to become the patron saint of the neo-evangelical cause—did adapt their eschatology to suit.[40] But, at the beginning of the twenty-first century, the separatist mentality of fundamentalism can no longer be easily maintained. Ironically, it is the premiere cultural marker of that separatism—the prophecy fiction novels that speak most vociferously of believers' marginality—that most obviously indicates its eclipse. The enormous success of pop culture artifacts produced by dispensational fundamentalists provides a powerful argument that the former separatists have gone mainstream. Dispensationalism emerged and was appropriated to explain its adherents' minority status in a hostile social environment. But that marginality is no longer a tenable status. Fundamentalist subculture produced an aggressive counterculture, and, in evangelical prophecy fiction, the literature of that counterculture has provided a quintessentially American myth.

It was during the 1970s that evangelicals came in from the cold. During that decade, it was estimated, eight million Americans were "firmly committed" to dispensational premillennialism.[41] More recently, it has been suggested, there are perhaps between twenty-five and thirty million evangelical supporters of Israel, and Pat Robertson and the late Jerry Falwell, two of the more outspoken premillennial leaders, have claimed the support of a television audience of one hundred million.[42] These millions of dispensationalists and their sympathizers are not restricted to a social or political underclass. Evangelical millennialism resonates within the political arena. Throughout the 1970s and 1980s, for example, Ronald Reagan and several of those who were prominent in his administration, including Caspar Weinberger, his secretary of defense, and James Watt, his secretary of the interior, confirmed their belief in a literal approach to the interpretation of biblical apocalyptic.[43] In 1971, the future president stated his conviction that "the day of Armageddon isn't far off . . . Ezekiel says that fire and brimstone will be rained upon the enemies of God's people. That must mean that they'll be destroyed by nuclear weapons."[44] Similarly, Reagan's famous (and apocalyptic) reference to the "evil empire" of Soviet Russia was made in a speech delivered (significantly) to the National Association of Evangelicals.[45] As Paul Boyer correctly notes, "we cannot fully understand cold war politics and culture without paying close attention to this religious component" of political rhetoric, the distinctive kind of fundamentalist millennialism that pervades vast sections of American popular discourse.[46]

Apocalyptic ideas permeate America's sacred lexicon, but they resonate most powerfully within evangelicalism.[47] Prophecy fiction is the public face of a uniquely
American evangelical faith.

II

Of course, prophecy fiction is only one part of a much larger American culture of
evangelical consumption. The recent success of prophecy fiction is not an isolated
outburst of creative activity on the part of evangelical authors, but it is the most
obvious evidence that conservative evangelicals have moved from subculture to
counterculture to cultural dominance. That success obscures the often troubled
relationship between fiction and theology. The difficulty has been particularly
marked among dispensational believers, who have traditionally reiterated the need
for their adherents to withdraw from worldly entertainments (though one early
writer of prophecy fiction did long for "the pen of a Rider Haggard").[48] With the
exception of hymnody, it is not clear when creative responses to dispensational
theology began to emerge. But if there is some uncertainty as to the beginnings of
the prophecy fiction genre, there is no doubt about the elements that define it.

Prophecy fiction dramatizes several variants of an end-time belief that has
become common among American evangelicals. To qualify for membership in the
genre, novels and films must refer, however critically or obliquely, to the narrative
framework of dispensational belief.[49] Even those novels that critique dispensationalism develop their plots against a deep background that readers, schooled in the
exegetical tradition from which the genre has emerged, can readily anticipate: life
will be going on as normal in the everyday world until the moment when all true
believers disappear; their rapture will be followed by the rise of the Antichrist, who
will broker a deal that brings peace to the Middle East; this "covenant with Israel"
will inaugurate a seven-year period of unparalleled global suffering known as the
"tribulation"; a huge number of people will come to faith as "tribulation saints"
after the rapture;[50] the awful events of the tribulation will combine the Antichrist's
tyranny, the imposition of the "mark of the beast," and the persecution of Jews
and Christians with unparalleled divine judgments on the unbelieving; the tribulation saints will include a large number of converted Jews, "the 144,000," who are
often depicted as becoming missionaries to the Gentile world;[51] the Antichrist will
break the covenant with Israel, and Jews everywhere will become subject to a holocaust more awful than any ever previously known; and when, after the deaths of
two-thirds of the global population, the final destruction of the planet seems inescapable, Jesus Christ will return, with angels and resurrected believers, to execute
judgment on sinners and to establish an earthly kingdom that will endure for the

one thousand years of the millennium.[52] When these structural props are taken into account, the novels are often very simple stories, lacking narrative complexity or a difficult range of points of view. Their purpose is essentially didactic, and so, with a tiny number of exceptions, they identify the narrative voice or an identifiable leading character with the authorial—and purportedly biblical—perspective.[53] They are also, almost exclusively, self-conscious in their use of dispensational themes. Prophecy fiction assumes, to a greater or lesser degree, the structural motifs provided by dispensationalism and expects its readers to do so too.

Many of the novels assume that the standard dispensational account is axiomatic. *The Omega Project* (1981), for example, by Morris Cerullo, a self-identified "converted Jew," argued that the system's end-time framework was an entirely objective and rational deduction from the Christian scriptures.[54] The novel's characters—none of whom have any experience of reading the Bible—construct a massive computer bank to process the biblical "data" they enter and to answer the questions they ask. It was a calculated narrative maneuver. The novel's reference to biblical verses as quantifiable "data" ignores the degree of subjectivity involved in any act of interpretation, and the idea that technology could solve problems of biblical meaning lends the novel's conclusions an air of total rationality, as if the author's dispensationalism was the only result that could ever be logically affirmed from objective enquiry in the Scriptures. *The Omega Project* dismissed self-conscious and self-critical processes of interpretation in favor of ideas of self-evident truth: "we're computer programmers, not philosophers," one character explains, arguing for the rationality of the novel's claims.[55] Again, in *Apocalypse* (1998), by Peter and Paul Lalonde, the principal characters "had another [Jack] Van Impe video playing on the VCR, and all around them were books filled with page markers." One character was "using a Bible, scanning each page with his finger until he found the passages he was seeking. In front of him was a piece of paper divided into two columns. On the left was a column marked 'Prophecy.' On the right was a column marked 'Fulfilled.'"[56] In these and other novels, the interpretation of prophecy becomes a simple matter of quantification.

But the dispensational narrative is not consistently affirmed. Some novels adopt the opposite perspective, playing with and ultimately defying readers' expectations that their narratives will adhere to the standard dispensational framework. Jean Grant's *The Revelation* (1992), for example, is a novel of prophetic doubt rather than certainty. It focuses on characters who believe that the pre-tribulation rapture could be denied only by "some fuzzy liberals and modernists" and describes the trials of faith they experience when their own commitment to the dispensational system is critically undermined.[57] The novel's characters continue to wait for the rapture despite their fear that the events of the tribulation may actually have begun. Other novels, like Frank Peretti's *This Present Darkness* (1986) and Ken Wade's Seventh-day Adventist novel, *The Orion Conspiracy* (1994), flatly deny the dispensational account. The latter novel even argues for the danger of a false Christian millennial-ism with a political agenda—but still expects its readers to make assumptions of dispensationalism's truth.[58]

As these examples attest, there are a range of doctrinal commitments within the prophecy fiction genre. The most obvious differences between novels appear in the relationship between the rapture and the tribulation. Most prophecy fic-tion, like Left Behind and the Christ Clone Trilogy, has adhered to the mainstream orthodoxy of dispensationalism and has positioned the rapture before the tribula-tion. Others have disagreed. John Myers's *The Trumpet Sounds* (1965) and Jean Grant's *The Revelation* (1992) tentatively suggested that the rapture would occur midway through the tribulation. Pat Robertson's *The End of the Age* (1995) and Robert Van Kampen's *The Fourth Reich* (1997) both positioned the rapture after the tribulation; the latter novel explicitly denounced the standard dispensational narrative as a "false hope."[59] Milton Stine's *The Devil's Bride* (1910) also advanced a post-tribulation rapture, though, as we will see, Stine's preface claimed that the novel's position did not necessarily represent his own mature convictions. Others have shared his uncertainty. Kim Young, author of *The Last Hour* (1997), didn't want to presume whether the events she described would happen "before or after the rapture" and hovered uncertainly between the pre- and mid-tribulation posi-tions.[60] David Dolan gave up on the debate entirely in *The End of Days* (1995) and explained that he had omitted any reference to the controversy so as not to dis-tract readers from his central concerns, which related to the religious future of the Jewish people.[61] More radically, Joseph Birkbeck Burroughs's *Titan, Son of Saturn* (1905), Ernest W. Angley's *Raptured* (1950), and Jean Brenneman's *Virtual Reality* (1997) suggested that only the best Christians would be included in the rapture. This "partial rapture" doctrine has always been a minority position within dispen-sationalism, and its proponents have used it to promote high personal standards. One character in *Titan* explained to her son that he could only expect to go to heaven "if you are a good boy and don't say naughty words."[62]

Despite this range of convictions, prophecy novels signally failed to address the conclusion that each of them assumed—the conclusion that those who had rejected the gospel before the rapture would be given a second chance to accept it thereafter. Writers of nonfictional prophetic material emphatically denied the possibility. Peter and Patti Lalonde made the point explicitly: "If you refuse to become a Christian now for whatever reason, God's Word says that you will be deluded and will believe all the lies of the Antichrist and the false prophet on the other side. There is no second chance. We believe that those who become saints during the tribulation are those who have never heard or fully understood the gospel of Jesus Christ."[63] Todd Strandberg and Terry James have agreed: "God's Word says that God himself will send (or allow) strong delusion to come upon unbelievers at this time, and that those who didn't believe before the Tribulation began will believe Antichrist's lies. They will, in effect, never again be open to accepting the message . . . God's Word does indeed say just that."[64] The point was confirmed in Don Thompson's rapture movie, *Prodigal Planet* (1983). But most prophecy novelists have insisted on the opposite possibility. The genre depends on the theology of the second chance.

As this controversy indicates, disagreements in prophecy fiction go beyond the details of eschatology. While the genre allows a limited variation in eschatology, its negotiation with wider patterns of orthodoxy has often been significant. Early novels promoted the "gap theory," the belief, confirmed by the interpretive apparatus of the *Scofield Reference Bible,* that the earth was of incalculable age. The theory allowed for the conclusions of geological science, for it argued that the creation story of Genesis 1:3–31 referred not to an original creation but to a re-creation in the relatively recent past. The gap theory was a key component of early dispensational orthodoxy that fell out of fashion in the aftermath of the Scopes trial and the subsequent development of "creation science," despite its recent reappearance in Hal Lindsey's *Blood Moon* (1996).[65] Early novelists also bypassed the prophetic significance of Petra, though later novels, such as the Left Behind series and the Christ Clone Trilogy, reflected the growing popularity of a "sacred geography" of the Middle East by identifying its stone fortress as a critical site for the survival of a future Jewish remnant.[66] Few novels support the use of charismatic gifts, even though some have been written by Pentecostals, including Carol Betzer and Pat Robertson, who has described himself as a prophet and a worker of miracles.[67] Most avoid any reference to the sacraments, though Mel Odom deals with baptism in *Apocalypse Dawn* (2003) and Neesa Hart imagines her tribulation saints sharing bread and wine.[68] But many readers would be most surprised to discover the genre's sustained tolerance of an unorthodox Trinitarianism. Burroughs's *Titan* (1905) suggested that Lucifer might have been God's first choice as Messiah and proposed that the Holy Spirit could represent a principle of femininity within the Godhead.[69] *Blood Moon* likewise developed an unusual description of the relationship between the Trinitarian persons: one character converting to evangelical faith explained that he felt "a certain level of comfort in communing with the God described in the Bible, especially the one called Jesus Christ."[70] Tim LaHaye, likewise, has advanced a species of modalism in describing the Trinity as "sort of like three responsibilities . . . different functions at the appropriate time."[71] But perhaps the most surprising aspect of the genre is that some prophecy novels—like Morris Cerullo's *The Omega Project* (1981)—do not feature any conversions, and others—like Carol Balizet's *The Seven Last Years* (1978)—omit any exhortation for readers to become evangelicals themselves.

Other disagreements range far beyond theology. The role of finance, for example, has been particularly contested among evangelical prophecy novels. Many early examples offered a bold critique of unfettered capitalism. One early novel was so concerned by industrial excess that its cabal of international business leaders takes on the narrative role of the Antichrist himself. Dayton Manker, writing in 1941, was probably one of the last to point to the dangers of "greedy capitalists"—who, he claimed, had "demoralized youth with filthy movies, literature, art"—but he rapidly switched his target to identify American Communists and their secretive Jewish controllers as the real enemies of the faithful.[72] In later stages of the tradition, by contrast, capitalism provides a key component of the struggle against the Antichrist. Characters in Left Behind, Pat Robertson's *The End of the Age* (1995), and Lindsey's *Blood Moon* (1996) construct an underground economy that challenges the hegemony of the mark of the beast.[73] Other prophecy novels give marriage tips or advice about propriety in dress—and in one novel the raptured saints always leave their clothes neatly folded.[74]

These debates about doctrine and proper behavior have been driven by the competing aims of authors, but also reflect the competing aims of publishers. Evangelical publishers can often be positioned within the movement's spectrum of theological belief and denominational allegiance. In their role as "cultural gate-keepers," evangelical publishers grant "access" and "legitimacy" to the ideas they introduce to the market.[75] Some publishers, like This Week in Bible Prophecy, will only publish materials that conform to the traditional dispensational framework. Others, like Thomas Nelson and Word, have been prepared to publish material that directly contradicts that framework, either by modifying the relationship between the tribulation and the rapture, as in Jean Grant's *The Revelation* (1992), or by abandoning premillennialism altogether, as in Michael Hyatt and George Grant's *Y2K* (1998). Some want to have their cake and eat it: Tyndale House has published novels that confirm the traditional account, like Left Behind, as well as those, like the Last Disciple series, that entirely subvert it. Nonevangelical publishers have also begun to promote prophecy fiction, but they do so with no apparent support of any distinctive theological criteria. Warner's republication of the Christ Clone Trilogy (1997–98; republished in 2003–4) seems no more theologically significant than its earlier decision to publish Glenn Kleier's nonevangelical apocalyptic thriller, *The Last Day* (1997).

These social, political, and theological debates are linked to the cultural function of prophecy fiction. Prophecy novels, like other evangelical novels, are stories that believers "tell to themselves and about themselves."[76] Their primary purpose is to build a defined community by recruiting and instructing adherents.[77] Like other evangelical novels, prophecy novels "embody not only an evangelical perspective but also advocate appropriate behaviors and solutions to problems."[78] In that sense, they are quite different from evangelical prophetic nonfiction, which tends to be prescriptive rather than descriptive and often more emphatic in tone. This success has shaped the future of the dispensational movement. Until the middle of the 1990s, Hal Lindsey had been the most widely read expositor of biblical prophecy. By the late 1990s, the influence of his "nonfiction" work had been eclipsed by that of Left Behind. This turn to fiction represented a paradigm shift in popular prophetic consciousness. Nonfiction had been replaced by fiction as the most successful cultural conduit of dispensational faith.

This turn to fiction was hugely significantly for the developing purpose of popular dispensational writing. The unprecedented success of Left Behind demonstrated that fictional texts could be far more popular than nonfictional prophetic texts—even such staggeringly successful nonfictional prophetic texts as *The Late Great Planet Earth*. The turn to fiction heightened the role of the readers' imagination. It allowed room for speculation without ever requiring the author to invest his credibility in falsifiable claims. Earlier writers had thus invested their credibility: Hal Lindsey's turn to a limited historicism had hinted that the rapture might occur in 1988, and in so doing had provided the dispensational movement with a significant hostage to fortune. The turn to fiction provided dispensational authors with a strategy of survival after the credibility of Lindsey's suggestions had been undermined. Prophecy novels allowed dispensational authors to maintain the immediacy of near-future speculation while countering Lindsey's historicism, and they did so without requiring readers either to engage in theological debate or consciously to disagree with one of the most popular prophetic expositors in history.[79] Prophecy novels provided a prophetic hope that was immediate and nonfalsifiable. Simultaneously, their nonaffirmative speculation made prophetic claims open-ended and heightened the potential ambiguity of the texts they produced. Prophecy novelists could speculate without damaging their expository credibility. Some of their number took real advantage of the opportunity the novel form provided. In an "Important Note from the Author," James BeauSeigneur stressed that his work would focus more on characterization and voice while being less assertively didactic than previous prophecy novels. He also distanced himself from his novels' theological claims: "Never assume that the characters—any of the characters—speak for the author," he told readers.[80] It was a necessary point to insist upon if prophecy fiction was to rescue dispensationalism from Lindsey's move toward falsifiable claims. In addition, as BeauSeigneur's comments suggest, the turn to fiction heightened the authority of the author. Novels did not need to spend time detailing alternative explanations of contested passages. Like the computer operatives in *The Omega Project*, prophecy novelists could elide the role of the interpreter while presenting the "plain and undisputable meaning" of the biblical text. With a small number of exceptions, including Jean Grant's *The Revelation* and the Last Disciple novels, prophecy novels refused to admit that the meaning of Scripture could be contested, and unusual conclusions were rarely provided with any detailed exegetical defense. The turn to fiction also involved an important change in the criteria of readerly persuasion. The elements of a convincing novel, even a convincing prophetic novel, are quite different from the elements of a persuasive scholarly or pseudo-scholarly text. Prophecy novels attempt to capture the hearts and minds of their audience by description, not prescription, in the hope that engaged sympathies will lead to changed minds. Paradoxically, the turn to fiction also decreases the significance of this persuasion and makes textual influence very difficult to ascertain. Prophecy novels are highly rhetorical texts which aim to persuade audiences of the truth of their claims, but can also be "persuasive" in offering ephemeral entertainment. Readers can consume and enjoy their narratives without ever actually endorsing their distinctive points of view.[81] The turn to fiction has had a huge impact on the nature and purpose of a large segment of evangelical popular culture. The influence of this fiction extends far beyond the boundaries of the evangelical movement. But it is difficult to know exactly what its popularity means.

This question of the significance of success has been foregrounded by the fact that prophecy fiction has not only been produced by evangelicals. Other texts, from outside the evangelical world, use dispensational themes for quite different ends. Ken Wade's *The Orion Conspiracy* (1994) developed a Seventh-day Adventist alternative to the dispensational tradition, but gave no indication of its being alternative to that tradition during its first one hundred and sixty pages. Other prophecy novels have been written by Roman Catholics. Like their evangelical counterparts, Roman Catholic writers focus on many of the usual suspects in the conspiracy moving toward a one-world government, economy, and church.[82] Hugh Venning's *The End: A Projection, Not a Prophecy* (1948) imagined the Jewish reconstruction of the Temple in Jerusalem and warned against the dangers of a revived Roman empire, founded by a man known as 666, who would attack the autonomy of the United Kingdom—all standard dispensational tropes. *As the Clock Struck Twenty* (1953), by "S. M. C.," also echoed dispensational texts of the period in imagining that Western nations could be infiltrated by a Communist fifth column that would eventually undermine the existing balance of power.[83] By contrast, Dodie Smith's *The Starlight Barking* (1967), the sequel to *The One Hundred and One Dalmatians* (1956), which described a canine rapture, a "great swoosh" that would rescue dogs from an imminent nuclear holocaust, was entirely outside the broadest possible boundaries of the theological. The novel was published in the same year as Smith's adult novel, *It Ends with Revelations*.[84] Thirty years later, veteran science fiction writer Robert A. Heinlein published *Job: A Comedy of Justice* (1984) as a searing critique of fundamentalist Christianity, describing his protagonist's profound disappointment with the heaven he is finally allowed to enter. Similarly, Mark E. Rogers's

The Dead (1990, reissued 2000) invested zombie horror into a traditional dispensational framework, and Brian Caldwell's *We All Fall Down* (2000, 2006) described in detail the kinds of narrative situations that evangelical authors would generally rather not countenance. Lydia Millett's *Oh Pure and Radiant Heart* (2006) provided a satirical take on the American Christian Right when it transported three atomic scientists from 1945 to the present day, where their leader, Robert Oppenheimer, is mistaken for the hero of a messianic cult.[85] But perhaps the most extended series of dispensational references in a nonevangelical text can be found in Michael Tolkin's controversial film *The Rapture* (1991). Tolkin's film was "as authentic a premillennial vision of the end-time as Hollywood is probably capable of producing."[86] It dramatized the religious conversions of Sharon (Mimi Rogers) and Randy (David Duchovny), who find themselves bored by the emptiness of their "swinging" nightlife and, searching for lasting happiness, become involved with a secretive group of Christians. These believers, whose denominational perspective is never identified, conduct their lives according to apocalyptic prophecies made by their leader, "the boy." The film is entirely apolitical and not nearly as theological as those emerging from the Left Behind franchise: the religious culture of their movement is hardly described. There is no sense in which this film—which alludes repeatedly to the structures of the dispensational system—can be classified as even a broadly evangelical text, but it illustrates the extent to which mainstream American film audiences can be assumed to be familiar with the core elements of dispensational belief. And those audiences can also be assumed to be familiar with the most successful products of dispensational culture. The hit cartoon series *The Simpsons* included an episode entitled "Thank God It's Doomsday" (May 8, 2005), in which characters watch a spoof entitled "Left Below." These nonevangelical examples of prophecy fiction indicate the extent to which core elements of dispensational belief have crossed into the cultural mainstream. As these examples attest, the audience for prophecy fiction should not be consistently identified as passively receiving the "messages" of the texts—nor can it be consistently identified as evangelical.[87]

Prophecy fiction novels are not consumed by a stable popular mainstream and do not imply a stable evangelical readership. In fact, their implied readership appears to change from one novel to another. It is interesting to note that many of the novels, until fairly recently, emphasized their crossover appeal, as if they deliberately intended to introduce fiction to people who had little experience of reading it. The commendation on the back cover of Gary G. Cohen's *The Horsemen Are Coming* (1974, 1979) was typical of this approach: "I am not a dedicated reader of novels; however, if Mr. Cohen keeps on writing this way, he just might change my taste."[88] Similarly, very early editions of *Left Behind* (1995) featured commendations from lesser-known figures in the evangelical world, including Erwin

W. Lutzer, pastor of the Moody Church, Chicago, who noted that "even those who are not connoisseurs of fiction will be gripped by this book."[89] Before the eventual success of Left Behind, prophecy novels advertised themselves as novels for people who preferred not to read fiction.[90] Later examples were clearly intended for a more sophisticated audience: James BeauSeigneur's Christ Clone Trilogy (1997–98) took its place among the most "literary" examples in the genre. But while the novels vary in the kind of evangelical readers they aim to attract, their aspiration to address nonevangelicals has been consistent. Many prophecy fiction novels are clearly exhortatory and a number have advertised their evangelistic success. One of the most famous rapture movies, A Thief in the Night (directed by Don Thompson, 1972), cost only $68,000 to produce, but within fifteen years it had been "translated into three foreign languages," "subtitled in countless others," and had been shown to an estimated one hundred million viewers, resulting, its producers believed, in four million conversions.[91] The authors of Left Behind have likewise highlighted their series' effect in producing conversions, though in nothing like the same numbers as Don Thompson's blockbuster film.[92] Other novels provide little or nothing in the way of evangelistic exhortation. The Christ Clone Trilogy replaced an appeal for salvation with a number of unexpected and challenging theological twists, more obviously intending to instruct existing adherents than to recruit new converts to the cause. These varieties of purpose are indicative of the range of relationships that might be imagined between prophecy fiction, dispensational theology, and the evangelical movement from which both have emerged. But whatever the variety of their ideal reader, these prophecy novels return to invoke or revoke the same basic elements of plot. Because that plot is narrated in changing social contexts, prophecy novels have become an acutely sensitive barometer of the changing evangelical condition.

Nevertheless, the variety of beliefs among dispensational and evangelical believers illustrates the dangers involved in reading its literature as indicative of a homogenous religious culture. Prophecy novels do not provide privileged access to an unchanging cultural *mentalité*. There is no simple way of describing their relationship to a broader evangelicalism—or even, more precisely, their relationship to dispensationalism. We have already noticed that neither evangelicalism nor dispensationalism can provide a fixed point of reference to which the development of prophecy fiction can be compared. Instead, the fictional mode establishes a series of discourses that can be used to both consolidate and challenge dominant trends in the contexts of its production. Similarly, prophecy novels do not provide a micro-history of the movement that has produced and consumed them. Prophecy fiction justifies and challenges aspects of the wider evangelical culture.

Prophecy novels have certainly been designed to be supportive of a larger project. Didactic, nonfictional texts have used fiction to advance their ends. *Raptured*

(1975), by Tom McCall and Zola Levitt, had each of its chapters begin with a fictional scenario which the rest of the chapter attempted to explain. Morris Cerullo's *The Omega Project* (1981) interspersed its fictional narrative with episodes of direct exhortation from the author himself. Other prophecy novels insisted that readers actively engage with the theological debate. John Myers began his novel with an instruction for the reader to "STOP . . . if you have not read the book of Daniel, Chapters Two, Seven and Eight, and the thirteenth chapter of Revelation, get your Bible and read them . . . before you read *The Trumpet Sounds*."[93] These texts established the trend that dominated dispensational literary culture throughout a large part of the twentieth century: fiction was subservient to nonfiction and existed only to advance its predetermined ends. Nonfiction was paramount in the construction of theology.

But the trend is increasingly being reversed. More frequently than before, modern prophecy authors are working from fiction to theology, surrounding novels with a scholarly or pseudo-scholarly apparatus designed to consolidate or elaborate a broader doctrinal consensus. Carol Balizet's *The Seven Last Years* (1978), for example, contained an appendix listing ninety-four prophecies relating to the events of the tribulation.[94] Morris Cerullo's *The Omega Project* referred readers to an appendix which listed proof-texts for the development of the plot as well as a "chart portraying God's plan for the ages."[95] James BeauSeigneur's Christ Clone Trilogy also advertised an accompanying study guide.[96] But the most significant para-textual culture has been generated by Left Behind. Authors associated with the franchise have produced a swathe of study workbooks, devotional materials, and associated exhortatory material. One of the most important of these associated texts is *The Truth behind Left Behind* (2004) by Mark Hitchcock and Thomas Ice.[97] But these texts, and others like them, defend dispensationalism by assuming that the fictional narratives around which they have gathered represent a normative theology within the dispensational tradition—which often they do not. Prophecy fiction emerged at the beginning of the twentieth century from a predefined dispensationalism, but, at the beginning of the twenty-first century, is increasingly attempting to reshape it.

Throughout the history of the genre, therefore, dispensationalists have responded to growing market forces that have simultaneously blurred the distinction between exposition and fiction and that have called for a continual recasting of prophetic expectations in the light of current social and political concerns. Prophecy fiction—like other expressions of dispensational theology—has rarely functioned merely as an indicator of eschatological concern. Because of this, the popular reception of prophecy novels is, at least partially, indicative of the extent to which the distinctive elements of their various worldviews have been endorsed, or at least generally sympathetically consumed, by a largely, but not exclusively, evangelical reading public. Because they blur the boundaries of edification and entertainment, prophecy novels can be read, with due qualification, as a barometer of cultural and political attitudes within the evangelical movement and as significant but not determining representation of the changing face of a distinctively American faith.

III

It is the longevity of the prophecy fiction tradition that makes possible this reading of its content. Most critics who comment on the phenomenon assume that prophecy fiction emerged with the publication of Left Behind.[98] Others have looked for an earlier date. Paul Gutjahr dated the rise of evangelical prophecy fiction to the 1980s; Glenn Shuck and Frederic Baumgartner dated its emergence to the 1970s; Paul Boyer identified examples from as early as the 1930s; and Amy Johnston Frykholm has found examples from as early as 1905.[99] These uncertainties about the genesis of the genre are indicative of the lack of serious attention it has received. Millennialism has become a growth area in recent scholarship, but the study of evangelical millennialism—and especially the popular culture of dispensationalism, evangelicalism's most significant millennial subculture—has been largely overlooked.[100] Paul Boyer argued as recently as 1992 that evangelical millennialism has received "little scholarly attention."[101] Two years later, Stephen O'Leary noted that evangelical prophecy writing had "received no thorough analysis."[102] Even those scholars who specialize in evangelical history have tended to overlook the movement's eschatological interests in favor of enquiry into its politics and cultural engagement. This scholarly gap reflects a wider lack of interest in evangelical popular culture, which Heather Hendershot's work has done so much to correct.[103] But prophecy novels should be central to the investigation of that popular material culture. While evangelicals appropriated the forms of romance, the western, and the historical novel, prophecy fiction is something they invented.[104]

Nevertheless, there are a number of difficulties in describing the origins and development of prophecy fiction. It is not easy to decide upon the optimal terminology. Prophecy fiction has often been described as "rapture fiction," but this term seems appropriate only for those novels actively representing the expectations of dispensational believers. Similarly, from time to time in this book I use the term "genre," but always with some degree of hesitation. *Writing the Rapture* is not the history of an identifiable genre. Firstly, the novels do not themselves constitute a genre in the strictest sense of the word. They do not exist in a straightforward canon, and most appear unaware of the existence of other examples of their kind. Where the novels do appeal to existing texts, it is almost exclusively to other material by their own authors or to denominationally approved texts.[105] Ken Wade's Seventh-day Adventist novel cited *Steps to Christ,* "a Christian classic that had been translated into dozens of languages and sold in millions of copies," and a staple of denominational piety, for example.[106] *Apocalypse,* by the Lalonde brothers, referenced Jack Van Impe's *Left Behind* video and radio broadcasts by Marlin Maddoux, who was also the author of a prophecy novel called *Seal of Gaia* (1998).[107]

But this lack of overt genre consciousness should not conceal the fact that there are a number of similarities between prophecy novels. Both Benson and "S. M. C." suggested that the protagonists of their novels will bear an uncanny resemblance to the Antichrist.[108] "S. M. C.," the Lalonde brothers, Ken Wade, and the Left Behind novels suggested that believers will use subterfuge to hijack broadcasting technology and use it against the Antichrist.[109] Manker and Cash both began their novels with the future Antichrist meeting a Jewish cabal in an underground bunker somewhere in Europe.[110] Two prophecy novels identified the Antichrist as "Mr. Natas" ("Satan" in reverse)—Jean Brenneman's *Virtual Reality: It's No Dream* (1997) and Judith Gale's *The Promise of Forever* (1997). Most strikingly of all, a journalist protagonist appears as Tom Hammond in Watson's trilogy (1913–16), George Omega in Salem Kirban's *666* (1970), Marshall Hogan in Frank Peretti's *This Present Darkness* (1986) and *Piercing the Darkness* (1989), Cameron "Buck" Williams in Left Behind (1995–2007), Ken Walters in *Virtual Reality* (1997), Yuri Kagan in Robert Van Kampen's *The Fourth Reich* (1997), Bronson Pearl and Helen Hannah in the Lalondes' *Apocalypse* (1998), Stephen Wallace in Jonathan R. Cash's *The Age of the Antichrist* (1999), Decker Hawthorne in the Christ Clone Trilogy (1997–98), and Cat Early in *The Prodigal Project* (2003), by Ken Abraham and Daniel Hart.[111] Similarities between novels can most often be explained on the basis of shared nonfictional sources, rather than direct influence between fictional texts, but occasional examples of obvious influence can be discerned. Prophecy fiction is less of a discrete genre than an imaginative mode that provides an overlay for texts that could also be accommodated in other genres. Many of the prophecy novels that are discussed in this book could also be considered as science fiction or dystopian fiction, as thrillers or romantic fiction. Very few prophecy novels would fail to fit into other generic categories. Nevertheless, as the final chapter explains, a sense of a self-conscious genre status has emerged in more recent publications, especially in the aftermath of Left Behind, whose success has stamped an identity on a tradition that was previously ephemeral and variegated. But prophecy novels can only be described as a "genre" in the loosest sense of the word.

The second reason why *Writing the Rapture* cannot be considered a history of prophecy novels is that it can only be an incomplete survey of surviving material. The most basic difficulty in developing this project has been in building a bibliography of primary sources. There is, sadly, no archive of prophecy fiction. There are large collections of items from the material cultures of popular dispensationalism—such as that hosted in the Christian Brethren Archive at the University of Manchester, the collection formerly held by the Center for Millennial Studies at Boston University, and the collection housed at the Pre-Trib Research Center at Liberty University. These collections contain a number of important examples of prophecy fiction, but they are far from being exhaustive in scope. Prophecy fiction novels have been produced and consumed within subcultures that kept few records. Many of the early novels, in particular, were privately published, had limited circulation, and became so entwined with the popular culture of one variant of evangelicalism that they were regarded as uncollectible ephemera by insiders and outsiders alike. Nevertheless, from a historian's point of view, a good bibliography must precede a good chronology, and a good chronology is foundational to any kind of literary or cultural study. Readers will notice that I hesitate to build any kind of argument on the relative absence of prophecy fiction from the 1920s and 1930s: it is impossible to know what has not survived; similarly, it is possible that the future discovery of additional prophecy fiction will complicate the argument this book advances. My research in this book has therefore been based on the bibliography of primary sources appended to Frykholm's *Rapture Culture,* to which I have added other titles collected by Doug Cowan and myself.[112] Perhaps most interesting among the latter are the texts serialized in a German Pietist magazine in 1901; two prophecy novels in Faeroese, both written and published by Victor Danielsen (1927, 1941), a Lutheran-turned-Plymouth Brother whose importance as a Bible translator was recognized in 2007 when his portrait adorned a Faeroese stamp; a Dutch novel, *De Laatste Week* (1999), by Erik de Gruijter; and *Countdown to Armageddon* (2006) by George Patterson, a Plymouth Brethren missionary in Tibet who assisted in the escape of the Dalai Lama during the Chinese invasion of 1959 and worked subsequently as a journalist and drug therapist, treating some of the most famous rock musicians of the 1960s and 1970s.[113] Nevertheless, while a large part of this book's reconstruction of the history of the tradition will be based on educated guesswork, some conclusions are in order. It is likely that relatively few prophecy novels have been published. In the last century, around one hundred examples may have appeared, including the various Left Behind spin-offs, and around half these examples have been published in the aftermath of Left Behind. I have listed every example with which I am familiar in the bibliography of primary sources. Other difficulties in my pursuit of this project have been related to the many kinds of contexts into which prophecy novels should be inserted. The limitations of this book's survey of the prophetic fiction mode prohibit the deep archival work required by a sustained study of a single author or period. There is a great deal more that could be said about the backgrounds of Milton Stine or Joshua Hill Foster—and certainly a great deal more that could be said about Jerry B. Jenkins and Tim LaHaye.

Similarly, accurate sales statistics have been virtually impossible to obtain, though information on the number of editions through which a novel may have passed is certainly available. This information has been used to make vague calculations as to each novel's popularity.

This study's relative lack of context is related to a third difficulty, the problem of establishing the reception of these fictions, both within and outside the communities they attempted to address. Large parts of the literary culture of early twentieth-century American and British evangelicalism have not survived. Evangelical journals may have featured publishers' advertisements and reviews of early novels, but, in the absence of proper archives, these have been almost impossible to access. A study of the reception of prophecy fiction would seem particularly important in view of the fact that the genre's authors and implied readers are, almost without exception, white American men. It is important to emphasize, therefore, that *Writing the Rapture* is not and makes no claims to be an exhaustive study. Instead, it provides a basic map to the territory that future work will qualify and redefine.

Nevertheless, *Writing the Rapture* does provide a series of analytical and descriptive readings of some of the most significant evangelical prophecy novels. The nature of their significance certainly varies: some novels are important because they are early examples of prophecy fiction, though their sales statistics are entirely unknown; other novels are important because they advance innovative theological or social perspectives; and other novels are important because of their vast sales. While *Writing the Rapture* attempts to engage with the most significant evangelical prophecy novels, its coverage of material produced before Left Behind seems much more comprehensive than its coverage of material after Left Behind. This book argues that these novels sometimes parallel and sometimes oppose wider trends in dispensational culture and evangelical eschatological thinking. In the interests of concision, this book reads prophecy novels in isolation from rapture movies and from the Left Behind children's novellas within the wider context of the evolution of dispensational premillennialism and alongside broad trends in popular evangelicalism across the Atlantic world.[114] In the interests of elucidation, it describes some of the most important aspects of these hard-to-trace texts, though for practical purposes it assumes that most readers will already be familiar with the narrative contour of Left Behind. (Chapter 6 will therefore focus on the reception of the Left Behind phenomenon.) *Writing the Rapture* focuses on the evolution of the genre and its status as a palimpsest upon which the tensions and conflicts of the last century have been inscribed. The book will historicize the genre and present it in parallel with the evolution of dispensational premillennialism and the changing cultural status of American evangelicals. This book will explore prophecy fiction's reflection of the political and cultural concerns of evangelicals as they have evolved throughout the twentieth century, documenting the variety of social and cultural positions that evangelical prophecy fiction has inscribed. Prophecy novels enact the movement of dispensationalism from the evangelical subculture to the cultural mainstream, indicating the increasing influence of evangelicalism's cultural power and the increasing eclecticism of the contemporary American imagination. What is certain is that, throughout their history, prophecy novels have reflected and challenged the changing contexts of dispensational culture. It is increasingly obvious that, with the success of Left Behind, prophecy fiction is now shaping dispensational culture and is even reformulating the tradition they once attempted only to represent. But prophecy novels are also shaping the culture of the "secular" mainstream. For all their expectation of increasing marginality, writers of evangelical prophecy fiction now find themselves defining the mainstream in a way that earlier prophecy novelists could never have imagined. But perhaps we shouldn't be surprised. Whatever their expectations of the future, as James BeauSeigneur once explained, "the conclusion is by no means foreordained."[115]

1

The Eclectic Roots of
Prophecy Fiction

This is the twentieth century . . . make haste and keep up with the times.
—Joseph Birkbeck Burroughs, *Titan* (1905)

At the beginning of the twenty-first century, "Christian fiction" has
for many readers become the public face of evangelicalism. The sudden popularity of novels and movies concerned with biblical prophecy
disguises the extent to which evangelicals have wrestled with the ethics
of fictional prose. Throughout their history, evangelicals have maintained an uneasy relationship with literary fiction. When the millennial
thinker John Bunyan published *The Pilgrim's Progress* (1678), a text that
many critics have identified as the first novel in the English language, he
appeared ambivalent about the value of this mode of writing and noted
the uncertainty of his peers: "Some said, John, print it; others said, Not
so; / Some said, It might do good; others said, No." When he did print
it, the title page of *The Pilgrim's Progress* quoted Scripture in its defense:
"I have used similitudes" (Hosea 12:10).[1] Of course, Bunyan was not
the only seventeenth-century Puritan to express ideas in fiction, and
growing evidence suggests that nonconformists—and, later, evangelicals—were eager consumers of the new literary mode.[2] But, despite
Bunyan's appeal to Scripture, the uncertainties of his critics persisted.
One generation later, as *The Pilgrim's Progress* was being established as a
devotional classic, Cotton Mather was warning young ministers in New
England against literature produced by the "powers of Darkneß," literature which he believed included "most of the Modern Plays, as well as

the Romances and Novels and Fictions."[3] Some eminent Americans maintained a critical distance from his claims. The daughters of Jonathan Edwards, for example, were enjoying Samuel Richardson's rather racy account of eighteenth-century life in *Pamela* (1740).[4] But their eager consumption of fiction became increasingly unusual within the emerging eighteenth-century cultures of transatlantic evangelicalism. Uncertainty about the value of the fictional mode gave way to widespread disapproval of its method and its scope.

By the middle of the nineteenth century, preachers and writers on both sides of the Atlantic were regularly fulminating against the dangerous proclivities of prose fictions and their effects on those who consumed them. These criticisms were regularly voiced within the premillennial communities that most vigorously insisted upon separation from the rapidly perishing world. J. C. Ryle, the conservative bishop of Liverpool, epitomized the response of many fellow prophecy believers when his *Practical Religion* (1878) listed "novel-reading" alongside such sins as "worldliness . . . flippancy . . . frivolousness . . . time-wasting . . . pleasure-seeking . . . bad temper . . . pride . . . making an idol of money, clothes, hunting, sports, card-playing . . . and the like." Ryle argued that novel readers ought to be "ashamed" of a pastime that "makes the angels sorrow, and the devils rejoice."[5] Their sentiments were more commonly expressed within the stricter confines of the Plymouth Brethren. In *Father and Son* (1907), a memoir of his Brethren childhood, Edmund Gosse remembered that "storybooks of every description were sternly excluded" from the family home; "no fiction of any kind, religious or secular, was admitted into the house."[6] Gosse's comment was an important indication that religious fiction had begun to be produced, even as it signaled that it continued to be dismissed by many evangelicals who, like Gosse's father, an eminent geologist, were otherwise culturally engaged.[7] Sydney Watson, one of the most successful English evangelical writers, would have shared many of Gosse's father's prophetic conclusions, but even his work would not have been acceptable within the confines of this milieu. Premillennial believers' ambivalence about fiction continued into the middle part of the twentieth century. A. W. Tozer, one of the movement's most respected devotional writers, put the position starkly: "If it's Christian, it's true; if it's fiction, it's false. So there can't be Christian fiction."[8]

Nevertheless, as we have noted, many evangelicals combined this preference for otherworldliness with an obvious subservience to the cultures they rejected. David Bebbington has described the prevailing influence of Romanticism on the development of the evangelical movement throughout the nineteenth century—ironically, an influence that its world-denying premillennial cultures made especially evident.[9] Perhaps inevitably, evangelicals came to reconsider their earlier hostility to fictional writing. The catalyst appears to have been the work of Sir Walter Scott and his increasingly respectable genre of historical fiction.[10] By the end of the nineteenth century, evangelical writers had become significant producers of narrative fiction, using short stories of several hundred words to advance the cause of temperance and their preferred version of the Protestant faith. Their ideas were co-opted elsewhere, as a wider range of nineteenth-century writers drew evangelical imagery into novels of sentiment, social reform, and anti-Catholic polemic.[11] This evangelical culture was often severely utilitarian in tone, but it grew increasingly imaginative. Most of these early evangelical novelists concentrated on adapting the genres that they knew would sell. Ralph Connor, for example, was publishing evangelical cowboy novels from as early as the 1890s.[12] But other writers grew increasingly inventive. In the same decade, prophetic and literary interests combined to produce the only fictional mode that evangelicals can rightly claim to have invented—the mode that would become known as "rapture fiction."

The social context of the first appearance of dispensational prophecy fiction was to dominate its later evolution. Rapture novels emerged out of nineteenth-century American culture that often deferred to a particularly virulent species of ethnocentrism. In the 1880s and 1890s, for example, popular American writers were constructing a national religious culture on the basis of a shared Anglo-Saxon ethnicity and Protestant faith. It was a culture that gave birth to a distinctive "civic religion" and that imagined the certain dominance of the Anglo-Saxon race.[13] These points of view were espoused in texts like Josiah Strong's *Our Country* (1885) and Theodore Roosevelt's *Winning of the West* (1889–96). The Protestant nationalism of these writers homogenized readers and consolidated a community identity around the rapidly developing culture of Bible veneration.[14] But the identity provided by this Protestant nationalism appeared to be under threat. Non-Anglo-Saxon Roman Catholics were increasing in cultural significance, and, in 1908, Pope Pius X recognized their new standing when he withdrew "mission status" from the Roman Catholic Church in America.[15] Contextualized by the large-scale immigration of Mediterranean Roman Catholics, white northern European Protestant nationalism no longer provided an obvious creed for America.

Early dispensational prophecy novels offered a critical response to these social and religious concerns. They attempted to homogenize their readers on the basis of race and religion even as they questioned the period's dominant ethnocentric narrative. Their texts were pervaded by assumptions of the racial supremacy of white Americans and nervously wondered how their society might be affected by the sudden reversal of their progress. But the novels also argued that theories of racial unity were deeply unsatisfying as a basis for international union. They suggested that the "Anglo-Saxon world" could be prized apart and imagined that the United Kingdom and the United States could find themselves on opposing sides in an unparalleled global war in which American citizens could suffer the violent assaults of terrible ethnic "others." These prophecy novels were creating an imagined community of the faithful but imagined this community facing the greatest of all tests.

I

George Eliot was the best prophetic novelist evangelicalism never had. As a young evangelical, Eliot praised Edward Bickersteth's *Practical Guide to the Prophecies* (fourth edition, 1835) and prepared a chart of the prophecies of Revelation in 1840.[16] She was certainly not alone in combining her interest in eschatology with her interest in popular fiction. Although it is difficult to know when a recognizable "genre" of prophecy fiction can properly be said to have begun, it is clear that Christian creative writers have long been interested in eschatological themes. In *The Antichrist* (1900), the Russian Orthodox theologian Vladimir Solovyov identified the Japanese as Gog and Magog, and imagined that the Antichrist would rise to power with the help of major Christian churches and the Jews.[17] Similar themes had been considered by Protestant writers such as William Hill Brown, in *The Power of Sympathy* (1789), Charles Brockden Brown, in *Wieland* (1798), and Elizabeth Stuart Phelps, in *Beyond the Gates* (1885).[18] Novels with specifically dispensational interests emerged in the popular literary culture of late nineteenth- and early twentieth-century Protestantism, throughout and beyond the transatlantic world. The ephemeral nature of many of these publications suggests that earlier examples—as well as other examples from the same period—may well have disappeared. The limited circulation of these publications militated against the development of a self-conscious genre. Early authors of prophecy fiction appeared to write without any knowledge of other similar texts. Despite their apparent independence, however, these early novels established the parameters that would govern the tradition until the end of the twentieth century.

There is no evidence to suggest that evangelical prophecy fiction emerged as a distinctively English-language phenomenon. One of its earliest examples was serialized in *Sabbathklänge,* a weekly paper of German Pietism, in 1901. The story's inclusion was certainly controversial, and its challenge to the traditional commitments of German Pietist eschatology was highlighted in its juxtaposition with a series of articles on J. N. Darby, a leader of the Brethren movement and a chief proponent of dispensational premillennialism on the Continent. It was hardly surprising, therefore, that the letters pages of successive issues of the magazine were filled with complaints that it had become a vehicle for Darby's doctrinal innovation. This was a most unlikely charge. *Sabbathklänge* was edited by Ernst Modersohn, a Reformed churchman unsuspected of any dispensational sympathies. His response to the criticisms did not defend the theology of the dispensational rapture, but rather focused on his strategy of religious pragmatism. The serialized novel could serve an evangelistic purpose, he hoped, by warning the unconverted of the imminence of the end times. Modersohn's argument made an important and regularly repeated point in the debate about the reception of these novels. In the culture of early twentieth-century German Pietism, and for many decades after, prophecy novels could be consumed without necessarily being endorsed.[19]

Nevertheless, if prophecy fiction emerged outside the English-speaking world, it certainly consolidated within it. Most of the earliest examples of prophecy novels—and perhaps its first individually published titles—appeared in the United States. They were published independently, without any hint of mutual awareness. Like other literary texts of the period, they emerged in response to a widespread sense of political, social, and cultural collapse. Some of their secular Modernist peers came to revel in that chaos—James Joyce's movement from *Dubliners* (1914) to *Finnegans Wake* (1939) was an extreme example of that trend—but prophecy novelists, like other writers of the period, attempted to impose an order on the chaos they discerned.[20] They found that order in the dispensational scheme. Though these texts emerged from the slowly evolving dispensational mainstream, they offered a surprising variety of social and theological perspectives. Joseph Birkbeck Burroughs's *Titan* (1905) and Joshua Hill Foster's *Judgment Day* (1910) were both concerned by the rising tide of immigration and its implications for the future stability of the United States. The narrative of *Judgment Day* imagined that the tribulation period would herald a second civil war, a racial conflict between blacks, "Orientals," southern Europeans and "Anglo-Saxons" that would precipitate the final destruction of America. *Titan* anticipated a wider clash of civilizations, pitting Islamic and European armies against the meager forces of the United Kingdom, climaxing with the invasion of America and the destruction of its "Anglo-Saxon" way of life. This concern for the American future went hand-in-hand with criticism of business excess. Milton H. Stine's *The Devil's Bride* (1910) bypassed concerns about the false religion of the end times to focus on the totalitarianism of an international capitalist cabal whose beastly mark would be required for any kind of economic transaction. In *Titan*, by contrast, the exploited masses were imagined to overthrow their masters in a series of revolutions that would be led by the emerging Antichrist. *Titan* was happy to support the unionization of the masses; *The Devil's Bride* understood unionization as an unfortunate response to the exploitation of modern industrial life. As this range of opinions suggests, early prophecy novels responded in a variety of ways to the material contexts of their production.

Neither were early prophecy novels theologically uniform. In fact, some of the early titles displayed a surprising distance from traditional patterns of doctrine. *Titan* and *The Devil's Bride* demonstrated a considerable difference from the six-day creationism of a great number of later evangelicals by endorsing the "gap theory" and suggesting that demons were the disembodied spirits of the pre-Adamite dead. But *Titan* went significantly further in its doctrinal deviation. While one leading conservative clergyman had "no hesitation" in commending the novel, praising its "deep reverence for the sacred Scriptures," *Titan* was actually developing a radically unorthodox Trinitarian theology.[21] Nor were these novels uniform in their eschatology. *Titan* suggested the possibility of a partial and pre-tribulation rapture, and *The Devil's Bride* described a post-tribulation rapture that would involve all surviving believers, while *Judgment Day* and the trilogy of novels by the English author Sydney Watson provided an exposition of the standard dispensational paradigm. Despite their theological and thematic variety, these early novels shaped the direction of the emerging tradition, developing the basic themes and stock characters that would be developed in later texts.

It is difficult to estimate the influence of these early novels and difficult to access the responses of their first readers. *Titan* appears to have been very successful. Later editions claimed that the title had sold over ten thousand copies in its first twelve years; these editions were commended by influential clergy from across the Protestant denominational spectrum. But there is no evidence to suggest that a large number of the novel's readers adopted its heterodox Christology and Trinitarian theology, nor that a substantial proportion of evangelical prophecy believers adopted its theory of a partial rapture. It is nevertheless significant that the first English-language prophecy novel should have advanced ideas so different from those of the evangelical mainstream. Its popularity suggests that these early novels were regarded as no more than edifying entertainment, as the editor of *Sabbathklänge* had suggested prophecy fictions could be, and not as serious theological interventions, and that future fundamentalist leaders were willing to indulge theological latitude before the crisis of American Protestantism. Alternatively, *Titan*'s popularity suggests that prophecy novels could be read actively against their authors' didactic intentions, as Amy Frykholm has demonstrated of the genre's more recent examples.[22] Early prophecy novels illustrate the social and theological breadth of evangelical prophecy commitments in the years after the collapse of the conservative postmillennial consensus and before the public emergence of Anglo-American fundamentalism. With the consolidation of dispensational orthodoxy after the success of the *Scofield Reference Bible* (1909) and the publication of *The Fundamentals: A Testimony to the Truth* (1910–15), the political and theological variety of these novels was rapidly eclipsed. Early prophecy novels established the basic narrative contours of the tradition, but whatever their popularity, they may have had much less of a theological impact than their authors might have hoped. Prophecy fiction in evangelical America has some very eclectic roots.

II

The longest and best-publicized of the early prophecy novels appears to have been *Titan, Son of Saturn: The Coming World Emperor: A Story of the Other Christ* (1905). The novel was written by Joseph Birkbeck Burroughs, a medical doctor from Oberlin, Ohio, about whom hardly any biographical information appears to have survived.[23] *Titan*, his only book, was certainly alive to the narrative potential of the dispensational scheme. Early in the novel, one character described its literary potential: the belief that "a king is to win great power and become Antichrist and cause a terrible persecution of Christians" would make "a good foundation for a story," he believed.[24] Burroughs evidently agreed and wrote his novel with a deliberately stated intention: "The book Titan has been written in the form of a religious story that these coming events may be vividly real to the reader, and lead many to search the Scriptures to see whether these things are so."[25] This prophetic study was to be facilitated by the notes appended to each chapter of the novel, which summarized biblical evidences for elements of the plot, and by material in the appendix, which provided an extensive defense of Burroughs's claim that the future Antichrist would be a resurrected form of Antiochus Epiphanes, the Seleucid king who destroyed Jerusalem and desecrated the Temple in 167 B.C.[26] These Scripture "helps" demonstrated that Burroughs was not writing fiction for its own sake, but a theological polemic invested with unusual fears for the future of America. The plot, after all, described "coming events."

Whether or not its readers found these proofs convincing, *Titan* certainly sold well. It reached its sixth edition in 1909, was revised and "emphasized" in 1914, and reached its tenth edition, and ten thousand sales, in 1917.[27] Burroughs was keen to advertise its orthodoxy, and later editions marshaled a series of commendations from prominent pastors whose names, by 1914, included that of the respected evangelical James M. Gray, an Episcopal clergyman who had become a leading figure in the Moody Bible Institute, a contributor to *The Fundamentals* and editor of the *Scofield Reference Bible*.[28] Gray's commendation was certainly surprising, for *Titan*, despite its occasional literary power, betrays a number of theological positions that traditionally minded evangelicals would have regarded as deeply unorthodox.

Setting a pattern for the emerging genre, *Titan*'s plot begins as the end approaches. The novel imagines an unexpected surge of interest in eschatology, an enthusiasm that, like the dispensational movement itself, would begin "in the churches of England, and spread to America, Europe, and the foreign missions." This "tidal wave of prevailing prayer for Jesus to return" would sweep "around the world and up to Heaven"; "never before had there arisen, north, south, east, west, so many fanatics—selfish enthusiasts—proclaiming themselves to be Christ or Elijah heralding him coming." But, in *Titan,* this revival would not make an impact on every Christian. The majority of church members would dismiss it as "a repetition of the days of seventy years ago"—perhaps the genre's only reference to the eschatological enthusiasms and disappointments of the 1840s.[29] And, as in those days of the Millerites and other mistaken Adventists, this revival would prove to be "another false alarm."[30] *Titan* begins, then, in the aftermath of widespread millennial disappointment, but it goes on to elaborate its plot through the lens of a literal biblical hermeneutic.[31] The narrative develops the basic structural elements of the early dispensational consensus, from the "gap theory" at the beginning of biblical history, through the Christian age as a "parenthesis in the centuries," to the rapture and the tribulation.[32] But the novel made a distinctive claim when it argued that the "coming mighty conflict" would focus on "the question of *the deity of the Lord Jesus Christ.*"[33] *Titan* identified contests in Christology as a significant end-time sign.

This defense of the most significant of the "fundamentals" might explain Gray's decision to recommend the novel. But his decision was, perhaps, ill-considered. *Titan*'s articulation of the deity of Jesus Christ was highly unusual—not least in its claim that God's first choice for Messiah was actually Satan. In an extended soliloquy, Satan describes his original exaltation as "the Messiah of heaven and earth . . . God gave me liberty; I was made a free-moral agent, my will was my own. I could love God and serve Him who gave me such power and freedom; or I could, if I chose, rebel."[34] Satan did rebel, using his eloquence to carry other angels with him, but in his punishment, was stripped of his Messianic title, "and when amidst rejoicing, the Almighty crowned the Son of Man . . . to be Messiah in my place, I fled in rage."[35] Whatever the roots of this idea, it had few exponents among respected evangelicals at the beginning of the twentieth century. But Burroughs's unorthodox Christology also contributed to an unorthodox doctrine of the Trinity. *Titan* identifies the "Bride of God" as the Holy Spirit, not the church, and so moved from the orthodox mainstream to reimagine the Trinity as a marriage of male and female principles.[36] Again, the doctrine had seventeenth-century origins, but few supporters in early twentieth-century Protestantism.[37] Other of the novel's ideas were equally unusual, such as its claim that election is based on the individual's good works, which had been foreseen by God; its claim that those Christians who have not formally joined a church excluded themselves from the possibility of immortality; and its suggestion that salvation would ultimately be almost universal.[38] *Titan* was a most unusual defense of the Protestant fundamentals.

It is highly ironic, therefore, that the novel should identify unorthodox theology as a latter-day challenge to the Christian faith. But Burroughs developed the idea with no apparent embarrassment about his own position. In fact, the novel's assumption that Christology could be the most important factor in defining truth and error is used to justify its surprisingly ecumenical ambitions. *Titan*'s extremely optimistic assessment of the state of contemporary Christianity was made possible by its decision to represent the Roman Catholic Church—the traditional enemy of the faithful in the Protestant apocalyptic tradition—as a truly Christian denomination. The novel's positive attitude toward Roman Catholicism was signaled by its including at the heads of chapters quotations from such representative figures as Cardinal Newman and Thomas à Kempis.[39] Burroughs might have been "sound" on one of the most tenaciously defended of the fundamentals—but not on much more.

Burroughs's refusal to denounce the Roman Catholic Church allowed him to present the latter-day situation of Christianity in terms that were entirely untypical of the wider dispensational tradition. *Titan* suggested that, at the end of the age, Christians would not be a marginalized minority. Burroughs suggested that the true faith would continue to advance in both numbers of adherents and in political clout. No generation before the final one would contain "so many devout followers of Christ," he claimed; their enemies would be "alarmed" by their large numbers and their holding the "balance of power in every city."[40] But the novel also suggested that the growing popularity of Christianity would finally be reversed. Burroughs highlighted biblical texts that appeared to show that "when Jesus returns for his people wickedness will be in power and rapidly preparing for a new evil."[41] Secularization would achieve a victory—but a sudden one, in the final years of this age.[42]

Perhaps surprisingly, given these novelties, *Titan* begins by confirming the expectations of many of its first evangelical readers: "No people have been more faithfully taught the truths of the coming of our Lord than the Baptists of America, and Great Britain," one character opines.[43] Most Baptists are included in the rapture, therefore, though one minister, the Reverend Truman Gordon, is not.[44] A popular preacher of another denomination, the Reverend Doctor Abundance, is also left behind, partly because of his adherence to the "social gospel," the progressive and postmillennial *bête noir* of early twentieth-century fundamentalists. The social gospel is shown to be the antithesis of authentic and therefore otherworldly faith. *Titan* uses the popularity of these aversions from the truth to explain why the rapture would only remove a "small proportion" of church members.[45] It would include all children, "for of such is the Kingdom of Heaven," but only a tiny minority of Christians—the "faithful Christians," the "Wise Virgins," those who would be deemed sufficiently worthy.[46] Unlike many later prophecy novels, therefore, *Titan* was optimistic about the possibility of salvation outside the evangelical denominations, but often skeptical of claims to faith within them.

Burroughs's novel confounds evangelical expectations. *Titan* argued that the revival of true spirituality that would follow the rapture would stimulate to "renewed zeal" the members of the "great Roman Catholic Church."[47] Readers are never informed how Roman Catholic theologians would abandon their centuries-old rejection of premillennialism to recognize that the rapture was in fact a divine work, nor are readers informed of the means by which the centuries-old schism between East and West would be resolved before the pope could be appointed head of the Russian Orthodox Church.[48] During the tribulation, the Roman Catholic Church would be stripped of its wealth and prestige and "thrust back into the centuries of her poverty, that she again might live the life of Jesus, the Son of Mary."[49] At the same time, the Greek Church would be "cast down" and the Protestant churches "swept together."[50] *Titan* was advancing an end-time ecumenism. But far from being developed by the Antichrist, this latter-day one-world church would be a glorious work of God: "one Shepherd, one Flock; one Head, one Body of Christ—one Holy Universal Christian Church."[51] In *Titan,* this one-world church would unite all Christians in the sparest of fundamentalist creeds: "one common belief in the infallibility of the Bible, the divinity of Jesus Christ, and man's accountability to God."[52] The united denominations would "carry the Gospel unto every soul in the heathen world, and . . . put down every unrighteous practice and pleasure in the nations at home."[53] A stripped-down confession would drive unprecedented missionary zeal.

This end-time ecumenism would be based not on doctrine but on shared moral conviction. The novel's doctrinal apathy justified its radically ethical rewriting of Christian history. *Titan* reduced the Reformation to a revolution in manners, a period in which the Protestant example of "the ideal home" challenged "impurity of life" among the Roman Catholic elite.[54] This rewriting of Reformation history included no reference to the central doctrinal disputes of the age. The novel's preference for morality over theology, and its reduction of essential dogma to the divinity of Jesus and the infallibility of the Bible, allowed it to represent Marian devotion as an authentically Christian spirituality.[55] With no sense of doctrinal difference or historic dispute, with no acknowledgment of the apocalyptic rhetoric that had divided the denominations, the novel imagined that Roman Catholics and Protestants would "die together for their common faith" as the end of the age approached.[56] Of course, some doctrinal differences were still thought to be important—the novel mounts a vigorous polemic against Christian Science, for example—but the elements of theology that were believed to be most important did not include the central themes of the Protestant Reformation, the evangelical movement, or mainstream dispensationalism itself.[57]

Titan's pan-Christian community was being defined as much by race as by faith. The novel consolidated Anglo-Saxon Christendom by "other"-ing the peoples of the Asian East. In *Titan,* the tribulation begins slowly. Life continues much as normal until the appearance of Satan in Babylon, "that once mighty city, whose kings, priests, and people worshipped Lucifer, Angel of the Dawn, and called him Baal, Lord of the Sun."[58] In the midst of a storm, Satan identifies a lost tomb, opens it, revives the "mummy" of Antiochus and promises to restore to him the kingdom he once possessed.[59] The incident consolidates the basic political parameters that would govern the tradition until the end of the cold war. Following a long line of nineteenth-century expositors, Satan identifies "the people of Rosh, Meshech and Tubal" as "Russians, and their cities . . . Moscow and Tobolsk."[60] Russians are most suitable company for the Antichrist, for their ambition is to "grasp all of Asia and . . . rule the world," and the destiny of their leader is to become the "Chief Prince of Rosh, Meshech and Tubal," the "King of the North."[61] But the secret of his strength is clear. In a moment of horror, "the coming man for whom three hundred million people await, to unite Europe in a union of nations to conquer the world, bows down and worships the Devil."[62] Satanic religion becomes the overlay for an amalgam of anti-American political dangers. In a moment of astute prescience, *Titan* imagines that Russia would erupt in a revolution that would spread to urban centers across the Western world.[63] This expanding "kingdom of Socialists" would generate a "Confederation of Ten States" in which the Antichrist's political ambition would be realized—and, ultimately, "Europe would rule the world."[64]

Titan understands that the contest of race and faith would be ultimately for world domination. The novel contrasts European socialist countries with the Anglo-Saxon nations and describes the manifest destiny of the United Kingdom and the United States as "the lofty task of civilizing the world."[65] The novel provides a polemic for the "special relationship" of white Christian nations: "United, Saxondom will stand; divided we shall fall."[66] In fact, the novel goes so far as to identify the "twenty-five million" southern European immigrants in America as opposing this alliance with the United Kingdom and as standing in the way of national and racial destiny.[67] But ultimately the European/Anglo-Saxon dichotomy would boil down to the competition between Russia and the United States.[68] The Monroe Doctrine is cited but is argued to be outdated: "The days of American isolation and neutrality are passed forever."[69] When America fails to engage in the final civilizational conflict, volunteer "Saxons of the United States" swarm to the aid of "England," but cannot withstand the onslaught of the Islamic armies of Europe, Asia, and Africa.[70] The army of the United States of Europe invades the United States and exploits the moral paralysis of "the great middle class, the bulwark of the nation," which "refused to volunteer in defense of the country."[71] The result would be chaos. America would be gripped by a race war in which white Protestants would be defeated and the work of "the Saxon people" would suddenly end.[72] No one would be unaffected: "When the coming antichrist conquers the world, great changes shall take place in many an American home."[73]

And yet, the novel argued, these "coming events" would have their roots in contemporary theological debates. Like liberal Protestants, against whom fundamentalists were beginning to organize, the Antichrist's clergy would deny "the deity of Jesus Christ; man's sinful condition; his need of forgiveness; and accountability to God."[74] Instead of the old dogmas, his theologians would promote "the Universal Fatherhood of God" and "the Universal Brotherhood of Man," the sentiments that had dominated the World Parliament of Religions, which had met under the banner of the "Fatherhood of God" and the "Brotherhood of Man" in Chicago in 1893, in a gesture that unsuccessfully attempted to understate the differences between religions.[75] These sentiments were the same demonic impulses that necessitated *The Fundamentals*. The Antichrist had become the patron of the "Protestant iconoclasts."[76] It was the conservative conclusion of a novel that challenged many of the central components of evangelical thought. But *Titan* was not enough to stem the skeptical tide. Its warnings would need to be repeated, for, as Burroughs realized, "terror is soon forgotten and men never wonder long."[77]

III

Burroughs's words might have seemed prophetic in 1910, when *Titan* was followed by another prophecy novel that emerged from an equally surprising source and that also adopted a series of unorthodox positions. This time its eschatological presentation was at odds both with the orthodoxy of the developing dispensational consensus and with that of its author's Lutheran background. Milton H. Stine (1853–fl. 1930) was the only son of a German immigrant tailor, and he had struggled to provide himself with an education at Pennsylvania College and Lutheran Theological Seminary, in Gettysburg, Pennsylvania. Stine graduated from seminary and was ordained in 1880, taking up pastorates in Maytown (1880–83) and Lebanon (1883–92), Pennsylvania, and in Los Angeles (1892–95) before returning to Harrisburg, Pennsylvania, in 1895.[78] By then he had become an author of some reputation, having published *Studies on the Religious Problem of Our Country* (1888) and *A Winter Jaunt through Historic Lands: Embracing Scotland, England, Belgium, France* (1890). It was in the Harrisburg pastorate that Stine began to publish novels—*The Niemans* (1897) and *Baron Stiegel* (1903) were followed in 1910 by his prophetic novel, *The Devil's Bride: A Present Day Arraignment of Formalism and Doubt in the Church and in Society, in the Light of the Holy Scriptures: Given in the Form of a Pleasing Story* (1910).

The Devil's Bride represented a sea change in Stine's eschatological thinking. His earlier work, most notably *Studies on the Religious Problem of Our Country*, had embraced a robust postmillennialism, an eschatological optimism that identified him with the progressive "American" Lutheranism being promoted by Samuel Schmucker, president of the Gettysburg seminary.[79] Writing twenty-five years after the end of the Civil War, Stine showed no dismay at the prospect of the American future.[80] Although the Civil War had generated "relatively little millennial speculation," its outcome did confirm the postmillennialism that Stine shared with many of his Northern counterparts.[81] Northern postmillennialists—in contrast to post-millennialists in the South—tended to link the abolition of slavery to the beneficent social influences of Christianity.[82] They understood the Northern victory in the war as confirming the progress of goodness within the United States. Stine's early ebullience was clear: "I believe the world is surely but slowly getting better."[83] He believed that America was "destined, in the providence of God, to lead mankind into that second Eden, where no destroying angel shall ever enter."[84] America was "the hope of the world, civilly, morally, religiously," "the grandest country upon which God's sun ever shone."[85] Stine poured vitriol on those misinformed Christians who did not believe that "good was ever designed to triumph over evil in the present dispensation," who held that "the end of this dispensation is near, and that in these closing years of the nineteenth century the conflict between good and evil will be more fierce than ever with a decided preponderance in favor of evil."[86] These premillennialists expected "nothing but persecution and bloodshed," he lamented. They expected the triumph of evil and the destruction, in "blood and shame," of the "Christian institutions" for which "our fathers endured so much."[87] The errors of the premillennialists were obvious, he continued, for the "millennium of sacred Scripture" involved the overthrow of "idolatry and superstition" and the "proper recognition in this world" of "the beautiful and the good."[88] In fact, he was certain that the blessings of the future period were already being anticipated: "The Church of Christ was never stronger or more glorious than to-day . . . instead of beginning to wane she is in the ascendancy of power."[89] The true church was "just awakening to the great work of converting the nations to God," and Stine was sure that the end result would amount to the "conversion of the world."[90] The outcomes were there to see. At home and abroad, "the growth in the thoroughly evangelical denominations has been most rapid in the last few years," while "the growth of Unitarianism and Universalism is scarcely perceptible."[91] But Stine was also prepared to believe that the immediate future was open and that America's destiny was not guaranteed: "the hand of the Lord is still extended in benedictions over our land. The progress it will yet make before we chronicle the year of our Lord 1900 may be more stupendous than that of the last two decades; or yielding to the evil forces at work in our midst, it may fall like a statue from its pedestal to lie forever a broken ruin on the shores of time."[92] Stine's caution was justified by his citation of a series of native vices, and so "the battle between good and evil is not ended. There are mighty barriers to be leaped, severe battles to be fought, many foes to be smitten, before the victory over sin in all its hideous shapes is complete."[93]

Like Burroughs, Stine was concerned by the threat represented by the rising tide of immigration. He believed that the Christian character of "the first settlers of our country" had made possible the development of "Christian civilization" in America.[94] Its aspirations were not shared by more recent immigrants, who appeared to have come from "the mines of Siberia and from the dungeons of every state in all Europe, and from the darkness of Asiatic and African heathendom."[95] These "foreign vultures" were prominent among those controlling the trade in alcohol, and as such, he believed, they "prey[ed] upon American society."[96] Alcohol was an expected target: it "wields the club of the socialist . . . throws the bomb of the anarchist, and drives the blade of the assassin."[97] "Every murderer's hand," Stine claimed, "is nerved for the fatal deed by the demon Alcohol."[98] Similarly, he argued against exploitative capitalism, condemning the "avariciousness of capitalists" as being responsible for "the suffering of the poor who must work for starvation prices."[99] Capitalism was also to blame for the desecration of the Sabbath, which, he believed, was "God's greatest gift to man."[100] Stine feared that the final overthrow of this day of rest would have significant religious and economic consequences. Those who sought to overthrow the Christian Sabbath would "rob us of all the hallowed associations of christian intercourse and christian worship" and "confine the laborer to his toil, until the vital cord snaps from over tension."[101] History taught that "God chastises the nations which forget the Sabbath," he believed, remembering that England's fall into Sabbath desecration had preceded the loss of her American colonies.[102] But as Stine surveyed the dangerous growth of vice, he was equally concerned by the growing popularity of fictional writing, the "trashy novels" that were being "literally devoured by the American youths."[103] He had no doubt that "the modern novel" was exercising a profoundly "evil influence," and provided a graphic description of its worst example: "What the pen feels its inability to accomplish in these descriptions the artist's pencil fully supplies. . . . They are carried to our front doors and literally thrust into our homes."[104] The wide distribution of unsanctified fiction was nothing less than a sign of the times.

Stine appears to have rapidly changed his mind, for fiction became central to his literary career. In 1897, he published *The Niemans,* which, though it was "not a religious novel," claimed to preserve "the highest moral tone," and he followed it with *Baron Stiegel* in 1903.[105] But when Stine came to publish *The Devil's Bride,* he found himself adopting the very techniques of the "trashy novels" he had earlier condemned. Sold by subscription only, *The Devil's Bride* was "carried to . . . front doors" and "thrust into . . . homes" by his publisher's representatives. Like the novels he despised, and unlike his earlier work, *The Devil's Bride* depended for its initial effect on a lurid, colorful cover. Simultaneously with Stine's reconsideration of the medium of fiction had come a dramatic rethinking of his postmillennial hope. By 1910, Stine had abandoned his optimism about church growth and his pessimism about prose fiction; now he was pessimistic about church growth and optimistic about prose fiction. He had moved from postmillennialism to premillennialism and from opposing to encouraging the consumption of novels. In *Studies on the Religious Problem of Our Country,* Stine had argued that America's "heaven-born institutions" could never be destroyed.[106] In *The Devil's Bride,* by contrast, Stine was to participate in the apocalyptic reimagining of the nation whose future glory he once thought certain.

The Devil's Bride was published by a local publisher, Luther Minter of the Minter Company. Like other of Minter's books, it was illustrated by Paul Krafft and shared an opposition to rapacious capitalism. Minter was well-known as the publisher for a series of works by another local clergyman, the Reverend W. S. Harris, who is best known for his early interest in science fiction, notably his *Life in a Thousand Worlds* (1905). But Harris's writing, like Stine's, was eminently serious. His *Capital and Labor* (1907), also published by Minter and illustrated by Krafft, provided an overview of the history of labor conflict from a socialist and prohibitionist perspective. Stine's prophecy novel combined those political concerns with an unusual dispensational worldview.

It is ironic that *The Devil's Bride* was written and published by Lutherans. Since the Reformation, the confessional constitution of the Lutheran churches had consistently rejected the possibility of an earthly millennium. At Gettysburg, however, the seminary president, Samuel Schmucker, had been promoting an expansive "American Lutheranism" which combined traditional patterns of denominational orthodoxy with the robust millennial optimism of a wide range of North American religious cultures.[107] This was a vision with which Stine had once identified. In *The Devil's Bride,* however, Stine opposed both positions, arguing, against the Lutheran confessions, that the church should expect an earthly millennium and, against Schmucker, that this millennium should to be expected after, rather than before, the return of Jesus Christ. Stine was on an eschatological journey, and there is some evidence to suggest that he had completed *The Devil's Bride* before finally committing himself to a specifically dispensational premillennial position. Most obviously, the novel never describes the rapture as preceding the tribulation, though, perhaps as a late addition to the text, its preface states that the author expected it would.[108] But this "Explanation" also served to outline Stine's other doctrinal emphases, literalism in biblical interpretation and the sorry state of liberal clergy, who, he expected, would be "utterly powerless . . . in the hour of trial."[109] Stine emphasized his evangelistic purpose: "The book was written to warn and enlighten men and women in the church and outside of it, in the hope that it may be the means of enlightening, convincing and convicting souls 'Dead in trespasses and Sins,' in these closing years of the Church Militant."[110]

In 1910, Stine was sure the "closing years of the Church Militant" were not far away. The plot of *The Devil's Bride* begins in a northern American city racked by a lust for acquisition, when "for a month the sun had been shining with more than its usual power and brilliancy," leaving many dead.[111] Notwithstanding the heat, "the driving lash of greed and necessity kept man and beast at work until both alike gasped for breath or sank helplessly to the earth. The great blocks along city streets radiated the heat like so many glowing furnaces, silently expressive of the fact that behind their walls, men and women, and above all, helpless children, were enduring the anguish incident to the combined causes of poverty and the great heat."[112]

This unusual heat was the first of a series of signs with ominous significance. It was followed by the rising of a red moon, "an orb of blood, dark, dim, portentous, awe inspiring."[113] Sudden darkness accomplished what the heat had failed to accomplish: business was "terrorized" and "paralyzed" by the sudden plunge into darkness.[114] But the situation grew worse when the darkness was illuminated by a shower of meteors, which destroyed buildings and started "devastating fires" across the city.[115] The meteors were "like the fearful cannonading of hell's minions before their charge upon the defenseless inhabitants of earth."[116] Some crashed into the sea and created a massive tidal wave.[117] Stine's description of the scene was vivid in its present tense: "The network of wires is fused and broken and a perfect entanglement of subtle death litters the streets, as though the demons had set cunning snares of copper cable, and then charged them with a thousand volts of intangible death."[118]

Stine's novel consolidated a number of the stock characters whose ghosts would haunt the tradition. His liberal-minded clergyman is the Reverend Doctor Knowit, a distinguished and well-connected graduate of leading American and German universities who had become pastor of a large and influential city church.[119] Nevertheless, the narrator opines, Knowit's "theology was not as noble as his bearing. He had been taught that the Bible is full of inaccuracies historically, that the statements with regard to the miracles are necessarily overdrawn, because they were the product of a superstitious age."[120] Knowit is certainly not an evangelical—and even his Protestant credentials are in doubt. He "preached the doctrine of salvation through works. Every man within himself has the power to save himself . . . because of his liberal views men of the world heard him gladly and joined his church in great numbers."[121] He advanced a creed that "was broad enough to comprehend every cult which embraced in it God as the universal Father."[122] Knowit's creed echoed that of the World Parliament of Religions, which, in Chicago in 1893, had identified the "Fatherhood of God" and the "Brotherhood of Man" as core components of Protestant liberal expectation.[123] Knowit became a paradigm of faithlessness.

Knowit's function in the narrative is therefore to link this "liberalism" to a series of recent developments among the clergy. His ministry preferred biblical criticism to emotional worship.[124] As a consequence, his pulpit, like that of many of his peers, "began to give forth uncertain sounds. Ministers of the faith became the chief doubters of the times."[125] As a consequence of this ubiquitous articulation of doubt, parishioners needed some alternative reason for attending church. Their pastors found that reason in new styles of liturgy: they substituted written prayers for real ones and "formality constantly increased. Men turned themselves into priests, wearing garb very much like that worn by Old Testament priests, and offi-ciated before altars of their own building."[126] True spirituality rapidly declined: "As society became more heartless and depraved, the difference between the church and the world was in no way perceptible except that some still continued to pay pew rents. . . . Yet with it all the Church of those days boasted that she was rich and increased in goods and had need of nothing."[127] Stine's novel was illustrating to his readers the "uncertain sounds" of many of his clerical peers.

Stine's identification of theological liberalism and the power of wealth were significant in terms of his novel's thematic development. His allusion to Revelation 3:17 linked the situation of latter-day liberalism to that of the church in Laodi-cea, a standard trope in the emerging dispensational jeremiad and in the literature of Victorian social pessimism.[128] The allusion provided a hint of the judgment to come: "Because thou sayest, I am rich, and increased with goods, and have need of nothing; and knowest not that thou art wretched, and miserable, and poor, and blind, and naked: I counsel thee to buy of me gold tried in the fire, that thou may-est be rich; and white raiment, that thou mayest be clothed, and that the shame of thy nakedness do not appear; and anoint thine eyes with eyesalve, that thou may-est see. As many as I love, I rebuke and chasten: be zealous therefore, and repent" (Revelation 3:17–19). The novel's criticism of the links between wealth and liberal theology justified its contrasting material accumulation with authentic Christian devotion. This came to a focus in the novel's description of Sunday trading. The narrative constantly highlights the disparity between the church's complacency and the recent repeal of the "beneficent" blue laws, which had restricted Sabbath desecration.[129] Knowit, as the occasional friend of workers, favored the relaxation of these laws.[130] But the narrator opines that "the repealing of the Sunday laws, the observance of which had contributed so much to the integrity and advance-ment of society in the Nineteenth Century, must bring disaster to the people of the Twentieth Century."[131] That disaster was marked in the sudden collapse of civic religiosity and decreasing church attendance: "With the repeal of the Sabbath laws came the disregard for . . . God's house also. The attendance upon the services in the sanctuary diminished more and more."[132] With the collapse of the church there came a moral vacuum in the home: it "lost its sanctity and hallowed influence. The ruin of the family altar brought about the destruction of family affection and family virtue."[133] Nevertheless, among the "great horde who had a name yet were dead," a remnant had been preserved, "a great company of true believers . . . who waited for their Lord."[134] The wealth generated from seven-days trading had come at great cost.

It is hardly surprising, therefore, that the end-time economic revolution lead-ing to the mark of the beast is headed, not by communists, but by dreamers of the American dream. *The Devil's Bride* imagines an international cabal of capitalists, "money barons" who would "dictate the price of bread and meat, of salt and sugar," enacting "any laws we desire" to create "a new aristocracy the like of which the world had never heard."[135] The cabal's power would be consolidated in a system "more powerful and more sweeping in its control than anything the world had ever known or ever even thought of."[136] Their total control of trade would constitute "a direct stroke at the liberties of the people . . . the Trust had not only arrogated to itself the right to say what a man should eat and drink and wear, but it was an easy matter to decide what a man should say, what political cause he should espouse, what church, if any, he should attend."[137] The novel admits that this possible future would be some time in coming: "the capitalists were not yet sufficiently hardened to allow their scheme to go into effect."[138] But their power was beyond dispute. There is no Antichrist in *The Devil's Bride,* and no latter-day universal religion. Its revived Babylon is a business empire with a religious devotion to trade, a religion "whose high priest is the devil . . . whose religious acts are robbery and murder and whose results are starvation and death."[139] The great danger of the latter days is the tyranny of international capital, not that of a one-world church.

But *The Devil's Bride* was also concerned by the recent rise of spiritualism and Christian Science, its more respectable equivalent.[140] The narrator, clearly positioned with the authorial voice, explains that he believes "that it is possible to open communication with the spirit world; that such communication is now taking place in an ever-increasing number of instances. We believe also that in not a single instance is there communion with a pure spirit. We believe that every one of them belongs to the kingdom of the devil."[141] He engages in some speculation as to the identity of these impure spirits, and suggests, as Burroughs had done, that they may be the spirits of pre-Adamite men, a suggestion he links to the gap theory.[142] Stine, like Burroughs, is vitriolic on the popularity of Christian Science: this "so-called church," which "numbered its votaries by the millions" and "seemed to be growing by leaps and bounds," was trying to "rob Christ of His claims as God manifest in the flesh."[143] He devotes a full chapter to an exposé of the cult and provides an extensive analysis of Mary Baker Eddy's *Science and Health with Key to the Scriptures.*[144] In marked contrast, and again like Burroughs, Stine refused to attack the Roman Catholic Church, evangelicalism's traditional "other," even when describing a gateway to hell that opened near Rome.[145] Its criticism of the Roman Catholic Church was minimal and implicit while its criticism of Christian Science was overt. Like Burroughs's *Titan,* Stine's novel imagined a latter-day deterioration of Christianity from which the Roman Catholic Church would be observably exempt.

Stine must have realized that many elements of his plot would appear bizarre to his listeners: "I do not wonder much that the great mass of men think themselves ready for heaven because they can laugh at the exploded superstitions of their forefathers, and read by the electric light."[146] Nevertheless his conclusion was exhortatory, warning his "kind reader" that "the signs of the times point clearly to the fact that this great apostasy is near and that the consequent fearful events described in this book will soon come upon the children of unbelief."[147] It was imperative, he argued, that every reader of *The Devil's Bride* should ask themselves "whose betrothed are you? Let your own conscience in the light of Scripture give you the answer."[148]

IV

With all of their disparities, and their distance from the emerging evangelical and dispensational mainstream, the Burroughs and Stine novels must have appeared unlikely to begin a new genre. Perhaps their eclecticism militated against their contributing to its cohesion. It is certainly the case that many of their areas of agreement were to rapidly disappear from the evolving dispensational imagination. Yet the similarities appeared accidental: Stine made no reference to Burroughs, and later editions of Burroughs's novel made no reference to *The Devil's Bride*. But neither could these novels have referenced each other if they had regarded as important the interpretive and theological differences that kept them apart. At the beginning of the prophecy fiction tradition, as throughout its history, theological diversity would frustrate the development of a self-conscious tradition. Stine could not own the model provided by *Titan,* for to do so would have been to draw attention to and identify with the heresies the book contained. And yet, for all their surprising theological eclecticism, the early novels were ethically conservative. Both Burroughs and Stine called attention to the evils of Sabbath desecration in a gesture that distanced them from dispensational orthodoxy, which, in the *Scofield Reference Bible* and elsewhere, was to undermine the sacred status of a weekly day of rest.[149] Nevertheless, the doctrinal aberrations of the early novels were to demonstrate how rapidly the genre consolidated within the boundaries of dispensational orthodoxy.

But the genre was consolidating without the ongoing help of Burroughs and Stine. Burroughs never published another novel, and Stine seemed to move from premillennial pessimism as rapidly as he had embraced it. In 1930, compiling his account of a journey around major European cities, his was still prepared to consider the prophetic future of America as an open question: "If this civilization, the noblest the world has ever known, fails, it will be because doubt in the inerrancy of the Scriptures gains the ascendancy and materialism triumphs over spirituality," he declaimed.[150] "This failure is sure unless Atheism in our institutions of learning is curbed."[151] Nevertheless, he insisted, it was the "faith and prayers of the Christian people" that would decide America's destiny.[152] The future—and the genre of prophetic fiction that sought to describe it—looked very open indeed.

2

The Orthodox Consolidation
of Prophecy Fiction

Every sign of the times to-day is surely but a sound of the returning footsteps of Him for whom we wait and watch.
——Sydney Watson, *Brighter Years* (1898)

Milton Stine's cautious optimism about the prophetic future of America
seemed quite out of step with the mood of many of his fellow prophecy
believers in the decade immediately following the publication of *The
Devil's Bride*. His insistence that the "faith and prayers of the Christian
people" would decide the immediate future of the nation was not widely
shared among those evangelicals who most closely adhered to his novel's
prophetic scheme.[1] By the second decade of the twentieth century, many
prophecy believers felt decidedly pessimistic about the future progress
of the evangelical faith. As they surveyed the ecclesiastical landscape,
comparing its contours with those they saw mapped out in the prophetic
Scriptures, they concluded that grave dangers loomed on the horizon.
Their prophetic literature—and the prophecy fiction it influenced—
reflected increasingly pessimistic themes.

By the second decade of the twentieth century, conservative Protestants had agreed on the need to defend the "fundamentals" of their
faith. As the character of Doctor Knowit had suggested, the traditional
assumptions of their faith appeared to be under serious threat from the
Modernist liberalism that concealed in religious veneer the "assured
results" of biblical criticism and the new evolutionary science. Evangelicals found themselves being positioned in opposition to intellectually

respectable forms of knowledge. They responded to these trends with real concern, most famously in a series of twelve paperback booklets edited by A. C. Dixon, Louis Meyer and R. A. Torrey and sponsored by two California oilmen, Lyman and Milton Stewart. These booklets, presenting a compilation of mostly prepublished material from a wide range of authors, addressed a series of subjects of immediate concern. *The Fundamentals: A Testimony to the Truth* (1910–15), as the booklets were collectively known, advertised themselves as being sent to "every pastor, evangelist, missionary, theological professor, theological student, Sunday School superintendent, Y.M.C.A. and Y.W.C.A. secretary in the English speaking world, so far as the addresses of all these can be obtained."[2] The project was nothing if not ambitious. In the fourth volume, the sponsors reported that the 128-page booklets were being sent gratis to some 250,000 subscribers.[3] In the fifth volume, this figure had risen to 275,000 subscribers, and Roman Catholic priests were specifically listed among the recipients.[4] But the booklets seemed to parallel prophecy novels' flirtation with and eventual rejection of the Roman Catholic Church. By the tenth volume, as the circulation figures had begun to decline, the project was advertising itself as dealing with Protestant essentials.[5] Anti-Catholic rhetoric was noticeably stepped up in volume eleven, which contained essays on "Is Romanism Christianity?" and "Rome, the Antagonist of the Nation."[6] Nevertheless, *The Fundamentals* addressed the needs of the hour. The series' sponsors—who were never named in any of the booklets—reported that they had printed a total of three million copies of the booklets.[7] Reflecting the most important of the contemporary challenges to evangelical belief, the booklets' articles dealt with the inspiration and authority of the Bible, the challenge of evolution, and the theology of the person and work of Jesus Christ. Eschatological themes were significantly absent from the titles of their essays. One of the few essays that made any kind of eschatological reference addressed the theology of Jehovah's Witnesses. Despite being written by William G. Moorehead, who had edited the *Scofield Reference Bible,* the essay concentrated on Jehovah's Witnesses' attacks on Christological orthodoxy.[8] Therefore, while *The Fundamentals* encouraged the development of a distinctively subcultural mentality, and motivated believers to defend the issues they addressed, they did not define the boundaries of the movement whose name they provided. They became notably anti-Catholic, but remained eschatologically agnostic. Ironically, given the future preferences of self-styled "fundamentalists," these seminal documents made almost no reference to the prophetic teaching of Scripture.[9]

As the contents of *The Fundamentals* suggest, the rise of a fundamentalist movement was not a determining factor in the evolution of prophecy fiction. Many themes in the emerging tradition were shared by other fictional accounts of Christian apocalyptic. One of the most famous nonevangelical responses to the ecclesiastical crisis of the early twentieth century was provided by Robert Hugh Benson (1871–1914). Benson, the youngest child of Edward White Benson, the Archbishop of Canterbury, had followed his father into Anglican orders before converting to Roman Catholicism in 1903.[10] He was, as a recent biographer has put it, a "supreme catch of a convert."[11] Benson's conversion had been influenced by Charles Gore, the Anglo-Catholic and politically radical future bishop of Oxford, whose lectures on the sacraments convinced Benson that he faced no alternative between total skepticism and a radical submission to the authority of the church. Benson's conversion was also, significantly, contiguous with the beginnings of his literary career. His early outputs were in historical and contemporary fiction, but four years after his reception into the Roman Catholic Church he responded to the general sense of ecclesiastical crisis by publishing a startling account of the rise of the Antichrist in a novel entitled *Lord of the World* (1907). The novel encoded his fears for the future of conservative Christianity. It began with the admission of its being "a terribly sensational book" but advanced into a startling description of the technologically advanced and dystopian culture of twenty-first-century England.[12] Benson imagined that a worldwide conspiracy of Freemasons would engineer the Communist dominance of Europe and the final decline of the Christian faith.[13]

Lord of the World prophesized that the Church of England would collapse in 1929, and that Nonconformity, which "was, after all, nothing more than a little sentiment," would collapse under the assault of "German attacks" on the integrity of Scripture and liberal attacks on the divinity of Jesus Christ.[14] Only the Roman Catholic Church would resist these demonic trends. The novel had no doubt that the conflicts at the beginning of the twentieth century had begun "with the rise of Modernism."[15] But Modernism's erosion of traditional Christian truth was paving the way for the coming of the Antichrist, who would emerge to "lead the Communist movement and unite their forces" while saving the world from a "duel of East and West," the kind of civilizational conflict that Burroughs and Stine thought inescapable.[16] Nevertheless, *Lord of the World* demonstrates that the fear of a pan-European dictator and a subsequent clash of civilizations were not unique to American evangelicals in the later decades of the twentieth century, nor to evangelical or fundamentalist prophecy believers in any part of their tradition. Instead, fears of international conspiracy, Freemasonry, Communism, and skeptical biblical criticism can be identified as pivotal tropes in an early twentieth-century English Roman Catholic text. Evangelical prophecy fiction was taking part in a much larger conversation as it responded to a broadly conceived sense of religious and political crisis.

I

The crisis of Christendom was given a distinctively political spin by the author of the first recognizably orthodox dispensational novel. The author, Joshua Hill Foster (1861–1947), was a colorful character in Southern society, a Baptist minister and university professor whose novel, *The Judgment Day: A Story of the Seven Years of the Great Tribulation* (1910), was published in Louisville, Kentucky, by Baptist World Publishing. Foster had been born into a distinguished family in Tuscaloosa, Alabama. His father, who bore the same name, had also been a farmer, Baptist minister and professor.[17] Foster followed his father to the University of Alabama, graduating with a M.A. in 1880 before moving to the Southern Baptist Theological Seminary, where he studied under some of the denomination's most respected academics—Basil Manly, John A. Broadus, James P. Boyce, William H. Whitsett, "and some lesser lights."[18] After his graduation in 1887, Foster moved through a series of pastorates. His standing in the Baptist community can be gauged by his being invited to address the state's annual denominational convention in 1908. His theme was celebratory, applauding Baptist interventions that had identified "Jesus Christ as the moral leader of the world and . . . the supreme ideal of individual character," and that had assisted the Anti-Saloon League in "sweeping" the public sale of alcohol from the state.[19] The speech provided a surprisingly upbeat context for the publication, two years later, of *The Judgment Day,* and its social optimism provided a stark contrast to the novel's concerns about apocalyptic violence, race war, and the latter-day destruction of America.

Foster was certainly aware of the controversy his novel might begin. His novel's preface admitted that many readers might consider it "presumptuous for any one to understand the Book of Revelation."[20] It was a point worth making, for while his novel bore the imprimatur of denominational respectability, it also presented an eschatological scheme quite different from the approach traditionally adopted by evangelicals across the range of the Southern denominations.[21] Their shared postmillennialism had reinforced a wide range of conservative social and political positions for, as its ablest historian has explained, it provided "an appropriate eschatology for an activistic people who believed in the essential soundness of their civilization and who saw the future as an arena for its indefinite improvement and extension."[22] Even as the Civil War began, those postmillennial believers who supported slavery felt that they were "riding the wave of destiny."[23] The ultimate defeat of the South shattered their social optimism and imploded their hopes of conservative progress.[24] In the decades following that defeat, southern evangelicals abandoned postmillennialism as a theology that could no longer explain their social situation, but they developed no clear consensus on what ought to replace it.[25]

Introducing *The Judgment Day,* Foster deflected the charge of exegetical presumption by claiming that his research for the novel had continued over a period of fifteen years. During that period, he had been "using the best helps available" in eschatological study, postmillennial and otherwise.[26] Such a defensive position was a practical necessity for an influential Baptist in the Southern states. In the decades after the Civil War, Southern Baptist theologians developed a number of possible revisions of their earlier postmillennial consensus, but none of these came close to endorsing Foster's variety of dispensational premillennialism. James P. Boyce (1827–88), who had studied at Princeton Theological Seminary with Charles Hodge, moved a significant distance from traditional postmillennialism in his developing emphasis on the imminence of the second coming, an emphasis he shared with other eminent Southern Baptists including John L. Dagg (1794–1884), president of Mercer University, and James M. Pendleton (1811–91), a founder of the controversial "Landmarkist" grouping.[27] John Broadus (1827–95), who taught Foster, developed an alternative eschatology that eventually evolved into an idiosyncratic amillennialism.[28] Even the *Abstract of Principles,* a document that had governed teaching at the Southern Baptist Theological Seminary since 1858, repudiated central claims of the premillennial position.[29] Of course, the Baptist tradition had eminent premillennial spokespersons, and English preachers and writers like John Gill (1697–1771) and Charles H. Spurgeon (1834–92) had been among their most eminent representatives. But these would not have been convenient figures for Hill to cite. Both men were unpopular in the Southern states—Gill for his High Calvinism, and Spurgeon for his public opposition to slavery.[30] In any case, the support that could have been provided by citations of Gill or Spurgeon would have been of limited value, for neither theologian had endorsed the "secret rapture" that dominated Foster's narrative. His movement toward dispensationalism was unprecedented among the major theologians of his denomination.

In 1910, therefore, Foster was driven to look significantly beyond the boundaries traditionally maintained by his Southern Baptist brethren. In *The Judgment Day,* he listed Smith, Sayce, Seiss, Warren, Rolleston, and Carter among the most useful eschatological writers he had consulted. This was evidence of very wide reading: these writers, some of whom paraded their premillennialism, ranged far beyond the traditional orthodoxy of the Southern Baptist faith. And that wide reading led to a widening of associations. Three years after the publication of the novel, Foster spent a "great" summer at the Moody School, in Northfield, Massachusetts, and later celebrated his friendship with R. A. Torrey, the noted premillennial preacher and editor of *The Fundamentals.*[31] As the postmillennial consensus was dying, Foster was moving far from the tradition of his denomination and into a wider and more obviously fundamentalist evangelical scene.

Foster's eschatological opinions may have been controversial, but he was certain that coming events would justify his claims: "the time is imminent when . . . the fearful judgments of God will begin."[32] He emphasized that imminence by beginning chapters with present-tense descriptions of events in the tribulation; this stylistic decision invited readers to imagine the events of the tribulation as occurring within their own world. But Foster's writing was far from realistic. Like other early prophecy novelists, Foster chose to save time on characterization: *The Judgment Day* is populated by such characters as Julian Goodenough, Emily Trueheart, Nancy Snobby, and Doctor Bland, "the popular pastor of the most aristocratic church in New York."[33] But, while other early prophecy novels focused on the impact of the rapture on a typical American middle-class home, Foster, true to his privileged roots, concentrated on an aristocratic circle in New York. This choice of characters was designed to illustrate Foster's conviction that the rapture would remove only a tiny number of people.[34] Burroughs had been confident that latter-day Christianity would enjoy unparalleled social success, but Foster reversed his optimism and argued that the true church would decline in numbers and prestige to such an extent that authentic faith would almost disappear before the rapture.[35] As a consequence, its impact would be concentrated in only two demographic groups: all children under the age of eight, and many of "the best people in New York," who were, overwhelmingly, white and Protestant.[36] In a sign of the genre's increasingly Protestant self-consciousness, the novel included only "one aged Roman Catholic priest" among the disappeared—but even he was unrepresentative of his church, an unpopular preacher who was "always making the people angry by insisting upon what he called practical, every-day religion."[37] Nevertheless, while latter-day believers were to be a marginalized minority, the wider culture still reverberated with their faith: the dispensational rapture is the only explanation offered for the disappearances and none of the novel's characters disputes the truth of this explanation's claims.[38]

The Judgment Day was the first English-language prophecy novel to clearly articulate the theology that had come to define the dispensational mainstream. Its emphasis on a literal hermeneutic was primary to its development of plot.[39] The novel complained that "men have not taken Revelation for what God gave it to them. . . . The very title of the book should have prevented any such mistake as that."[40] This didactic process is concentrated in the character of Doctor Bland, who is among those left behind.[41] Unlike others among the clergy, Bland does not abandon his pastoral career when it becomes obvious that clerical salaries would soon be reduced.[42] Instead, he becomes an evangelical and a dispensationalist whose preaching, throughout the tribulation, grows plainer and less oratorical.[43] After his conversion, Bland develops a prophetic scheme that clearly borrows from the *Scofield Reference Bible* and merges theological and political concerns as he anticipates "the most terrible drama of the world's history."[44]

The Judgment Day suggested that its American Protestant readers had good reason to be concerned. In stark contrast to the novels by Burroughs and Stine, *The Judgment Day* revealed that the Roman Catholic Church was a "fraud"—no more than a "political organization, without any power to absolve from sin or save the soul."[45] Foster presented the Roman Catholic Church as a threat to America, which, in the novel, is a nation in the process of rejecting its Anglo-Saxon and Protestant past. But that traditional identity faced many other threats. The nation had elected as president "a foreigner and a Mohammedan," and his ungodly government abandons the legal protection of the Sabbath even as it welcomes an unstoppable tide of immigration.[46] His policies plunge America into social crisis: "Men were afraid to leave their homes. In the South the Negro problem was no nearer a solution than fifty years ago. If the people of the West should leave home their property and families would be at the mercy of Mexicans, Chinese and Japanese, who swarmed the land. In the North, Italians were waiting their opportunity to wrest the government from the hands of the native-born Americans and rule or ruin."[47] But "native-born Americans" were certainly not Native Americans. *The Judgment Day* constructed the tribulation as a war against white Anglo-Saxon supremacy, a second civil war, with "Negroes in the South," "Italians in the North" and "Chinese, Japanese and other foreigners" in the West all "pillaging, dynamiting and committing the most atrocious outrages."[48] Those "native-born Americans" who become evangelicals after the rapture fall victim to homegrown terrorism and are martyred in unprecedented numbers.[49] Polite society in New York gives itself up to immorality and the occult and sponsors a grand ball in honor of the devil.[50] America's evil is inescapable and worse even than the most notorious scenes of excess: "Sodom would have blushed and Gomorrah would have hid her face from the disgraceful and revolting scenes . . . Even Coney Island in its wickedest days had never dreamed of such shame."[51] Perhaps Foster was engaging in some kind of Southern revenge fantasy when he imagined that the gates of hell would appear in the center of a Northern city, when Satan appears in Central Park to open a "rent in the earth . . . half a mile square" that leads to the bottomless pit.[52] But this rejection of Northern urban life is not unbalanced. The same New York park becomes the center of a great revival and the focus of the worldwide conversion of Jews.[53]

As the latter reference suggests, Foster's text mixed its robust patriotism with an evident philo-Semitism. *The Judgment Day*, for all its racial concerns, was the first obviously philo-Semitic novel in the genre. Foster expected the Jews to return to Israel during the tribulation but, when war breaks out between the United States and the United Kingdom, imagined that it would be the American military that would save Jews from the aggression of the British.[54] The resolution of American philo-Semitism is contrasted with the unstable sympathies of "Anglo-Saxon" Europe.[55] Foster's Euro-skepticism is particularly reflected at the end of the novel, when events move from New York to the Middle East. As in *Titan*, Babylon becomes the "chief city of the world," the origin of the new world under the Antichrist's control.[56] But while *Titan's* Antichrist was identified as the resurrected Antiochus Epiphanes, Foster's Antichrist is the reincarnation of Nero, and his assistant is a Judas Iscariot resurrected from the dead.[57]

Despite this evidence of philo-Semitism, the novel's description of the Middle East appears to lack some local color. Unlike Stine, Foster does not appear to have traveled to Palestine, and his descriptions of Jerusalem exhibit a surprising degree of historical and geographical ignorance. He imagines that the Dome of the Rock had existed since the days of David and sidesteps the competing claims for ownership of the Temple Mount site by imagining that the mosque could be "used by the Jews and all Christians for worship."[58] Likewise, his narrative entirely fails to consider the status of displaced Arab Muslims. But at least he does not include Muslims in an end-time one-world faith—for in *The Judgment Day*, as in the novels by Burroughs and Stine, there is no one-world religion to fear.

That exception aside, *The Judgment Day* established the basic pattern of the prophecy fiction genre. The conservative articulation of the dispensational scheme depicted in Foster's novel would supplant the eccentricities of Burroughs and Stine. *The Judgment Day* provided the emerging genre with theological respectability, confirming its Protestant and evangelical credentials and establishing its stock themes and a number of stock characters.[59] Crucially, Foster's novel made it possible for American evangelicals to imagine their own political eclipse, for his believers were depicted as being much more marginal than those of other early novels. And, by rooting his chapters in present-tense description, *The Judgment Day* made it possible for evangelical readers to imagine that they were already in the end-time conditions their leaders had encouraged them to expect. The last judgment was an imminent possibility.

II

That assumption that evangelical prophecy novels were being read in the final days of the church age was confirmed by the most thematically enduring and regularly reprinted of the early prophecy novels. Published by a British author called Sydney Watson (1847–c. 1918), these novels, *Scarlet and Purple* (1913), *The Mark of the Beast* (1915), and *In the Twinkling of an Eye* (1916), constituted the first series in the genre and were widely distributed in America.[60] By the mid-1910s, Watson was in the third decade of a hugely successful career as a writer of pietistic and polemical prose. His request that readers should pray for Christian writers reflected his sense of the importance of his work in the defense of the Protestant fundamentals: "when do we hear Christian authors and publishers prayed for in our public services? Yet who, in these days of uncertain sounds, need it more?"[61]

Watson had begun his writing career in the late 1880s, preparing "penny stories" for the evangelical press.[62] These tales were polemical from the beginning: an early contract with the Drummond Tract Depot, Stirling, provided Watson with an outlet for a "good, strong line of temperance stories."[63] Looking back on these modest beginnings, Watson believed that the early texts would have provided him with a "small fortune" had they generated any royalties: "As it was, I had to be content with £5 each for the copyright of the first thirteen stories, though I succeeded in getting £7 10s. for each of the next twelve MSS."[64] But, despite not having "the pen of a Rider Haggard," Watson soon found himself addressing a regular readership of "over a million a week."[65] He wrote at a phenomenal rate: one thousand words per hour, five thousand words per day, and one million words per year.[66] The statistics were considerable: "In eleven years I have written *three hundred twenty thousand word stories*; a dozen serials of a hundred thousand words each (many of these have since become volumes); a hundred or more tracts and booklets; besides hundreds of short articles."[67] Watson was modest about the value of his work, refusing to believe that it qualified as proper literature.[68] Nevertheless, it was evidently making an impact. Watson wrote to sell—as well as to be "entertaining and useful to the saved reader" and "useful to the unsaved."[69] And many of those "unsaved" readers appeared to make the response he desired: although he kept "no record of numbers—God does that, and He makes no mistake, while we are apt to make wholesale blunders"—Watson was certain that God had "blessed" his stories "to the known conversion and blessing of hundreds of souls."[70] These conversions, of course, were no guarantee of the author's fame. "To thousands of reading people my name . . . will be absolutely unknown," he admitted.[71] Watson's provision of a biography was designed to redress their ignorance.

Watson's two volumes of autobiography were published as *Life's Look-out* (1897) and *Brighter Years* (1898). A third volume, *From Deck to Glory* (1920), was prepared by his wife, Lily Watson, sometime after his death.[72] The volumes were written in a "gossipy style" and reflected the new mood of the reading public, anxious for information about their favorite writers: "We live in days when people are ever curious to know certain things about the writers whom they read, —about their methods of work, their output, the influences (human and otherwise) which have chiefly affected them, etc."[73] Watson prepared his autobiography after receiving "requests from many of my readers in many lands, for such a book."[74] But it is possible that these volumes blurred the boundaries of fact and fiction. Watson's writing combined autobiographical anecdotes with excerpts from his evangelistic tracts and stories. He admitted that his fiction borrowed from his own experience, but it is not clear how far his fiction influenced the autobiography.[75] Watson certainly admitted that his autobiographical narrative was far from complete. Despite his rambling and baggy style, he confessed that he had "not been able to put in *one fourth* of the events and incidents which found place in my actual life *up* to this period . . . Truth *is* stranger than fiction!"[76] "I cannot find room in this book for a tithe of the experiences that crowd upon me as I write," he complained.[77] Watson's life, as documented in his autobiography, included repeated desertions from the navy, an addiction to gambling, three months as a stowaway on a ship bound for Australia, and being lost without water in the Australian outback. This remarkable catalogue of events in the life of a man who had not yet reached twenty years of age had plenty to offer the storyteller.[78]

Watson's journey toward evangelical faith was peppered with references to C. H. Spurgeon, the most famous minister in Victorian London. Even before his conversion, Watson remembered Spurgeon's "wonderful" preaching had "thrilled" him.[79] After his conversion, the two men found common ground in an opposition to Modernism. Watson stood solidly with Spurgeon in hostility to the rising tide of biblical criticism, refusing to admit that God's revelation could include mistakes.[80] But his developing theology showed itself to be far broader than Spurgeon's Romantic infusion of Calvinism.[81] Watson applauded the efforts in "sacred song" of P. P. Bliss and Ira D. Sankey and documented incidents of "holy laughter" and "holy mirth" that the Particular Baptist minister could never have countenanced.[82] Neither could Spurgeon have tolerated Watson's wholesale rejection of congregational life.[83] The references to Spurgeon may have been designed to buttress Watson's fundamentalist credentials; paradoxically, they epitomized his denominational independence.

After an early brush with Methodism, Watson kept himself at some distance from denominations, explaining that God had "plainly set me to be a free-lance as regards the Churches."[84] His preaching activity, similarly, was highly interdenominational, involving "almost all sections of the Christian Church: Salvation Army, Baptists, Methodists (of all types), Bible Christians, Evangelistic Societies, Independent missions, etc."[85] Most controversially of all, Watson was prepared to accredit the preaching of women.[86] He believed that the Holy Spirit had led his wife, Lily Watson, to begin a preaching career and recalled that she had taken over his preaching ministry to enable him to devote himself more fully to writing.[87] This regendering of evangelical patriarchy was perhaps assisted by his conviction, which unconsciously echoed Burroughs's Trinitarian speculations, that God could in some sense be understood as "our mother."[88] Nevertheless, his listing of the denominations in which he had been active actually emphasized the extent to which these innovations had limited his ministry: he appears not to have been active among Presbyterians, Congregationalists, Plymouth Brethren, or Anglicans, and was therefore probably restricted to a fairly narrow territory of dissent in the rural south of England.

But it is its relative lack of interest in biblical prophecy that makes Watson's autobiography most surprising. The first words he heard spoken by his future wife were a quotation of an eschatological hymn, but his memoirs made no more than a handful of apocalyptic references and only once referred to predictions of Israel's future.[89] Even at the end of the 1890s, Watson did not seem to be particularly interested in eschatology. But the closing pages of the second volume of his autobiography made clear that some sympathy for premillennialism had begun to develop. Watson noted that the "last twenty years" of the nineteenth century had seen a "blessed" growth of interest in "the near coming of the Lord, *into the air,* to gather up His Church—the Bride—when the dead in Christ and the living believers shall be caught up together, and so be ever with the Lord."[90] This premillennial coming, he explained,

> has grown and is still growing to be the great *hope* of the Church. It is not the hope of Christendom, it never will be, since Christendom, in the mass, has no living union with Christ. But the Church composed of truly regenerated souls, wherever found, —and there are some such in every section of the Evangelical Church (by which I mean, of course, so-called nonconformity and dissent, as well as Episcopalian, with some who are not identified with any section of the Christian Church)—is in more or less a waiting, watching attitude for the return of the Lord to the air.[91]

Watson concluded that "there is no truth which God has blessed in its preaching to the unconverted half so full of conviction and conversion as this truth of the Lord's near coming in His second advent."[92] No doctrine could do more to "quicken the life and service of God's real people like that of the near coming of the Lord," he believed.[93] Every "sign of the times," he concluded, "is surely but a sound of the returning footsteps of Him for whom we wait and watch."[94]

Watson later claimed that his prophetic beliefs had been settled around 1900, shortly after the completion of his second volume of autobiography.[95] His earlier prophetic convictions had been entirely conventional: "for the first twenty years, or more, of my own converted life, I held the view held by myriads of professing Christians, that there was but ONE *General Judgment,*" an opinion that lent itself equally to a postmillennial or amillennial position.[96] By the turn of the century, however, Watson had become a decided premillennialist. His comments were made in retrospect and sit somewhat uncomfortably with the content of his rapture novels and some later prophetic materials. Nevertheless, his series of prophetic novels—the trilogy, *Scarlet and Purple* (1913), *The Mark of the Beast* (1915) and *In the Twinkling of an Eye* (1916), and a later novel, *The New Europe: A Story of To-day and Tomorrow* (1918)—showed that Watson was prepared to be emphatic about his newfound faith.

Watson's prophecy trilogy was constructed to promote standard dispensational paradigms. It was published into a culture of intense prophetic concern. The novels reflect a situation in which the study of prophecy was burgeoning: there are now "myriads" of prophetic textbooks, according to one of Watson's characters.[97] But despite the popularity of the subject matter, Watson felt the need to defend his choice of genre. In fact, he noted, "the first and only real problem I had to face" when contemplating the production of prophetic fiction "was . . . the principle involved in using the fictional form to clothe so sacred a subject."[98] As Edmund Gosse remembered, the rejection of prose fiction was a significant element in the piety of many of Watson's fellow dispensationalists. And there is evidence to suggest that not all of Watson's readers were convinced by his approach. His preface to the second novel in the series continued to defend the fictional mode by appealing to a policy of pragmatism, asserting that "many thousands have read, and have been awakened, quickened, even converted" by the first novel and other evangelistic fictions.[99] Citing divine utility ("how wondrously God had owned and blessed" another example of Christian fiction) and the example of the parables (a book "written in the vein our Lord himself suggests . . . could not have been written in any other way"), Watson did more than any other to establish the basic contours and the stock characters and events of the prophecy fiction genre.[100]

Watson's characters set up a series of enduring precedents. The protagonist of the third novel, *In the Twinkling of an Eye,* is a thirty-year-old bachelor, a journalist named Tom Hammond, whose characterization is closely followed by his narrative equivalent in Left Behind.[101] Faced with sudden unemployment, Hammond is given the opportunity to launch a new daily newspaper, which rapidly becomes the most successful media outlet in the world.[102] One of its most popular features is a daily column, which Hammond writes, entitled "From the Prophet's Chair": "every editor," Hammond notes, "ought to have a strain of the seer."[103] Despite his interest in biblical prophecy, Hammond only slowly comes to embrace evangelical faith. His spiritual interests are quickened through his attending a number of afternoon lectures on biblical prophecy and through his increasingly romantic relationship with Zillah Robart, a Jew associated with a scheme to rebuild the Temple in Jerusalem. It was a signal of Watson's early commitment to political Zionism. The novel argues that "the first sign of [Christ's] return is an awakening of national life among the Jews, that shall immediately precede their return—in unbelief—to their own land."[104] Thus is established the genre's pattern of focusing on Jewish concerns—and Watson's portrayal of Jewish life is more extensive than any of the earlier novels.

Although the novels are optimistic about the future of the Jews, they reiterate the social pessimism of contemporary premillennialists. "The Bible nowhere gives a hint that the world is to be converted before the return of the Lord for His Church," one preacher opines in an overtly didactic passage in *In the Twinkling of an Eye;* "as a matter of fact, the world—the times—are to grow worse and worse; more

polished, more cultured, cleverer, better educated, yet grosser in soul, falser in worship."[105] This pessimism shapes Hammond's concern about the small numbers of
those likely to be involved in the rapture: "'If Christ came this instant,' he mused,
'how many of those Commoners and Peers would be ready to meet Him? And
what of the teeming millions of this mighty city? God help us all! What blind fools
we are!'"[106] Watson's reference to the "teeming millions" indicates his concerns
about urban deprivation and industrial squalor. His autobiography had claimed
that "my heart is in London," but Watson took no pleasure in the city's crowds; his
distrust of crowds had been influenced by his being involved as a boy in a riot.[107]
But Watson's memoirs and fiction are haunted by the thought of "London's teeming population."[108] The "hurly-burly of town and city rush," he claimed, was more
of a challenge to spirituality than the "silences and restfulness of rural scenes."[109]
The same pattern emerges in his prophecy novels, where London is described as
a "mighty Babylon" of vice and misery, and where, after the rapture, "the hordes
of the vicious that festered in the slums" would creep from their "filthy lairs" to
become a "menace to public life and property."[110] There is a hint, too, of social
critique in the narrative's note that "Hell had no shadow of terror to people who,
for years, had suffered the torments of a life in a literal hell in London."[111] Despite
these indications of social concern, the implied reader of Watson's novels is, to say
the least, socially conservative, expected to endorse the narrative's other references
to "coons" and "half-breeds."[112] Unlike evangelical leaders of the earlier nineteenth
century, however, Watson's novels proposed no remedy for the tensions of urban-
ization; the rapture was the only possible answer to the degeneration of society he
lamented.

The rapture is also presented as the only remedy to problems in the church.
Watson's novels complain that lower standards of holiness were crippling the evangelical denominations. "Certain religious and semi-religious journals," for example, discussed whether "*true* Christians could attend the Theatre and Music-Hall,"
but the fact that no one from "these London houses of amusement" was involved
in the rapture answered that question "as it has never been answered before."[113]
(Watson's autobiography had lamented his early exposure to music hall culture:
"I would have given my right hand, my right eye, to be delivered from the smirch
of these remembered things."[114]) Perhaps more serious were the explicit denials of
historic orthodoxy that were being tolerated in the name of theological Modernism.
In the "early part of the first decade of the twentieth century," Watson explained,
"men calling themselves Christians, taking the salaries of Christian ministers,
openly denied every fundamental truth of the Bible—Sin, the Fall, The Atonement,
The Resurrection, the Immaculate Birth of Christ, His Deity, the Personality of
Satan, the Personality of the Holy Spirit, and everything else in God's Word which
clashed with the flesh of their unregenerate lives."[115] This downgrade in doctrine

was accompanied by the loosening of distinctive denominational commitments, as ecumenism fostered changes in historical hymnody and tinkered with traditional liturgical texts.[116] Worse, however, was the Modernists' abuse of the Bible. Higher critics had brought about a "gradual decay of reverence for the Word of God," the novel complained; these were "men who broke Spurgeon's heart."[117] The rise of Modernism, with its denial of "every fundamental truth of the Bible," was a telling sign of the times. Watson, like many other evangelicals on both sides of the Atlantic, was acutely concerned by the ascent of liberal theology.

Watson's novels therefore emerge from an English evangelicalism that, at the beginning of the twentieth century, retained the social concern—if not the improving ambition—of the nineteenth-century evangelical reformers even as it was beginning to define itself in opposition to the social and theological mainstream. The novels identify their heroes as "ultra-protestants" adhering to a "Moody and Sankey religion."[118] But this evangelicalism is not associated with any particular denomination. Watson had earlier proclaimed his preference for being a "freelance" instead of a denominational stalwart. In the novels, any kind of denominational commitment is made impossible by the extent of ecclesiastical decay. "The Devil is a Ritualist," he claimed, but the sacramental trends of the Church of England were paralleled in the "Rationalism, Unitarianism, Socialism, etc., of Nonconformity," and "in many cases," he continued, the D.D. that adorned the titles of so many Nonconformist clergy might well indicate their status as "Deliberate Deniers."[119] This dismissal of the value of denominations was accompanied by Watson's increasing sense of the importance of a generic Protestantism—a trend which was also reflected in *The Fundamentals* and other prophecy novels. The term "Protestant" occurs only once in the two volumes of his autobiography, in which his spiritual development was partly traced in relation to Roman Catholic devotional material.[120] Twenty years later, in his prophetic fiction, Watson's opposition to Roman Catholicism had grown far more stringent: "no man breathing hates the foul *system* . . . more than the present speaker."[121] The novels vilify the Roman Catholic Church, and those "ultra-protestants" who resist her claims are represented as patriots as well as Puritans, for, echoing the language of an essay in volume eleven of *The Fundamentals*, "Romanism" had declared "its aim to win, or coerce Britain back into her harlot fold."[122] Watson's reading of the future was essentially Protestant and nationalist. "Rome's ultimate purpose," he claimed, "is to break the power of Britain."[123] Adhering to a long evangelical convention, Watson's "Romanism" was identified as an apocalyptic beast which had deliberately played down the eschatological consciousness of the early church fathers to stifle any recognition of her diabolic role in the latter times; and, as its influence advanced, "the looking for Christ's return died down."[124] The Roman Catholic Church had proved itself to be the inveterate enemy of prophetic truth, and Watson's prophecy fiction denounced its interventions.

In Watson's novels, therefore, the denominations can offer no solution to the decline of Christianity. The series imagines the pre-rapture faithful being led not by clergy but by the kind of respectable middle-class laity that had emerged to lead the Brethren and organize the major prophetic conferences. Conventional leadership roles were attributed to "a well-known military officer, a writer on prophecy" and "a well-known West End Christian doctor," but, as in other cultures of radical religion, Watson's prophetic movement also offered opportunities for female leadership.[125] As in his volumes of autobiography, Watson's novels allowed significant space for the autonomy of his female characters. Not many of Watson's clergy would be raptured, by contrast, and their failure to understand either the evangelical gospel or the dispensational paradigm would become one of the distinctive tropes of the genre; their post-rapture public confessions would emphasize the importance of prophetic knowledge and evangelical conversion.[126] Watson's second novel, *The Mark of the Beast,* for example, was dedicated to the Reverend G. Campbell Morgan, a contributor to *The Fundamentals* and a pulpit hero of London evangelicalism in the early decades of the twentieth century; but even then, on the first Sunday after the rapture, when one character goes to "a great Nonconformist church where one of London's most popular and remarkable preachers had ministered," he is surprised to discover that the church secretary is among the many left behind.[127] It was a narrative trope grounded in Watson's own experience: "I number among my personal friends, more than one devoted churchman, clergyman, who were not converted, not Born Again until years after they had been ordained."[128] Future writers would elaborate the theme.

Watson's novels were pessimistic about the political future, and their narratives echoed the concerns of the implied white, English, and middle-class reader. Despite Hammond's growing interest in Judaism and his romance with Robart, the novels' depictions of the tribulation dramatizes contemporary fears of Jewish internationalism and economic conspiracy even as they reflected with evident admiration on Jewish influences in politics, finance, and art.[129] Nevertheless, their description of the emerging political Zionism was evidently sympathetic, and they insisted on the importance of the Jewish future: "the politics of the world, of Europe especially, which ignores the Jews and Palestine, are politics which ignore God, because God's word is so plain as regards the final future of the world, that it is all centered in the Jew."[130] Nevertheless, the future of "the Jew" was bleak. *Titan*'s Antichrist had been identified as the resurrected Antiochus Epiphanes; Foster's Antichrist had been identified as the reincarnation of Nero; but Watson's novels were the first in the genre to present the Antichrist as a Jew, and they thank Campbell Morgan for the idea that the Antichrist would be Judas's reincarnation.[131] Whatever his identity, the Antichrist's rule would undercut the distinctive political identity of Britain. The "peoples of all the world" associated Britain with "safety and liberty," but the onset of the tribulation would put the British throne "under the supreme rule of a Jew" whose empire would be governed from his capital in Babylon.[132] Because his empire would be limited to the actual territory the Romans controlled, Ireland would finally gain home rule and, to fulfill other biblical prophecies, Jews would return to control the land of Palestine.[133] But they would be returning to intense persecution. Toward the end of the tribulation, "all the reigning Powers of the world will . . . be even more indebted to the Jews, financially, than even they are to-day, and whatever may be the *ostensible* cause for an almost universal out-break of Anti-Semitism, the *real* cause may either be an inability to pay their debts, or an unwillingness. The nations instigated by Antichrist, will therefore make a common cause against the Jew, in Jerusalem."[134] The tribulation would make clear that, whatever Watson's speculation about an international Jewish cabal and the power and influence of its wealthy elite, anti-Semitism was a hellish creed.

But the tribulation presented dangers for peoples of all faiths and none. Its changing political paradigm would be accompanied by religious and moral chaos. Women would almost universally take up smoking and marriage would be scorned, while the religious world would continue its drive toward a one-world religion mixing "Romanism, Spiritism (demonology), Theosophy, Materialism and other kindred cults" with liturgical music of a "sensuous, voluptuous character."[135] It is against this background of idolatry that the Antichrist would take his revenge on those whom the rapture had left behind and who had subsequently adopted the evangelical faith. Watson echoes the tradition of Reformation hagiography, recounting the "trio of Protestants" being taken "up the steps of the scaffold" to be beheaded.[136] The link between the Antichrist and the guillotine—emerging from the evangelical response to French revolutionary terror, echoed here, in successive rapture movies and in Left Behind—is explicit: "let's call a blade a blade."[137] No wonder the series provoked "hundreds of people" to contact Watson for further information.[138]

The question continually posed by Watson's novels therefore has more than theological overtones: "Think of what it will mean, unsaved friend, if you are . . . Left! Left behind!"[139] The appeal was urgent, for this terrible future was imminent. Writing in 1918, just two years after *In the Twinkling of an Eye*, Watson argued that the "approximate time" of the rapture could and should be calculated.[140] And he made public his conclusion: Christ's coming, he calculated, could not be any further than five years away.[141]

Watson's claim indicated that his prophetic trajectory was pushing him beyond dispensational orthodoxies. His admiration for the recently published *Scofield Reference Bible* was evident. It was, he claimed, "the last word in Bibles, until we get a perfect translation. The Notes and divisions of the 'Scofield Bible' seem, to the present writer to be as near perfect as can be."[142] Furthermore, in his prophetic novel *The New Europe* (1918), Watson used Scofield's notes to elaborate the dispensational scheme.[143] And yet, as his end-of-the-world calculations indicated,

Watson had definitively moved from the futurism of traditional dispensationalism to the system of historicism it had sought to replace. He calculated that the "times of the Gentiles" had ended in 1914 or 1915, and noted the "consensus of opinion of most prophetic scholars" that "a great European War would take place probably between 1912 and 1919, which should alter the whole map of Europe."[144] This was an easy claim to make in 1918, especially when the prophetic scholars on whose work the claim depended were not named. But, by combining this historicism with openness to the possibility of extra-biblical revelation, Watson was basing his claims on foresight rather than hindsight. *The New Europe* paid attention to a prophecy, reportedly dating from 1871, which predicted that

> in a score of years—perhaps a few more—there will be a great, last, gigantic struggle, which will be fought out to the death, amid scenes of carnage and bloodshed . . . The war will be between the Germanic nation on the one side, and . . . France and some of the Latin nations on the other side, with such decisive results that Germany will be completely defeated, and driven altogether across the Rhine; so that all the left bank of the Rhine, including Belgium, Luxembourg, and the Rhine provinces, will be annexed to France; for there is a revival of the old Roman Empire predicted in the Book of God—the Bible—and that prediction necessitates the extension of France to the Rhine, as its original frontier.[145]

The publication of this prophecy in *The New Europe* allowed Watson to confirm its truthfulness retrospectively in the aftermath of World War I. *The New Europe* was a late appendage to Watson's prophetic sequence and advanced a significant revision of some of his earlier claims. Unusually, Watson presented himself as a character in the final novel and presented his lectures on prophetic themes as profoundly impressing his learned and sophisticated audience. Twenty years after his two volumes of autobiography, Watson was still concerned to shape his public image. In his final prophetic novel, and as he calculated the date of the end, Watson fashioned himself as a prophet who could use the Bible with "unerring instinct."[146]

But infallibility was, of course, too large a claim to make. Watson's fictional avatar in *The New Europe* was shown to predict the coming and impact of World War I: "here we are in April of 1914 . . . Yet, probably before 1914 is out, certainly before 1915 is out, Europe will be in the throes of a war so awful; so general in its entanglements of the nations; so diabolically, hellishly cruel and hideous, that all the wars of all the previous world's-history [sic] will prove to have been but as school-boy play-ground fights compared with the coming great struggle."[147] The results of the struggle were certainly immense—but the novel's specific predictions were ultimately undermined. *The New Europe* claimed that the First World War would "change the Map of Europe, and make way for a great Super-man whom the

Bible calls the Antichrist," and that, after its conclusion, France would become "the most powerful nation in Europe, and, consequently, in the world."[148] But British Christians should be reassured, Watson continued. Christ's coming would be personal and premillennial, and the Bible never encouraged them to expect to die.[149] The rapture could not be far away.

Not everyone was convinced. Writing in the year in which *The New Europe* was published, a number of theologians at the University of Chicago argued that evangelical millennial hope was now "open to serious question. Can men today continue with confidence to expect a cataclysmic reversal of present conditions, or does the light of experience and present knowledge demand the adoption of a more constructive, though less spectacular, program for the renovation of the world?"[150] Watson would have found the sentiment only too familiar. "Traveling with the gospel, and speaking on this great Truth of the Second Coming continually," he considered, "one's heart is at once gladdened and saddened. Gladdened at the spirit of inquiry in so many, on this theme, but saddened at the rank infidelity on this subject, as well as the positive railing out against its preaching, by many, and even leaders of so-called Christian Churches."[151] Watson's prophetic trilogy, and *The New Europe*'s revisions of their earlier claims, provided the genre with its standard tropes and demonstrated its potential as a medium for an evangelical jeremiad. Even as Watson moved into historicism, the genre had completed its consolidation.

III

While these early prophecy novels illustrate the growing conservatism of the genre, they also demonstrate the extent to which many of its early authors were moving between and beyond eschatological paradigms. The American Civil War had confirmed Northern postmillennial hopes at the same time as it challenged Southern ideas of postmillennial progress, but Milton Stine, a Northern Lutheran, and Joshua Hill Foster, a Southern Baptist, both moved from postmillennialism to premillennialism in its aftermath. Watson moved from an undefined but conventional millennial tradition to an eccentric dispensationalism which combined admiration for the *Scofield Reference Bible* with elements of the date-setting historicism it deplored. Authors were also moving between ecclesiological positions. Foster abandoned his denomination for the emerging fundamentalist network, while Watson abandoned churches altogether and positioned himself as an ecclesiastical "free-lance." But these shifting eschatological and ecclesiastical loyalties merged with robustly patriotic themes. Foster wrote as an American, concerned by the threat of Southern European immigration to his national identity; Watson wrote as a Briton concerned by the threat of European Roman Catholicism, a politically powerful Judaism, and a militarily resurgent France. Foster wrote as an educated and conservative Southern gentleman, concerned by the fragility of the social status quo; Watson wrote as an uneducated Englishman whose ecclesiastical indifference was being contoured by an eccentric individualism and a lack of patience with such evangelical norms as the liturgical silence of women. Foster had been on a journey to dispensationalism; Watson and Stine were on a journey through it. Foster and Watson were evidencing the consolidation of dispensationalism; but Watson's *The New Europe* was paying homage to the *Scofield Reference Bible* even as it was deconstructing its central ideas.

But that is not how Watson has been remembered. Of all the early prophecy novels, it was Watson's earlier trilogy that was most widely distributed and, as the century progressed, most often reprinted.[152] Burroughs, Stine, and Foster never gripped the imagination of the evangelical reading public in quite the same way. Perhaps the issue was theological—although the commendation by James M. Gray provided a degree of respectability to Burroughs's earlier eccentricities, the increasing scholasticism of dispensational thinking and its regular identification with a well-defined fundamentalism pushed conservative evangelicals away from the kind of intellectual latitude that Burroughs's novel had embraced. Evangelicals could not allow any speculation about alternative varieties of Christology when the foundations of their faith were under serious attack.[153] This was certainly a transitional moment. Early prophecy novels were published in a period in which it was still possible for evangelicals to imagine that the dispensational explanation for the rapture would be easily accepted by the social and political mainstream. Nevertheless, the cultural inflections of the novels by Burroughs, Stine, and Foster demonstrated that their work was emerging from "the last years of Protestant America," and Watson's novels demonstrated that British evangelicals were also being increasingly identified as "superstitious, ignorant fanatics."[154] In Britain and the United States, traditionally minded evangelical believers—like characters in their prophecy novels—had "never known of conditions so alarming."[155] And so they must have seemed. These early prophecy novels were being published as an old American world—the world of white, Anglo-Saxon Protestant dominance— was coming to an end. And, despite the popularity of Sydney Watson's claims to the contrary, no one knew what might happen next.

3

Prophecy Fiction and
the Second World War

We do not know what the next news flash will bring.
—Ernest W. Angley, *Raptured* (1950)

The social uncertainty of the early writers of prophecy novels was reflected by many outside their conservative Protestant world. Other writers, sharing few of their religious commitments, were using similar language to narrate their concerns about modernity—and they also discovered that disaster sold. Sidney Fowler Wright (1874–1965) was one of the most successful writers of secular apocalypse. His novel, *Deluge* (1927), was a tale of survival after rapidly rising water levels destroyed vast swathes of civilization. The novel had been optioned by RKO Radio Pictures and, largely on the strength of this market potential, was published to commercial success and significant critical acclaim.[1] Press releases boasted—erroneously, as it later emerged—that this was the first book to have an initial American printing of 100,000 copies. In England, reviewers claimed that 70,000 copies had been sold on the day of publication. London's *Daily Express* hailed Fowler Wright as one of "the ten best brains in Britain." Yet the biblical and cultural contexts of his novel were obvious. Fowler Wright had been brought up as a Baptist but had moved toward agnosticism. His fear of a "deluge" may not have emphasized the dangers of the "sea of faith," but neither did his agnosticism construct any hostility toward organized religion. *Deluge* drew on Protestant expectations of apocalyptic disaster—and nowhere more obviously than when identifying one character as a "Plymouth

Sister."[2] In a fictional description of a global apocalypse, the reference was a significant nod toward the end-time speculations of the movement from which dispensationalism had emerged. In one of the best-selling novels of the period, Protestant fundamentalists were identified as possessing a significant—and often controversial—apocalyptic imagination.

The fundamentalist imagination developed rapidly through the early decades of the twentieth century, and prophecy fiction increasingly reflected the movement's new orthodoxies. Sydney Watson's novels were regularly reprinted throughout the 1920s and 1930s, but they appeared increasingly anachronistic in those decades of change and challenge—and not only because of Watson's failed prophecy of the second coming. Shocked by public responses to the Scopes trial, evangelicals on both sides of the Atlantic began to retreat from the cultural mainstream to develop alternative institutions and media. But the movement was evolving through a period of momentous social change. In the later 1930s, the Great Depression swept through Europe and North America, and Western nations were preparing themselves for the possibility of another European conflict. In the aftermath of the Scopes trial, and the creeping influence of the Modernism the trial was believed to represent, popular Protestantism had begun to fragment. Fundamentalists retreated to the cultural margins, building a reactionary orthodoxy out of the materials of *The Fundamentals,* which they wedded, increasingly, to dispensational premillennialism. Others regrouped as neo-evangelicals, developing a series of institutions such as Wheaton College and *Christianity Today,* preparing to rethink at a foundational level the cultural implications of the dispensational faith.[3] Some of the movement's most significant voices were beginning to emerge, including Billy Graham, who was to preach to more individuals than anyone else in history, and Carl F. H. Henry, whose study of *The Uneasy Conscience of Modern Fundamentalism* (1947) was to underpin the new mood of faith-based cultural engagement. Prophecy novels took sides in the division of popular conservative Protestantism. They reflected the times from which they emerged. Those novels published after the 1910s worked hard to invest in the genre a higher degree of theological respectability. They were significantly less likely to refer to the "gap theory" and were much more likely to carefully follow the increasingly codified dispensational scheme. This doctrinal redaction was a sign of the slow eclipse of the original *Scofield Reference Bible.* Later novels were much more likely to be published by mainstream or denominational publishers, had clearer cross-denominational networks in which to circulate, and enjoyed a generally higher media profile that meant they were much more aware of each other. As the 1940s developed, a distinctive genre of prophecy fiction was beginning to emerge.

These were fruitful times for prophetic study. Prophecy novels, which had always acted as barometers of evangelical cultural change, provided evidence of their authors' deep uncertainties as to the relationship between fundamentalism, neo-evangelicalism and the evolving cultural mainstream. The changing expectations of the number of those who would be included in the rapture emerged as a significant indicator of the degree of tension perceived by the novelists and the culture they sought to represent. None of these novels sold as many copies as *Deluge*, but they reinforced Fowler Wright's connection between conservative Protestant religion and an acute sense of social despair.

I

In 1937, *Be Thou Prepared for Jesus Is Coming* was published by Forrest Loman Oilar (1880–1971). Oilar, who was in his late fifties when his novel appeared, was a conservative Presbyterian whose writing reflected an eclectic fundamentalism, the antiformal theology that marked so many of the prophecy novelists of the period and that was institutionalized in the militantly anti-Modernist Bible Presbyterian Church.[4] Like many other Bible Presbyterians, Oilar appeared skeptical of claims to faith within the ecclesiastical mainstream. His characters attend "missions" rather than denominational churches, for example, and it is in mainstream churches that they believe doctrinal heresy can most clearly be observed.[5] Modernism seems ubiquitous in his narrative world. The novel writes off denominational clergy as those who "served for material gain and . . . denied the Deity of Jesus Christ."[6] They are also represented as those who shirked their pastoral task. "Millions" of the members of mainstream denominations "had gone through the form of being baptized and had tithed and . . . given alms to the poor," but, the novel laments, had never been "born again."[7] It was a depressing analysis of the state of the Christian church. Oilar, like many other Presbyterian fundamentalists, was writing in self-conscious opposition to the denominational mainstream and the theological decay it seemed to represent. Like many other writers in the genre, he had some experience of publication before his turn to prophecy fiction. That experience does not seem to have been directly related to the prophecy fiction project—his only other book appears to have been *How to Buy Furniture for the Home* (1913)—but there is some evidence that this interest in interior design made an impact on his eschatological thinking. He had no hesitation, for example, in believing that John 14:2 implied the existence of literal "mansions" in heaven, though this aspiration for heavenly possessions might also reflect his concern about the effect of the Great Depression.[8]

Be *Thou Prepared* was published by the Meador Publishing Company in Boston, and sold at two dollars per copy. An advertising flyer produced by Meador was a clear signal of the publisher's total lack of genre consciousness: it suggested that the novel represented "something new and entirely foreign in the scope of fiction."[9] Of course, this claim, if it represented anything more than publishers' hyperbole, was not true, but it could hardly have been made if the publishers expected that the novel would be compared with earlier examples in the genre. Oilar's novel, like others that preceded it, described in fairly standard terms the impact of the rapture and the subsequent rise of the Antichrist. It was evidently creative, containing some of the most unusual prose in the genre, and was regularly humorous. But it is not clear, even on its own terms, how Oilar's novel could have been described as "new and entirely foreign." The novel pushed into the foreground its dependence on existing publications and emphasized its utilitarian purpose. When Oilar paused to explain his dispensational theology, he, like Joshua Hill Foster and Sydney Watson, drew explicitly on the *Scofield Reference Bible*'s language.[10] Elsewhere, his chapters end with explanatory notes that quote specific expositors, such as Walter Scott and A. C. Gaebelein, in support of unusual ideas.[11] *Be Thou Prepared* was advertised as providing a "synthetic panorama of the countless analytical works of the most outstanding Bible students."[12] Like Foster, Oilar was prepared to list their names, but if Foster's work reflected the conclusions of a broad range of prophetic writers, Oilar's list was more clearly dominated by popular premillennialists. Pre-eminent among their number was W. E. Blackstone, author of the best-seller *Jesus Is Coming* (1898), but the list also included such luminaries as C. I. Scofield, James M. Gray, who had commended Burroughs's *Titan,* R. A. Torrey, D. L. Moody, A. C. Gaebelein, "C. H. M.," the Plymouth Brethren writer, and among the younger generation of prophecy scholars, Charles E. Fuller, an increasingly influential radio evangelist, and Louis Sperry Chafer, who had founded the Evangelical Theological College (which was to become Dallas Theological Seminary) in 1924.[13] Only one of the authors listed by Oilar was identified as anything other than premillennial, and that was Matthew Henry, the late seventeenth-century Bible commentator. But while Oilar's narrative listed these influences, it was quite prepared to go beyond the strict futurism they tended to share. Oilar described contemporary America as a nation in the grip of economic distress and a land in which ancient predictions were coming to pass. Witnessing the breakdown of traditional authority, it seemed to Oilar as if "prophecies are being fulfilled every day before our blind eyes."[14] *Be Thou Prepared* was not intended to be read for pleasure. "Every Christian will read it with delight and inspiration," but "every non-Christian who reads it will receive a new line of thought" and "every Jew will learn the scriptural teaching as to Israel's part in God's great plan after the Church is removed from the world."[15] It was a significant undertaking and Oilar recognized the research contributions provided by his wife and son. Harold Randolph Oilar had provided "gleaning material" for his father's novel, but, almost two decades after its publication, in late December 1954, as a rug dealer at the age of thirty-nine, and after his family's carol singing with the daughter of a professor at the dispensational and Presbyterian Highland College, he gained a wider notoriety when he murdered his wife and three children in Pasadena, California.[16] His father would never share the same degree of fame.

But that tragedy could not have been anticipated in the mid-1930s, when Forrest Oilar was researching the plot that he hoped would "synthesize" the best ideas of the most reliable prophetic commentators. Whatever Oilar claimed about his novel's dispassionate synthesis of the idea of eminent scholars, *Be Thou Prepared* made a number of calculated interventions of its own. Some of these were quite general in scope: one character learns from an angel that the crucifixion occurred on a Wednesday instead of a Friday, and that Jesus was resurrected on Saturday rather than a Sunday.[17] It was not a point that had any direct bearing on the prophetic narrative, but it was made repeatedly during the early part of the century by such hyper-dispensationalists as E. W. Bullinger and would continue to appear as the prophecy novel genre evolved.[18] Other interventions were specifically eschatological. The novel was pointedly uninterested in some of the key prophetic debates, including, for example, the debate about the identity of Antichrist. While many prophetic commentators suggested that the Antichrist might be "the Pope of Rome," Oilar believed their expectations were to be disappointed, for "the Pope received his exaltation and authority as the substitute of Christ, and not as His opponent."[19] Others had "thought that he might turn out to be one resurrected from the dead, perhaps Judas Iscariot reincarnated in the flesh"—as G. Campbell Morgan and Sydney Watson had earlier suggested. Others "thought he would be Emperor Nero brought to life by the devil"—as Joshua Hill Foster had claimed. But Oilar dismissed this "speculation." "No one could know what the all-wise God had seen fit to conceal in His Word," he explained, for before the rapture it was simply impossible to know who the Antichrist would turn out to be.[20] Similarly, Oilar was ambivalent about the possibility of the second chance for salvation for those who had rejected the gospel before the rapture. He did not rule out the possibility altogether, but was sure that those who had already rejected the gospel "will have little further hope of salvation."[21] There is "nothing in the Bible that promises any hope of salvation for those who have had their chance and refused it."[22] Only Jews could be given a second chance to respond to the faith they had earlier rejected—but even that second chance was a matter of serious doubt.[23]

Oilar was not afraid to pronounce on other, equally contested, issues. The material context of the Great Depression loomed large in his narrative, and, like other of the early prophecy novelists, he displayed deep hostility to the structures of market capitalism.[24] The novel explained that the mergers and acquisitions of big business had been foreseen and condemned in Isaiah 5:8–9 and that large-scale unemployment—which had become "nothing short of a tragedy"—was the fulfillment of another biblical prophecy.[25] In fact, the novel continued, the robber barons were even responsible for the rise of Communism and other political dangers of the period. "Capital had tried to rule labor, causing wars," and those wars had been "the result of selfishness since the beginning of time, until communism, socialism, fascism, bolshevism and radical unions all shared in the revolt."[26] The Great Depression therefore represented a peculiar series of dangers for small businessmen of Oilar's ilk: "competition was keener, unions were more exacting, strikes were raging; taxes, rent and cost of operating business grew in proportion each year."[27] Economic necessity drove Christian businessmen into Sabbath violation and ultimately pushed them out of business, as the robber barons initiated "a battle of brains and capital, until it seemed that the small independent dealer, with limited facilities, was doomed."[28] The unholy trinity of "taxes, interest and the insurance premium" was crippling small business, Oilar complained.[29] How attractive these conditions made the rapture, when "all of those who had believed in Christ" would be "released from worries, poverty, sickness, disease and all other irritating thorns, which included mortgages, taxation and loss of material possessions."[30] And how terrible would be the fate of those left behind, when insurance companies would refuse to pay out life insurance for those whose bodies had disappeared during the rapture, when bank failures and associated privations would drive Oilar's characters into pyramid fraud and Ponzi schemes, and when the Antichrist's rule would be marked by such specific evils as the impositions of additional taxes.[31] But economic changes could not be avoided—even in the millennium. Jesus Christ would adopt many of the same policies that had caused misery in the 1930s and again under the Antichrist's rule. He would become the new economic dictator, announcing a program for global currency, the nationalization of American industry and compulsory disarmament. The Savior of the world was being identified as a socialist. And yet, "as an economist," he would be "an adept. All enterprises such as manufacturing, shipping, mining, banking, and building" would be "under his jurisdiction." The "money of the world" would be "trusted to one exchequer."[32] But there would be one major difference between his regime and that of the robber barons: Jesus Christ would charge no tax.[33]

Economic difficulties were not Oilar's only signs of the times. Changes in the media were another indication of American moral decay. Before the rapture, the sober tones of Christian publications competed with the noise and glare of the jazz age, with all of its "dances, playing cards, smoking and tearing around."[34] The novel's believers are shown to be hostile to the moral impact of radio broadcasting. One character opined that the radio's "jazz-coughing gives my brain the galloping rheumatism."[35] Its "abominable, nerve wracking jazz" was "the curse of the age."[36] Nor were things any better in the newspapers. In a rare meta-textual gesture, one character is shown reading an article that shared the novel's title—"Be thou prepared."[37] And one major New York newspaper certainly followed its advice, printing an article on the rapture it had kept on file in case it should ever be required.[38] The novel complained that even those editors who "occasionally quote from the Bible" rarely offered any comment on the second coming. But even this rare moment of media sympathy for evangelical Christianity disappears during the tribulation, when newspapers would be dominated by the Antichrist, when editorials would be "stereotyped" to concur with his decrees, and when one popular newspaper would be known as the *Godless Gazette*.[39] *Be Thou Prepared* was therefore insisting on the need for the development of new media, whose moral content and editorial approach could be determined by believers. But they had a good substitute at hand if that project should fail: "My Bible is my newspaper and predicts, exactly, as to events and time."[40]

Oilar's insistence on "the Bible only" was highly problematic—not least in light of his earlier listing of recommended prophetic expositors, whose best ideas he claimed to combine. Oilar was prepared to use these texts to stand against the much longer tradition of Protestant apocalyptic thinking. We have already noted that the novel argued against the traditional Protestant opinion that the pope should be identified as the Antichrist—an opinion Oilar shared with the majority of the expositors he listed. Nevertheless, the novel reflected the increasingly Protestant identity of the genre by displaying overt hostility toward the Roman Catholic Church. Oilar remembered its persecution of Protestants during the Reformation and argued that later Catholicism had become a "most powerful force" alongside "apostate Protestant Christendom."[41] *Be Thou Prepared* suggested that the dangers of Roman Catholicism could be seen even by the Antichrist, who would attempt to destroy the "*Papal ecclesiastical system,* the Babylonic bride of Antichrist" some time before Jesus Christ would finally extinguish the "harlot . . . of Babylonic confederated religious systems" in which the Roman Catholic Church had played a principal part.[42] Oilar was also prepared to explore in thoughtful detail some of the less precise assertions of earlier writers. He agreed that the rapture would involve "all children below the age of accountability," but he recognized what this might mean for a mother delivering multiple births: "Twins were born. One came into the world a few seconds before the Rapture and was taken, the other, a few seconds after and remained."[43] He was also concerned by the impact of the rapture on animals and domestic pets. The disappearances of the rapture left many "horses running around without drivers and . . . many strange automobile accidents."[44] Similarly shocking was the discovery of "many pets . . . found dead, shut in the homes of the departed saints."[45] The emphasis on animals is made significant: the Antichrist's cruelty is particularly marked by his treatment of the pet animals of a poor beggar boy.[46]

For all its concern for animals, however, *Be Thou Prepared* was ambivalent on the question of race. The novel was occasionally forward-thinking. One white character remembers an "old, coloured Callicot" who engaged in date-setting speculations, but the link between African ancestry and religious unreliability is balanced by a description of the rapture of another "negro," who disappears at exactly the moment he is about to be lynched by an angry white mob.[47] An undertone in the novel is progressive on themes of racial justice, but it is less clear about the evils of anti-Semitism. While all of its major characters are Jewish or Jewish converts to Christianity, the novel is troubled by the issues raised by their characterization. It appears to straightforwardly condemn anti-Semitism, which, at times, is clearly identified as satanic.[48] Anti-Semitism is certainly opposed by Jesus Christ, who rescues one Jewish character from racial persecution.[49] Similarly, Jesus judges the Gentile nations according to their treatment of the Jews, and to those "goat nations" who failed to recognize their status as the chosen people he assigns the fate that Jewish people had formerly endured, as he scatters them among the nations.[50] But this reference to judgment suggests that the "unmerciful persecution" of the Jewish people had also been "a judgment sent upon them for their disobedience and for their denunciation of Jesus Christ."[51] The novel sympathized with Jewish people, but identified them as guilty of the ultimate crime. It was easy, therefore, for *Be Thou Prepared* to go on to imagine a high-level and international conspiracy, in which Jews "had for centuries secretly and underhandedly striven to control a world system which would overrule Gentile governments."[52] Even the "high finances" that brought ruin during the Great Depression "had been promulgated by their shrewd practices."[53] And the novel could not imagine that its Jewish characters could escape their guilt. One Jewish character remembers another "gazing blankly into the distance, probably thinking of the profit and loss account."[54] It is perhaps the novel's most singular moment of abjection, when a Jewish character himself perpetuates the ancient racial stereotypes. But the novel's final rejection of anti-Semitic violence is most clearly exemplified by its being associated with the Antichrist. In a litany of horrors—one of the longest lists in a book that is full of lists—Oilar records the persecution of those Jews who accept Jesus as Messiah:

> They've had the same terrible punishment as the early Christian martyrs did, suffering such things as being skinned or scalped alive, having hands cut off, eyes plucked out, being hanged in every possible position, stabbed, burned at the stake, having melted lead poured into open wounds, the baring of the shin bones, the cutting out of tongues for having preached the truth, and they deprived others of their sight, on account of them having read the Bible, and others were boiled ... thrown from tops of buildings or bridges, fed to hogs or wild animals, brains fried, nails of fingers and toes torn off with red hot pincers, tied and dragged by automobiles, with cords drawn so tight that the head came off; some had their breasts cut off and fried and fed to people, holes bored through heels, ropes put

through and dragged, legs of whole families cut off, points of swords bored through ears and feet, heads of suckling babies cut off and fastened to mother's breasts . . . heads paraded through the cities on long poles, and others were buried alive, noses and ears cut off, drowned, soaked in oil and burned, limbs pulled off, blown from cannon, hanged and quartered, teeth beaten from sockets, boiling tar poured on feet, faces smashed, ropes placed around necks of victims with the other end fastened to bridges and the body thrown off, heads snapped off . . .[55]

It was a litany of terror from the father of a future ax murderer. But while some Jews suffer this catalogue of extraordinary punishment, others find refuge in Moab—a version of the Petra myth, which emerges in later novels—where English missionaries had left Bibles for the Jewish remnant to find.[56] The novel insists that persecuted Jews would find safety in conversion to the Christian faith. But only in the millennium will the Jewish nation finally repent.[57]

Be Thou Prepared is perhaps the most overtly supernatural of the early prophecy novels. At times, its interest in angelic and demonic encounters makes it appear strangely similar to later work by Frank Peretti. There was no obvious source for these ideas in the literary culture of dispensationalism. When Jane Kolzon is locked up on the Antichrist's orders and is tempted to suicide by a demon who appears in her cell, for example, an angel takes her back in time to witness the crucifixion.[58] The angel then takes Jane to hell, where she learns about its geography and its population—over ten million and counting.[59] Jane is taken into heaven, to witness the "marriage supper of the Lamb" and raptured saints dressed in white, where she discovers that its population of over one hundred million is made up of "born again" Christians who, in a series of fundamentalist concerns, "had trusted for salvation in the virgin birth, vicarious death and the physical resurrection of the Lord Jesus Christ."[60] The number of the saved could not be counted. All in all, the novel reckons, when the population explosion of the millennium is taken into account, fully seventy-five percent of the human race will enter heavenly bliss.[61]

But Oilar was sure which nations would be under-represented. At the beginning of the novel, one character suggests that one quarter of global population could be involved in the rapture.[62] But this estimate—vastly greater than anything previously imagined in the prophecy fiction tradition—does not appear to be confirmed. Instead, a huge proportion of the global population unites in opposition to Jesus Christ. The Antichrist bases his world empire in Rome, revives and directs the old Roman Empire and, in a startling anticipation of the next world war, demonstrates an unhealthy interest in military technology.[63] It was a reflection of the tense years of the late 1930s and a reminder of the fascination with weaponry that had long pervaded the genre: "Every conceivable kind of scientifically made firearm and motor tank was being corralled by the Antichrist. The world's chemical factories, munitions plants and factories for the manufacture of arms were humming day and night. Such death-dealing instruments had never before been employed. Gigantic fast-moving aircrafts were built to transport whole armies. Electric death rays and powerful gases, capable of instantly destroying millions of men, whole cities, fleets of ships and planes, hundreds of miles away, had been patented."[64] These weapons are amassed for the final battle at Armageddon, which assembles "the greatest array ever . . . for warfare": "the supply of T.N.T., cyanide of potassium, phosgene, and thermite gases was unlimited. Big Bertha, of German fame, was a toy in comparison to some of the dinosaur weapons assembled for this war. There were miles and miles of tanks and armored cars, field guns and howitzers, and the air was dark with tens of thousands of airplanes, dirigibles and captive balloons equipped with powerful gas bombs."[65] But, even as he nodded toward the military technology of the First World War, Oilar anticipated the themes of cold war prophecy fiction. Satan's "communistic system" would continue to develop.[66] Even at the end of the millennium, when Satan would precipitate the final rebellion, he would find that the Russians were still his "most faithful servants."[67]

II

This insistence on the dangers of Communism was reiterated four years later, when Dayton A. Manker, president of the North Michigan Conference of the Wesleyan Methodist Church, published *They That Remain: A Story of the End Times* (1941).[68] Manker was an experienced evangelist, who had toured extensively as a preacher promoting the Wesleyan faith. But, in the depressed circumstances of the later 1920s, he experienced a number of events that confirmed his prophetic expectations. Social conditions were not encouraging: "in the last decade," he wrote, "greedy capitalists have demoralized youth with filthy movies, literature, art; demon inspired intellectuals have written text-books for the schools teaching that man is merely a higher type of animal—not a created, immortal soul; and parents relaxing home authority, have submitted their children to the trend of demoniacal influences, frequently taking the lead into the vortex of social debauchery."[69] The tide seemed to be turning against the faithful. In August, 1928, Manker and another Methodist minister were preaching in a "little Holiness mission" in Sault Ste. Marie, Michigan, when they met with "something that in all the four years of our extension work was new to us."[70] Manker's colleague reported that "souls were praying through"—a euphemism in his writing for the loud and sometimes riotous scenes of worship that characterized "revival" activities—when their tent was surrounded by an angry mob. Manker later reflected that "the laws of sin and death" would continue to "fill the world with the harassments common to man" for as long as "Jesus delays His return to earth."[71] And so it seemed that night. The police arrived, but instead of defending the rights of the worshippers they "joined with the mob, made a raid on the altar service and broke up the meeting." They threatened to jail the preachers, but, one day later, admitted that they had violated the rights of American citizens to worship "freely and in a respectable, open and above board manner."[72] Manker and his colleague had no doubt about the significance of the event: the suspension of constitutional entitlements proved that "the tribulation is near at hand."[73]

It was this kind of prophetic perspective that was promoted in *They That Remain*. The novel was, Manker later claimed, an unexpected success. The first edition, with a print run of "about 2,500 copies," sold out more rapidly than he had expected.[74] It had been published by Zondervan Publishing House, a young but rapidly growing company based in Grand Rapids, Michigan. The company had been established in 1931—soon after Pat Zondervan had been fired by his uncle, the eponymous director of the William B. Eerdmans Publishing Company, which was beginning to position itself as a major part of the newly reinvented evangelical movement.[75] The decision by Zondervan to publish Manker's book appears, in retrospect, somewhat surprising. Its founders belonged to the Christian Reformed Church, a denomination of composed mainly of Dutch immigrants that maintained a robust Calvinism alongside a confessional commitment to an amillennial eschatology. Manker's book, by contrast, was emphatically premillennial and clearly Arminian in tone. Elsewhere, he was quite prepared to denounce the faith articulated by his publishers' nonfiction titles. He wondered, for example, whether the Calvinist doctrine of "eternal security" was a heresy worse than those promulgated by the Roman Catholic Church, and he later described the Calvinist system as a "philosophy of fatalism" derived from ideas of a "relentless Sovereign, capricious and unpredictable."[76]

It is not clear why the Zondervan brothers should have found his prophetic narrative appealing. Perhaps they hoped its publication would intervene in the debate about prophecy that had recently preoccupied their denomination. The Christian Reformed Church had suffered a damaging split in the late 1910s, with the loss of a number of pastors who were committed to the dispensational faith, as the denomination came to understand itself as "an American church in the Reformed tradition."[77] But even in the aftermath of that debate, the denomination had refused to adopt an official position on dispensationalism, and the issue was to resurface later in the 1940s when Diedrich Kromminga, one of the professors at the denomination's college, Calvin Theological Seminary, wrote *The Millennium in the Church: Studies in the History of Christian Chiliasm* (1945) and *The Millennium, Its Nature, Function and Relation to the Consummation of the World* (1948). Both of these titles were published by William B. Eerdmans, and their advocacy of premillennialism prompted significant disquiet within the denomination, as well as the final possibility of a formal institutional response.[78] Zondervan's decision to publish Manker's novel may therefore have been intended to call attention to the doctrinal diversity that the Christian Reformed Church still maintained, or merely to signal the interest in fiction that would also be demonstrated in their decision to publish four hundred novels, and sponsor five international creative writing competitions, between 1945 and 1959.[79] Whatever its intention, Zondervan's decision to publish Manker's novel illustrates the steady movement of American evangelicals from ethnic toward generic theologies, just as Milton Stine's decision to abandon the progressive American Lutheranism had earlier suggested.

Whatever the reason for its publication, Manker's book was a resounding success, generating rapid sales and a number of reported conversions.[80] Manker eventually decided that the time was right for a second edition, but the Zondervan plates had been melted down, and a second, reset, edition was eventually published in 1946 by a smaller organization, the Sunshine Book and Bible House, in Cincinnati, Ohio.[81] The new edition was certainly directed at a very specific reading audience. In its preface, Manker emphasized that the decision to reprint had been supported by the Reverend William Beirnes, the editor of the premillennial journal *The Midnight Cry*, in an obvious gesture of appeal to that journal's readers. But this decision to operate within a much more specifically premillennial network required some justification of Manker's specific exegetical decisions. He wrote with some apparent awareness of the history of the genre. His Antichrist borrows titles from Burroughs's novel when he reveals himself as "Titan, son of Saturn, Apollyon, Beast, Man of Sin, Antichrist!"[82] But Manker was also quite prepared to diverge from the tradition he owned. "Opinions are jumbled as to pre-rapture events," he admitted, but he insisted that "the general pattern of Pre-millennial doctrine is clearly outlined in the word of God."[83]

They That Remain evidenced the first sustained fears of the rapture's impact on an increasingly irreligious America. Like the earlier novels, the rapture would involve "comparatively few" people but, unlike earlier novels, the character of the event would not immediately be understood.[84] Manker imagined that newspaper accounts would describe the rapture as "America's most baffling catastrophe," "our American Mystery," "something the like of which had been unheard of in all the annals of time."[85] It was a telling observation of an increasingly secular culture. Nevertheless, as in Oilar's *Be Thou Prepared*, one newspaper prints a preprepared article that explains the religious significance of the event.[86] *They That Remain* was also the first to imagine that the rapture would be followed by widespread accidents as a consequence of the disappearance of Christians. As the world grew more automated, the possible impact of the rapture began to increase: "Airplanes may drop pilot-less to the ground, horses may suddenly become riderless, automobiles may crash crazily into store fronts, trees, etc., locomotives may thunder in mad run-away past signal blocks, and, exhausting their power, stop or crash in some tremen-dous wreck."[87] Perhaps the impact of World War II had emphasized the dangers of the newly technological world. But these disasters also provided their Christian readers with a fantasy of their importance in this increasingly secular age—for, it explained, whatever their feelings of marginalization, Christian believers were an essential constituency that the world could not live without. The myth—which would be developed in future writing on the theme—implied that it was Chris-tians who held together the crucial infrastructure of society. *They That Remain* was the first example in the genre to work from clear assumptions of evangelical marginality.

Manker was in some senses an easy sell for a publisher—and not just because of his narrative innovations. He was established as an author long before the pub-lication of his first novel, and his prominence within the North Michigan Con-ference of the Wesleyan Methodist Church was long-standing. His earlier work had been uniformly exhortatory, though its interests in genre and subject had var-ied enormously. This earlier work had also been consistently ephemeral. *Danc-ing School Days, Open Letter to an Unsaved Youth of a Christian Home, Rings, Robes, and Righteousness, Parson Putter-heels* and *Old Wire-whiskers Gets a Shave* were advertised in the front matter of the novel alongside *Youth's Dreamtime*, a forty-six-page exhortatory booklet that, among other things, encouraged girls to wear dresses that had "sleeves enough to cover the fleshly upper arm," that were "high enough in the neck to cover the bosom completely in all positions" and that were "long enough to keep the legs covered as far as below the knees ALL THE TIME."[88] Like Sydney Watson before him, Manker was turning from the produc-tion of exhortatory, inspirational, and sentimental prose to stridently apocalyptic fiction. And Manker's interest in eschatology was to continue. Future books were to include a revision of his earlier eschatology in *Invasion from Heaven* (1979) and a consideration of eschatological anthropology in *The Return to Majesty: Essays on Original and Ultimate Man* (1989). But he did not witness the full impact of the genre to which he had contributed. Manker died in 1994, before the first signs of the dominance of the genre whose narrative patterns he had helped to shape.[89]

They That Remain clearly reflected its author's Methodist commitments. Like Oilar, Manker invested his narrative with discussions of his preferred spiritual-ity.[90] He emphasized emotional volatility. True repentance would be evidenced in "weeping and praying" and "shouts of holy joy."[91] One character's renewed commitment to Christ is displayed as she "laughed and shouted and cried with so many and inexplainable [*sic*] emotions."[92] As in Watson's autobiography, holy laughter—here described as "Holy Hilarity"—is represented as a key indicator of authentic spiritual life.[93] Manker's Methodist sympathies were similarly expressed in his novel's theology. Characters are described as losing their salvation, and one backslidden Christian finds that her sin had caused her to be excluded from the rapture.[94] But this Arminian theology exists in tension with the strongly deterministic character of the novel's prophetic narrative. God is shown to struggle to impose his will at an individual level—he makes "one last stupendous effort" to save one individual—but even the novel's Antichristian characters learn that it is "no easy task to defeat and destroy the influence of Jehovah God."[95] The novel never pauses to explain why God can be resisted by the individual but not by humanity in the collective, when, in both cases, human will is the only barrier to his achieving his ends. Nevertheless, *They That Remain* displays a clear trajectory in the restriction of human agency. The plot moves from the comic to the tragic form as characters discover that they possess decreasing volitional options. "In sober moments," one character began to realize that Apollyon was the anticipated Antichrist, but also discovered that "there was no way to turn for escape from the miserable present or threatening future."[96] Manker's novel was unable to maintain its theology of resistance to the divine will. Its plot drives toward increasing closure. Although humanity had been "free to choose . . . and unhindered in . . . wicked devices," God had finally "taken a decisive grip upon the affairs of men."[97] Manker's novel, the first to clearly address the problem of agency within the dispensational framework, illustrated the manner in which the mode of prophetic fiction could drive authors toward a kind of theological determinism they might elsewhere attempt to avoid.

Manker's authorial purpose did not appear to be evidently evangelistic. He denied the possibility of a second chance to those who had rejected the gospel before the rapture.[98] He introduced this innovation as one well-acquainted with the literature of the premillennial tradition. *They That Remain* reflected his concern that "sermons and literature concerning the Second Coming of Christ too often become obsolete" in this "rapidly changing world."[99] But his novel, Manker hoped, would be an exception to this rule. Its first edition had been published before the American intervention in World War II in December 1941. Its second edition—published soon after the cessation of European hostilities—addressed a markedly different environment.[100] Though the novel had been "copyrighted in 1941," Manker thought its contents still "very readable" in 1946. His insistence on the novel's continuing relevance indicated his refusal to read the world war or its atomic conclusion in the apocalyptic terms that others had come to adopt. The cessation of conflict did not require any changes to his proposed prophetic system or to the narrative he had woven around it. The world had endured "the greatest war in history," and had witnessed the deployment of weaponry of unprecedented power, but, Manker considered, "one may still read this book and feel up to date."[101]

Yet in some respects Manker did not appear "up to date." *They That Remain* was strikingly silent about its larger geopolitical context. While other writers of the period moved to alarmed conclusions about the prophetic significance of world affairs, Manker made no allusions to the war, its principal actors, or even to the German nation. His identification of the Antichrist as an Italian—rather than a Jew—was significant within the events of the period, but was still broadly within the premillennial tradition, which had often insisted on his Roman ancestry. This reticence about the political events of the early 1940s was matched by the novel's ambivalence about the morality of warfare. The novel condemned the pacifist movements as "ever Communistic," but balanced this with an observation that God's laws "were to love. His commands were that man should not kill."[102] Manker went so far as to insist that "every battle-cry that ever stirred the hearts of men has been a challenge to the ethics of the Eternal."[103] This could have seemed deeply unsatisfying as a comment on American participation in the Second World War. But then the puzzle increased. Though he was writing in the immediate aftermath of the discovery of Nazi death camps, Manker admitted that some of his narrative material did appear to be "anti-Semetic" [sic].[104] Of course, he rejected the charge: where racial bigotry did exist, he quickly explained, it was not so much his fault, as the fault of the international Jewish conspiracy that promoted it.[105]

They That Remain's hostility to American patriotism was perhaps its most significant cultural intervention. Manker was writing in a transitional moment, as America's enemy was being redefined. "Facism, Nazi-ism and Communism are all triplets of one blood," he argued, but "Communism is still the great agency of Satan in readying the world for the coming Antichrist."[106] Manker's earlier publications had condemned the "greedy capitalists" and "demon inspired intellectuals" who had "demoralized youth" with perverted ideas in literature and culture.[107] By the early 1940s, Manker was certain that it was Jews and Communists, not amoral capitalists, that were the hidden force behind the cultural war. In the final analysis, he was inviting his readers to imagine the apocalyptic defeat of their nation. The Antichrist may have been safely "othered" as an Italian, but *They That Remain* described the American government as capitulating to his conquest. Like other novels later in the tradition, the novel voiced nostalgia for the old America and "what remnant there was of American principle."[108] That nostalgia echoed the "elect nation" rhetoric of earlier evangelicals as well as the racial overtones of the earlier prophecy novels. Earlier in his career, Manker had paralleled "our Americanism and eternal safety," but *They That Remain* imagined the separation of the two, suggesting that paradigmatic national institutions would finally capitulate to the Antichrist's power.[109] The novel invited its readers to imagine that "the last several administrations were Communism's experiments" and the new president "was not in reality a President in the American sense of the word."[110] This kind of revolution was possible because Communists had already developed a "bitter, hostile attitude toward the time-honored institutions of America."[111] Patriots should already be wondering "if this is any longer *America*," for it certainly would not be for long.[112] America had a long history of religious commitment, Manker concluded, but before long it would take up arms against Jesus Christ himself.[113]

Manker's concerns about Communism dominate the novel. *They That Remain* bypassed fears of a one-world religion or an apocalyptic Roman Catholicism to prove that Communism would be the apocalyptic Beast. But Manker's Communism was an inflection of his fear of Jews—for Communism, he believed, had developed as a long-term Jewish conspiracy. One Jewish character even admits that Communism was the "child of the International Jew," a movement developed by a "little group of history makers" in their unfolding program for global domination.[114] This cabal controlled the world. Their predecessors had "taken control of the finances of most principal nations," had set in motion the events of the Russian revolution, and were now intending to undermine the "entire social order" and so fulfill the "old racial dreams" of the Jewish people.[115] They were "ever grasping for power" and had often "worked their way into centers of government."[116] Though most Jews did not realize it, "the master plotters . . . the secret leaders of the race directed them steadily toward a known and planned destination."[117] The cabal controlled a massive conspiracy with breathtaking aims, developing Communism as the "only way by which we could combat the Nazarene Christ . . . wear out the Gentile nations and ripen them for the reign of the true Messiah, for which we are so earnestly looking. Earth government will soon crumble. When our Messiah comes we will be the sovereigns of the world, and the simple Gentile will be our slave!"[118] Even political Zionism—which would dominate in later novels in the genre—was the result of a Jewish plot, having been sanctioned by the British government "for . . . financial favor."[119] Nor were Manker's suspicions of Jews eradicated by their conversion to Christianity. The conspiracy he described involved "even many so-called Christian Jews."[120] There was to be no escape from the racial type. Confirming his anti-Semitism in his repudiation of it, Manker's novel positioned itself at a critical distance from the emerging Christian Zionism that Foster, Watson and other prophetic authors had assumed.

But if Jews were to blame for Communism, then Communists were to blame for the final decline in American education and religious belief. Skepticism was a very immediate threat. Manker had first encountered Modernist ideas in 1928, and thereafter encoded his writing with a fundamental suspicion of its intellectual veneer.[121] He identified universities as key tools in the conspiracy that was at work to undermine America. *They That Remain* was particularly concerned by "the spiritual and moral downfall of young people" who "fell under the influence of the damning philosophies of the day as taught in the numerous centers of learning."[122] Educational institutions introduced theories that were working to undermine the American nation. It was a calculated strategy: "Bloody Bolshevism would have been too repugnant to find ready acceptance. Promiscuous immorality and free love would have been too sordid. The socialization of the home and of motherhood would have met with poor response within a God-fearing civilization."[123] Instead, the conspirators adopted a gradual approach: "Subtly, the world was made to discredit the purity and sacredness of the Virgin Birth. God was taken from His Book, leaving it the work of dreamers."[124] Modernists "entered the denominational schools with studies in philosophy and higher criticism, moderately at first . . . It was not long then until we had gone from Darwin to Nietzsche, and thence to Marx. Marxist professors at first had to conceal their true identity in our schools, until it became very clear that the people were ready for something in addition to the Modernism, which they had received enthusiastically. Then our Marxist professors stoutly declared themselves."[125] Manker worried that university education decimated the moral sobriety of younger people and uprooted "former convictions as to the worth of chastity."[126] He represents the university teaching of evolution as leading one Christian girl to godlessness and suicide: when her professor persuaded her that she was "only a high-grade ape, destined to perish like the meanest animal, she realized the futility of a character which must eventually be annihilated."[127] Even one of his novel's apostate believers "could curse the day I entered the University."[128] But as Manker's readers looked around them at the state of the churches and schools, it was imperative that they should realize what lay behind their rapid change. Modernist teachers were providing Communism with an "entering wedge into the civilized world."[129]

Manker believed these changes in education and theology were going hand-in-hand with a new economic order. In *They That Remain,* the Antichrist's initial impact is felt in the realm of economics. As in Oilar's *Be Thou Prepared,* taxes are represented as a burden that the godly should not have had to endure. Manker identified taxes as a sign of changing times. His concern is particularly directed to fears that churches were to lose their tax-free status.[130] But taxes are also represented as devastating to small businesses, and, as in *Be Thou Prepared,* are shown to produce a slump in the grocery business.[131] Higher taxes are paving the way for a "New Economic Order."[132] But that new economic order is believed to belie the real agenda of the American government. Tax hikes would be only the beginning, the first step toward "homes [being] broken, women ravished, ministers killed, and their churches confiscated or destroyed."[133] The New World Order was clearly being anticipated.

The tax hike certainly precipitates the fragmentation of evangelical churches. Church members lose confidence in their congregational leaders, and immorality and schism take errant members elsewhere.[134] "Self-appointed" laity set up their own congregations to compete with the lawful authority of the clergy and "the resulting competition was disastrous."[135] The confusion had an obvious impact on the spiritual condition of believers: "It had been months since there had been a shout heard or a tear seen in the meetings."[136] But this moral and spiritual decay was rooted in the new economic order: "A spiritual numbness had crept over them . . . The taxing of the property had loaded a burden upon them that seemed too heavy to carry."[137]

But just as Communists subverted homes, colleges, and churches, so they attempted to "communize the Negroes" in the South, agitating in favor of "a Socialist Soviet Republic south of the Mason and Dixon line and as far west as the Mississippi river."[138] Their rhetoric in the novel appeals to notions of racial equality that, Manker's novel strongly implies, will undermine the status quo. Communist officials declare "all men equal" in a gesture that is ultimately violent and sexual in tone, promoting the desirability of the "inter-marriage of the races" and the abandoning of "the delusion of 'White Supremacy'": "Negroes, get your white women. Marriage is not necessary, but to break the arrogant domination of the 'Capitalist' whites we recommend that you insult and defile the haughty women. Kill and maim the men as the occasion arises."[139] Manker identifies as "one of the leading points in the Communistic doctrine" the promotion of "promiscuous immorality, or free love." Communist clubs would permit "girls and young men" to mingle "freely together . . . in a bedlam of vice and profanity over which we must leave the veil of silence."[140] The fact that this sexual immorality involved couples of mixed race put it well beyond the pale.[141] Manker's narrative depended on racial stereotypes of the violent sexual agency of African-American men—but, even in their supposed autonomy, these men were being manipulated. Communists would stir up race hatred against whites while using "negroes" to bear the brunt of their violent struggle.[142] The conflict would become "America's all-time greatest tragedy": "Millions of colored people have, as though moved by a sudden signal from some secret source, lifted murderous hands against the white people of their intended 'Black Republic.' No-one knows the number of dead. Perhaps two million people have died. Murderous negroes marked their man . . . Only the fairest of women are spared, appropriated by their black captors as slaves to greed and lust . . . Many women have committed suicide rather than submit to the rapacious assault of these crazed brutes."[143] The language is evidently racist, emphasizing a stereotype of the violent sexuality of African-American men. And, as if to add insult to injury, the novel imagined the American Civil Liberties Union, or ACLU, providing Communist lawyers for the criminals of the African-American struggle. Manker's implied reader would hardly be surprised by their involvement, for the "chief purpose" of the ACLU had always been to "defend anarchists, bomb-throwers, attackers of women and destroyers of society."[144] But Manker was making his point clear. The race war that the novel imagined may have been in the future, but the institutions that would provide for its motivation and defense were already undermining America. The race war would be engineered by Communists, who already dominated the educational and theological world. The Communists were being developed by Jews, as part of a long-standing conspiratorial cabal. Powerful forces were arrayed against white Protestant America. No wonder Manker thought its end was near.

III

Manker was not alone in his fears, and neither were he and Oilar unique in expressing them in prophecy fiction. Hugh Venning, a Roman Catholic novelist, published *The End: A Projection, Not a Prophecy* (1948) to describe a conservative and dystopian England surrounded by a revived Roman Empire led by a man called "666." Five years later, *As the Clock Struck Twenty,* written by "S. M. C.," another Catholic writer, imagined Western nations being infiltrated by a Communist fifth column that would eventually undermine the existing balance of power.[145] These novels, despite their thematic variations, demonstrate that apocalyptic and conspiratorial concerns were not restricted to Protestant fundamentalists as they grappled with the aftermath of history's most terrible war.

Nevertheless, Oilar and Manker were shaping the narrative of the prophecy novel as it emerged into the geopolitical tensions of the 1950s and beyond. Both novels reflected the fundamentalist evangelicalism of their authors and signaled the extent to which the most militant of conservative Protestants were regrouping around apocalyptic themes. Both novels advanced a clear preference for small government. Oilar and Manker agreed that tax hikes should be resisted and argued that there would be no taxes in the millennium.[146] Both novels were acutely concerned by the threats posed by Jews, and, even as the Nazi holocaust was being planned and executed, Manker remained able to imagine an international Jewish conspiracy whose aim it was to subvert white Protestant America and to impose Jewish authority on the governments of the world. But the novels also demonstrated their authors' suspicions as to the safety of American institutions in a world which seemed to provide plausible evidence for this conspiracy's power. Within both narratives, the struggle against Nazism was just one aspect of a longer and much more critical conflict, in which Jews were criminals as well as victims. After all, Jews had invented Communism, and Communism—rather than Roman Catholicism—was being identified as the eschatological enemy of conservative Protestants. Communism was dangerous in its own right, they were arguing; but it was its Jewish roots that made its intentions most sinister. And Oilar and Manker were drawing that conclusion as the free world struggled with the Fascist bloc.

It is a surprising conclusion: both novels were much less skeptical about Communism and much more skeptical about Jews and the notion of a Christian America than their readers might have expected. In gestures of simultaneous reverence and pity, both *Be Thou Prepared* and *They That Remain* argued that American institutions were inherently weak and that they had already been vitally undermined. Their readers were being encouraged to imagine the failure of religious patriotism and the emptiness of the rhetoric that had often underpinned it. Americans were being invited to imagine the capitulation of national institutions to a Communist global dictator and a shadowy Jewish cabal. Oilar and Manker were setting the stage for the evangelical imagination of the cold war, but, significantly, their novels offered little prospect of American victory. Communism would certainly triumph, and Americans should brace themselves for the future, living as they did, as Manker later put it, in "an environment which [they] did not choose, in an existence which [they] did not determine and facing an end which [they did] not want at a time which [they] cannot predict."[147] Later cold war novels would be much more open about the outcome of America's immediate struggle. Sidney Fowler Wright may have been pessimistic about humanity's survival of a future deluge, but prophecy novels identified a much more immediate threat. A Jewish conspiracy was firmly in control, and the Communism it sponsored was evidently on the rise. In the middle decades of the twentieth century, evangelical prophecy fiction, in the hands of Oilar and Manker, displayed profound skepticism about the claims of the "redeemer nation" and the aspirations of the Jewish people with whom increasing numbers of prophecy believers had begun to identify.

4

Prophecy Fiction and the Cold War

Prophecy was . . . coming to life before his eyes.
                    —Tim LaHaye and Jerry B. Jenkins, *The Mark* (2000)

Manker's assumptions of an unchanging prophetic narrative were soon to be revised, for, in August 1945, the world entered its apocalyptic age. The American bombing of Nagasaki and Hiroshima unleashed destruction that was recognized as being unparalleled in the history of human experience. Mass death provided the most iconic images of the twentieth century. Global destruction was no longer the monopoly of an angry god. Human hands now controlled weapons of unprecedented power.

For many prophecy believers it was a moment of unparalleled opportunity. In 1946, Wilbur Smith, professor at Fuller Theological Seminary, addressed the topic of "This Atomic Age and the Word of God" in an article in *Reader's Digest*.[1] Almost one decade later, John Walvoord of Dallas Theological Seminary noted that "the whole world" was still "in a state of fearful expectation. The advent of the atomic bomb with kindred devastating weapons has brought the world face to face with the possibility of the doom of present civilization."[2] But not everyone was willing to capitalize on the beginning of the nuclear age. Some writers of prophecy fiction appeared to disregard the revolution in military technology. The second edition of *They That Remain* was published one year after the attack on Japan, but Manker reissued his text in the confidence that "one may still read this book and feel up to date."[3] It was a conclusion that many other writers of prophecy fiction were beginning to doubt. Many authors believed that an entirely new era had begun—and there was certainly evidence for that claim. The deployment of atomic weaponry seemed to dramatize many biblical predictions of mass destruction. Zechariah 14:12 described the fate of the armies that, evangelical prophecy scholars had often argued, would attack Jerusalem in the latter days: "Their flesh shall consume away while they stand upon their feet, and their eyes shall consume away in their holes, and their tongue shall consume away in their mouth." Never before had the prophet's claims been so closely matched by the ability of military technicians—a point that many dispensational writers were quick to make.[4] The horrific events drove one dispensational writer to verse:

> In Nagasaki's ruins lie the failures of the past,
>> For, the more we learn, the more we lose security and peace,
> The Ghosts of Hiroshima, disembodied in the blast
>> Are riding on the fire-storms, cry aloud for wars to cease.[5]

The biblical allusion embedded in the final line of the quotation was an appropriate response to the blasts that, to their observers, must indeed have felt like "the earth [being] removed" and "the mountains [being] carried into the midst of the sea." But the quotation was also a declaration of faith in the good purposes of the God who, in the midst of such destructive forces, "maketh wars to cease unto the end of the earth" (Psalm 46:2, 9). In August 1945, the "end of the earth" felt very near. But humanity might yet come to appreciate the danger of its new situation for, the poet continued, the ghosts of Hiroshima had "brought a cry from the scientists, not the preachers, but the weapons builders, for a revival of spiritual understanding."[6] Whatever the apathy of liberal Protestant clergy, dispensational theologians were certainly alert to the need for a "revival of spiritual understanding." The end was rushing upon them—and, three years later, the establishment of the state of Israel confirmed their hopes and fears.

The establishment of Israel, in 1948, energized many dispensational believers. Its impact was serious enough to lead to the reconsideration of the most elemental theme in the earlier writing of the movement—the strict futurism that insisted that the rapture was the next event that could be identified as a fulfillment of prophecy. Dispensational writers, like other evangelical prophecy enthusiasts, had long been interested in the fate of the Jews. The *Scofield Reference Bible* had identified the Jewish nation as "always the centre of the divine counsels earthward," but argued that prophecies of their restoration to the Promised Land would only be fulfilled after the tribulation, "at the return of the Lord as King."[7] Any earlier return to the land—and at least one earlier return to the land was required for the fulfillment of *Scofield's* panorama—would not fulfill the prophetic texts.[8] This standard position was being confirmed as late as one decade after the establishment of Israel, when J. Dwight Pentecost published his Dallas Theological Seminary doctoral thesis, *Things to Come* (1958). Pentecost admitted that Israel would need to be gathered to the land before the tribulation if the standard dispensational scenario were to be played out, but added that Israel would then again be scattered before their eventual, and prophecy-fulfilling, regathering, after the tribulation.[9] His Dallas colleague, John Walvoord, had been similarly reticent in *The Return of the Lord* (1955).[10] But, in the years after 1948, their careful and sober conclusions looked increasingly out-of-date. More and more voices were identifying the events of 1948 as the obvious fulfillment of prophetic hopes, and dispensational writers were ready to embrace the limited historicism demanded by that position. The subtle change in emphasis represented a foundational challenge to the mainstream of dispensational thinking, but the establishment of Israel was too tempting a prophetic fulfillment to ignore, especially when it appeared to confirm the movement's much-loved literal hermeneutic. For the first time in the history of the tradition, it became possible to point to events in the period of history before the rapture as fulfillments of biblical prophecy. A limited historicism was becoming fashionable among those whose prophetic system had done most to undermine it.

The establishment of Israel encouraged many dispensationalists to recontour their prophetic creed. By the later 1960s, those developments had been given an institutional form. A new *Scofield Reference Bible,* with substantially revised annotations, was published in 1967. While the earlier editions (1909 and 1917) had assumed that the rapture would precede Israel's restoration to the land, the *New Scofield Reference Bible* (1967) reversed the order of events.[11] Three years after its publication, the new view was massively popularized in Hal Lindsey's *The Late Great Planet Earth* (1970). Lindsey, together with other popular exegetes, began to revise traditional prophetic expectations to parallel trends in the world around him. He stated that the establishment of Israel had been a "paramount prophetic sign" and implied that the rapture would occur within forty years—one biblical generation—of 1948: "Many scholars who have studied Bible prophecy all their lives believe that this is so."[12] The emphasis on the significance of Israel's establishment was confirmed in *His Land* (1970), a feature film produced by the Billy Graham Evangelistic Association, which guided its audience into the prophetic significance of the Six-Day War and the recent Jewish occupation of the Old City of Jerusalem.[13] Never before had popular apologists for dispensationalism been able to point so clearly to current events and insist that these were nothing less than "signs of the times." There was, they claimed, a discernable providential order in the period before the rapture. The "present situation," as one prophetic novelist put it, "was not simply an accumulation of unfortunate accidents, but part of a vast, long-foreseen climax of history, cosmic in its implications."[14] By the end of the 1960s, dispensationalism had been substantially reformed. The new style of its most successful apologists—who became increasingly well-known for their "news-paper exegesis"—made its most eye-catching claims compelling. Israel and atomic weaponry were proof the end was near. Sales of *The Late Great Planet Earth* began to spiral as "pop dispensationalism" moved toward the American cultural main-stream. The conclusions of the new dispensationalists were clear: the second half of the twentieth century was the time of the signs, the age in which the providential clock restarted, and prophecies began to be fulfilled.

These claims were being made as the evangelical movement on both sides of the Atlantic struggled to come to terms with the changing social conditions of the Western world. Evangelicals in the United Kingdom reached their numerical peak in the later 1950s, while the numerical strength of American believers continued to grow, but the events of the next decade plunged believers on both sides of the Atlantic into situations they could never have foreseen.[15] A Catholic president, civil rights, women's rights, student riots, the sexual revolution, the Cuban crisis and the Vietnam War meant that the 1960s was not just a different decade—the 1960s was a different world. Conservative evangelicals struggled to come to terms with what the new conditions meant. Their prophetic textbooks were rewritten to take account of new enemies. Soviet Russia had begun to dominate Eastern Europe in the years after the Second World War, China continued to lower in the distance, and Reds were discovered under the American bed. But dispensationalists added some less fashionable enemies to the obvious political threats—the United Nations, founded in 1945 to replace the ailing League of Nations, and the emerging European Com-munity, founded on the Treaty of Rome (1957). Their world—both at home and abroad—seemed to be spiraling out of control. Civilization was unraveling, just as prophetic leaders had encouraged their followers to expect. Believers watched with fascinated terror as prophecy unfolded before their eyes. And they turned to books to explain it all, buying more and more as the 1960s and 1970s progressed. Between 1965 and 1975, the number of American Christian bookshops more than doubled, from 725 to 1850. Between 1972 and 1977, sales of religious books rose by over 112 percent. Between 1975 and 1979, average sales in American Christian bookshops grew at 16 percent per annum, well above the national retail growth of 9.7 percent.[16] And this growth rate was reflected in the sales of individual titles. John Walvoord's *Armageddon, Oil, and the Middle East Crisis* (1974) sold 750,000 copies.[17] But *The Late Great Planet Earth* was the most popular of them all, selling 7.5 million copies by the end of that decade, according to a survey by the *New York Times Book Review*.[18] Lindsey's book leaned heavily on the popular culture of the period. The chapter title for the rapture was "The Ultimate Trip"—an expression borrowed from the advertising posters for *2001: A Space Odyssey*.[19] Nevertheless, the fact that a dispensational textbook was the best-selling nonfiction text of that troubled and uncertain decade was a telling sign of the times.

Throughout the cold war period, prophecy fiction novels evolved to reflect the changing nature of dispensationalism and the world with which their writers were attempting to engage. Novels from this context illustrated profound changes in evangelical popular culture. Some endorsed the detailed ethical code that typified the social expectations of mid-century fundamentalists. Historically, these social codes illustrate seismic changes in evangelical culture and emphasize that the piety of dispensational believers was not necessarily being determined by the content of their end-time belief. Many other factors were at play. The eschatological thinking of Ernest W. Angley was broadly similar to that of more recent prophecy novelists, for example, but his characters' attempts to avoid worldly contamination contrast sharply with the social habits of the tribulation saints in Left Behind. Angley's characters abhor makeup and movies, but the details of the "sanctified lifestyle" of tribulation saints in Left Behind are subsumed within their wider commitment to beat the Antichrist at his own game, using all the material and physical resources they find available to them, including bribery, subterfuge, and attempted murder. The novels also illustrate changes in evangelical attitudes to specific forms of mass communication. Angley, for example, condemned the cinema. In 1950, he imagined that the widespread acceptance of evangelical prophecy belief would mean "no drinking, no card parties, no dancing, no blasphemy, no homes broken up by divorce, no prisons . . . no murders or suicides," and, of course, "no movies."[20] Fifty years later, but sharing exactly the same set of eschatological ideas, evangelicals had come to utilize the cinema in their quest to spread the truth.

Angley's novel reflected one element of a separatist, subcultural evangelicalism. His novel was as much about promoting a very distinctive variety of "clean living" as it was about encouraging widespread adherence to "the blessed hope." But his emphases could not survive as cold war prophecy fiction developed, as authors sought to reach an increasingly media-conscious audience, and as their exegetes moved increasingly toward a "pop dispensational" approach. Evangelical prophecy novels represented an increasing accommodation of modernity. Those examples published in the 1950s and 1960s demonstrate a basic commitment to cold war binaries and the political dangers of the East. They represented an obvious disengagement from and distrust of mainstream American culture. But they also demonstrated the deeply encultured nature of dispensational faith: while the core elements of belief remain the same, their expression changed entirely as the surrounding context evolved. Nevertheless, the cultural mainstream remained a source of continued fascination and concern for the implied readers of the novels. Their readers were not of the world, the authors hoped, but they were certainly deeply interested in it. And no wonder—the cold war period was the time of the signs, and "prophecy was . . . coming to life before [their] eyes."[21]

I

Despite that emphasis on contemporaneity, and in contrast to earlier writers such as Oilar and Manker, many of the writers of these novels were strangely reluctant to engage with Communism. Some dispensational writers appeared entirely uninterested in geopolitical concerns, while others, like John Walvoord, a writer of prophetic nonfiction, flatly denied that Communism could ever become a significant end-time threat.[22] And some novels embraced this creed. *Raptured* (1950) was written by Ernest W. Angley (b. 1921), a Southern evangelist then developing the "flamboyant and controversial" healing ministry that would be featured on his 1980s television show.[23] *Raptured* linked this pious political apathy to a well-developed and ethically precise theology of social withdrawal. The novel was one of the first prophecy novels to appear in the aftermath of the momentous events of the later 1940s. It made no attempt to play on the nuclear end to the Second World War and appeared to have been written before the establishment of the Jewish state, which would otherwise have done so much to confirm its expectations. "Since nineteen twenty-one there has been the greatest gathering in the history of the Jews," Angley noted, as he described Jews as still "fighting for Palestine" and still "trying to take over the Holy Land."[24] But *Raptured* had no doubt as to the ultimate significance of their struggle. The latter comment was juxtaposed with the archetypal metaphor of prophetic fulfillment in the pop dispensational tradition: "the swinging of the pendulum on the clock on the mantel shouted, 'The Lord's coming! The Lord's coming! The Lord's coming! The Lord's coming!'"[25] The link between Israel and the "prophetic clock" would have been evident to those readers schooled in the popular literature of the dispensational movement. Prophetic time would start again when a Jewish state existed in the Promised Land.

The casual placement of the metaphor was indicative of Angley's expectations of his readers. *Raptured*—which described the disappearance of hundreds of people from a small city in an unnamed state—is full of exhortations for characters to embrace a saving faith.[26] Nevertheless, it strongly implies a readership well versed in the norms of the subculture of prophecy belief. Like Oilar and Manker before him, Angley seemed to reflect and imply a readership that was familiar with and comfortable within the highly separatist, fundamentalist ethos of mid-century Pentecostalism. It was in many ways a naïve culture, which could imagine that women "always looked . . . prettiest" when they talked about Jesus.[27] But, in *Raptured*, this culture was being provided with a specific set of ethical and spiritual norms. As in Manker's novel, public worship was described as being informal, participatory, and often interrupted by joyful shouts, and at the end of services, large numbers of people would be expected to move to the front of the church "for prayer."[28] This style of piety was central to Angley's imagination of the evangelical faith and became a core component of the novel's spirituality, for a sure sign of sinfulness was that one did not believe "in the power of God and people shouting."[29] The novel's idealized church, Fairview, "was not a popular church with some of the town people," who "thought she was too quaint in her ways" by "preaching that people had to be saved through the blood."[30] The narrative did not pause to explain that "saved through the blood" had become an evangelical cliché linking conversion to the penal substitution theory of the atonement, but assumed that its readers could make that connection for themselves. The novel's believing characters would certainly have known what it meant. The members of Fairview were regarded as "fanatics," but all this meant, the narrative explained, was that they "still held to the fundamental teachings of the Word of God, and . . . lived pure, clean lives."[31] It would simply not be "Christian like" to "go to the movies and other lively places," and "wild parties," it feared, might involve their participants in playing bridge on the Sabbath.[32] Thus the godly lifestyle of believers is constantly contrasted with that of their moviegoing, tobacco-consuming, alcohol-drinking, cosmetics-wearing, card-playing neighbors.[33] Despite its title, *Raptured* was as much concerned with Christian living in the present as with the specifics of end-time belief.

But the novel certainly did have theological concerns. *Raptured* mounted a typically fundamentalist attack on theological liberalism, contrasting the faithful and energetic piety of the Fairview congregation with the cool and sophisticated polish of the educated unbelief that was promoted in the "large cathedral" in "another section of the city."[34] The pastor of this liberal congregation had not been born again.[35] His title and surname—Doctor Morehead—emphasized at one stroke the link between education, liberalism, and uncertainty and consolidated themes of respectability, religious infidelity, and wealth. Ministers in his unnamed denomination "used to believe" the standard tenets of evangelical faith, one character opines, but that was when they "did not have much education," some time before "this . . . day of enlightenment."[36] Morehead's self-proclaimed "enlightenment" was rooted in a hermeneutic that insisted that prophetic texts are "not to be used in a literal sense."[37] But he changes his approach when the rapture intervenes. Like other versions of this stock character, he readily admits that he had been "a blind fool" in uncritically accepting what he had learned in college—and, as a consequence, "here I am left behind."[38]

Morehead's skepticism is contrasted with the innocence and faith of the small remnant involved in the rapture. The rapture took "all the babies and small children"—without specifying an upper limit for the "age of accountability"— but involved only "thousands" of professing Christians.[39] This small number was involved because this was only a partial rapture. Those Christians who found themselves in a "lukewarm" spiritual condition, those who only followed Christ "halfheartedly," and those who "had been saved once" were all left behind.[40]

Angley's insistence that some believers had actually lost their salvation echoed the approach that Manker had earlier adopted, but it put him at a significant distance from the tradition and from its most eminent nineteenth-century spokesmen. Angley's tribulation offered these former evangelicals a final opportunity for spiritual renewal. Some of those who had "backslidden" and had altogether abandoned the faith once again "sought the face of God and prayed until the blood of the Son of God had covered their souls."[41] The novel does not pause to defend these assumptions in soteriology, which were certainly unorthodox by classical dispensational standards, but it does launch a vigorous polemic against the theology of a mid-tribulation rapture.[42] Presumably the audience for which Angley was writing was more in need of an exhortation to holy living and an argument against mid-tribulation theology than it was in need of being convinced that one's gaining of "eternal life" could be finally reversed.

Nevertheless, Angley's novel was altogether like others in the genre in imagining the impact of the rapture on the unbelieving world. It articulated the myth of social chaos that prophecy novels increasingly developed. The myth explained that believers were far more important to social stability than their enemies believed, and that their removal would result in widespread disaster: "People driving cars suddenly vanished, leaving their automobiles to stop as they could. Trains were wrecked without an engineer, and airplanes fell without a pilot."[43] Newspaper accounts of the rapture reported "train wrecks, ships at sea left without a pilot or captain, airplanes crashing because the pilot had disappeared and . . . no end of bus and car wrecks."[44] But even as it described these scenes of chaos, the novel affirmed the essential innocence of mid-century America. Like earlier prophecy fictions, but notably unlike Manker's *They That Remain*, *Raptured* implied that mainstream media would accept the biblical explanation within hours of the event. Even in 1950, Angley imagined that this could still be regarded as a possibility, that a conservative Protestant social consensus could still be expected to exist. The novel toyed with the idea that the religious community it represented was distanced from the wider culture, but in the final analysis, it believed that traditional patterns of Protestant evangelicalism still governed the popular imagination—dissolute though that imagination had certainly come to be.[45]

Angley interspersed his cultural critique and eschatological speculation with robust attacks on other evangelicals. *Raptured* imagined that the organization for one-world government would meet at a location called "Calvin Heights." The location's name signaled the novel's opposition to Calvinism (which the narrative clearly rejected) and cultural elevation (which it consistently linked to theological decay).[46] The novel assumed that its approach to Scripture was the only evangelical alternative to the Modernism that was otherwise sweeping the Protestant board. One character turns to the Bible after the rapture, to "read and reread the

Book of Daniel and Revelation." These most complex of biblical books suddenly reveal their confirmation of the dispensational faith: what "used to seem so complicated and far-fetched . . . was all clear . . . now."[47] But those who come to faith during the tribulation discover just how truly subcultural they have become. The novel represented the systematic persecution and martyrdom of believers, who are executed by fire, thrown to lions, thrown to snakes, and slowly dismembered.[48] When American police officers drink the blood of Christian martyrs they combine the cannibalism that appears elsewhere in the genre with a distinctive anti-sacramental twist.[49] The scene's horror made more than one theological point. The conditions of the tribulation allowed for this superbly Gothic innovation: "My God!" one character groaned, "this horror of being left behind!"[50]

Angley imagined this horror only for America. Despite the date of its publication, *Raptured* did not refer to the Communist world and imagined no political threat external to the United States. It made very few references to Jewish people and no mention at all of the new Jewish state. Its focus was clearly on small-town America and appeared more concerned to defend a distinctive spirituality and a regimented social code than to dwell on larger geopolitical trends. Almost sixty years after its publication, *Raptured* continues to be kept in print by its author's ministry organization.[51] But, as the cold war developed, its parochialism looked increasingly eccentric. Massive satanic forces were threatening America, and prophecy novels had to take account of the new and immanent threat.

II

Angley insisted that the threat was not necessarily Communist. While novels published in the 1940s had reiterated the dangers of the Soviet East, novels from the mid–cold war period continued to look beyond its immediate danger. They could not agree on the identity of their real enemy—for the United Nations, the emerging European community, and the Vatican were regularly identified with the final apocalyptic empire—but dispensational writers were sure the threat was real.

Many of these novels began their construction of external danger with the identification of internal decay. John Myers's *The Trumpet Sounds* (1965), like that of Angley's *Raptured*, presented a jeremiad for a formerly godly nation: America, "as we used to know it" in the 1940s, was "gone forever."[52] Like Angley's characters, Myers's characters position themselves in conflict with mainstream church tradition. The novel's tribulation saints—the "Gospel Group"—were entirely "separate from any denominational tie."[53] Their separation enabled them to preserve their grasp of truth in a wider context that witnessed the decay of orthodoxy and "the slow death of the spiritual life" within the denominational churches.[54] Like other fundamentalists in the period, Myers rejects as dangerously liberal the new Revised Standard Version of the Bible and positions his narrative in opposition to the neo-evangelical communities who were doing so much to reinvent an evangelical cultural presence.[55] He stated explicitly what Angley had only implied: "the Calvinist branch of the Christian Church" had "departed from the experience of salvation" and could not defend the truth.[56] It was an ironic exposure of the neo-evangelicals, who were throughout the period taking a renewed interest in their Reformed theological roots.[57] Like other fundamentalists of the period, the Gospel Group opposes materialism, Modernism, and ecumenism, but Myers was strangely reluctant to write against the Roman Catholic Church.[58] This was not a gesture toward ecumenicity—instead, the failure to critique the Roman Catholic Church allowed for the development of a critique of Protestant modernity. The Roman Catholic Church had produced "many of the choicest saints of Church history," he argued; so "if the great whore of Revelations seventeen contains Catholics, it also contains Protestants."[59] This suspicion of the ecclesiastical mainstream was certainly in order, for the religious symbolism of the mainstream was profoundly duplicitous. Myers imagined that the mark of the beast would exist in the shape of a cross, and he worried that those who were tricked into wearing it would end up losing their salvation.[60]

Like Angley, Myers matched an irregular soteriology with an innovative eschatology. His novel imagined the total destruction of the Christian church in the first half of the tribulation and argued that the rapture could be expected some years after the beginning of the Antichrist's regime.[61] This mid-tribulation position was exactly the kind of theology that Angley's novel had opposed. But both authors emphasized the period's dangers. Angley argued that believers could escape the tribulation if their sanctification had sufficiently advanced, but Myers argued that they could not expect to escape the conflict at all and warned that the conflict would imminently begin. Myers positioned his readers as "standing in the shadows of momentous coming world changes. The shadows are mighty with scientific achievement and at the same time black with war because of them; the shadows are bright with the hope of coming world peace, the promise of security and great wealth; and behind them is the haunting specter of tribulation without peace, the loss of security and worldly possessions, and the ultimate failure of every mortal hope."[62] The sonorous prose described a fundamental attack on the Western ideal of liberty.[63] Myers's plot, unlike that of Angley, was rooted in the geopolitical situation of the period of its composition. Myers believed that the decade in which he was writing—with its sudden cultural changes—represented "the last days of our system of national governments."[64] Communism was a serious threat, but it was not an eschatological danger, for all national governments were soon to be eclipsed.[65] Nevertheless, Myers thought it "probable" that the world would "still be divided between the Communist Bloc nations and the free world" when the Antichrist arose.[66] He believed that the "system of sovereign nations" that was then "banding together in a final and futile effort to perpetuate itself" would fail in the face of this final one-world government.[67] The "fourth beast," about which Daniel had prophesied and which Myers believed he could identify, was neither a revived Roman Empire nor the European Common Market that many thought it fore-shadowed.[68] Instead, he observed, the "fourth beast" was something that would "devour the whole earth" (Daniel 7:23). It was something that would draw to itself "all the nations of the world . . . in one huge organization." That fact, he thought, made its identification simple: "the only time in all history that every nation on earth has united in such a manner is right now, today, in the 1945–65 period in which we live. It has its headquarters in New York City and calls itself the 'United Nations.'"[69]

Myers had no doubt about the United Nations' power. Every member state, he reported to his readers, "must yield its sovereignty to the UN and submit to polic-ing by (possibly) a foreign power, if the UN says so."[70] He expected the organiza-tion to increase in power in the last days of American independence. But, Myers assured his readers, its attempt at one-world government would certainly fail—not just because of divine intervention, which he certainly expected, but also because of the racial divisions that continued to divide the member states. "Colonialism is dying in a blaze of rebellion, violence and gunfire as the races assert themselves," he observed. "Empires and kingdoms are breaking up, people are clamoring for free-dom, recognition, and their rights . . . Nations and people who have been content for centuries with an ancient way of life, are now leaping into the jet age, the space age, the age of nuclear war . . . and they do not intend to go back." But, he claimed, the inclusion of these nations within the one-world government undermined the coherence of its ideals: "Men who were born in the wilderness of backward coun-tries and grew up in savagery which still practices cannibalism in remote areas, now occupy seats and submit votes on an equal basis with the most modern and progressive of nations."[71] But the multiracial dream would fail. Daniel had foreseen it all: "the iron of mature peoples will not mix with the clay of immature peoples, and no amount of good intentions will make it do so."[72]

These kinds of political concerns about race and the United Nations were entirely absent from the novel prepared by a director of the United Kingdom's Atomic Energy Authority, and the eventual author of over seventy books, Doc-tor Frederick Albert Tatford (1901–86). Tatford, who was a lifelong member of the Plymouth Brethren, a traditionally apolitical but deeply conservative reli-gious community, was arguably one of the period's most significant writers of popular dispensational texts. He had a long interest in prophetic literature, and his work was published on both sides of the Atlantic. Many of his publications were exegetical and, despite his Brethren background, many of those exegetical works were deeply political in tone. His exposition of Revelation, *Prophecy's Last Word* (1947), was followed by *Climax of the Ages: Studies in the Prophecy of Daniel* (1964), *Will There Be a Millennium?* (1969) and *Daniel's Seventy Weeks* (1971). Others of his books and pamphlets developed a more topical approach. *The Rapture and the Tribulation* (1957) was followed by *The Middle East: War Theatre of Prophecy* (1959), *God's Program of the Ages* (1967), which had gone into its third edition by 1971, and *A One World Church and Prophecy* (1967). His political interests were made obvious in *China and Prophecy* (1968), *Russia and Prophecy* (1968), *Egypt and Prophecy* (1968), *The Jew and Prophecy* (1969) and *Middle East Cauldron* (1971). These interests were given a more local spin in a series of publications that emphasized the need for correct eschatological thinking in the politically charged environment of the early 1970s. *Five Minutes to Midnight* (1971), *Going into Europe: The Common Market and Prophecy* (1971), and *Israel and Her Future* (1971) were clearly the immediate context for Tatford's only prophecy novel, *The Clock Strikes* (1971).

Tatford's novel deferred to a growing sense of genre tradition. In his preface, he noted the continuing appeal of the novels by Sydney Watson and acknowledged that his own work was unlikely to and was not intended to replace the earlier trilogy.[73] *The Clock Strikes* would be "on similar lines to *The Mark of the Beast*, but with a somewhat more modern setting," he explained.[74] But Tatford was invoking standard tropes in prophecy fiction to attempt the refurbishment of the tradition. *The Clock Strikes* refused to echo the didactic detail that had by then come to typify the genre: "Those who come to this book, expecting to find a precise outline of the Bible's teaching on prophecy will be disappointed. One has attempted to do that in other books which are available."[75] *The Clock Strikes* did not embrace the modified dispensationalism of the *New Scofield Reference Bible* and *The Late Great Planet Earth*. Nevertheless, the discursive potential of the contemporary was very much in view; it had to be, as Tatford negotiated the fact that some of the events that Watson had reserved for the tribulation—such as the rebirth of Israel—had already taken place in normal time. When Tatford's novel did address political events, it highlighted the importance of "topical subjects and developments," including the evolution of the European Common Market and the significance of the ecumenical movement in the preparations for a one-world church.[76] The novel was far from being politically reserved. Its exponent of "prophetic truth"—Doctor Broughton—celebrated the establishment of Israel as the "most significant" proof of the reliability of Scripture.[77] Through Broughton's preaching, Tatford predicted that the membership of the European Common Market "may soon be ten nations and not merely six."[78] He anticipated a growing ecumenism, "the formation of a one world church with its headquarters in Rome," and these religious and political

concerns coalesced in his observation that eighty percent of the European population "professed to be Roman Catholic."[79] Nor were these events to be pushed
into the indefinite future. The reunion of the Christian churches was already far
advanced. The novel reported that "the Presbyterian and Congregational Churches
had come together"—as they would in the United Reformed Church one year
after the novel's publication—and anticipated their future amalgamation with the
Church of England.[80] The scientific dangers were similarly immediate. Tatford
argued that the apocalyptic language of Scripture included "semi-technical terms
which a nuclear physicist would employ today to describe what he expects eventually to happen—the dissolution of the world by some form of nuclear explosion."[81]
The Clock Strikes was a spirited attempt to update the genre to take account of the
realities of the cold war. But it included chilling speculation from the director of
the Atomic Energy Authority. It was "evident" that nuclear conflict would destroy
the planet, he warned, when "the God of battles" would visit the earth and find his
enemy in a political union of European states.[82]

Myers's concern with the United Nations, and Tatford's with projects for
European union, mapped out the basic territory of the genre's political engagement during the cold war. This version of the "evangelical world map" remained
in place despite the insistence on the dangers of Russian and Chinese Communism
in the decade's best-selling text.[83] Hal Lindsey's hugely significant reformulation of
traditional dispensationalism in The Late Great Planet Earth was far more significant than that of the New Scofield Reference Bible. The new Scofield annotations had
quietly adapted some important motifs in prophetic futurism but Lindsey's book
abandoned caution altogether and set an agenda that writers of prophecy fiction
struggled to maintain.

Nevertheless, the best-selling prophecy novel of the decade made no attempt
to follow Lindsey's path. Published in the same year as The Late Great Planet
Earth, Salem Kirban's 666 (1970) sold half a million copies in its first three years,
and, for a time, its sales must have been almost as impressive as those of Lindsey's market-defining text.[84] Critics have not made claims for its literary value:
one recent commentator described the prose as "cryogenically preserved in the
embalming fluid of Bible-speak and the abstract emptiness of a righteous religion."[85] But Kirban was already an established writer of prophetic nonfiction
when he published his prophecy novels. The first text, published by Tyndale
House, passed through ten printings in its first three years, and was followed by
a sequel, 1000 (1973).[86] Despite his being photographed with the revised Scofield
Bible, Kirban used his fiction to maintain the older dispensational paradigm. In
1000, for example, one character glances through J. Dwight Pentecost's Things to
Come, and a footnote in a preface encourages all readers to consult the text for
"a detailed examination of why these events are placed in this order."[87] Kirban

appeared to be downplaying the prophetic significance of 1948. And perhaps that was hardly surprising—for Kirban was an Arab.

It is not unexpected, therefore, that Kirban's extended description of the reasons "why I wrote this book" did not emphasize a philo-Semitic theme. Instead, Kirban reported that he had been disturbed by a number of trends in contemporary culture. It was an age of elitist thinking, he worried; he called on his readers to embrace herbal remedies instead of complex vaccinations—an emphasis which he would later develop in his ministry organization—and to abandon any interest in "art for art's sake."[88] But he was most concerned by trends within the conservative Protestant world. "Never before in human history has there been a greater need for the Gospel of the saving grace of Lord Jesus Christ," he observed, "and never before in human history has there been, comparatively speaking, less of an effort to reach the teeming billions with the Word of God."[89] Kirban was particularly concerned by the "growing lack of interest among churches to stress the missionary ministry and the need for evangelism."[90] Instead, the neo-evangelicals then attempting to reinvent the evangelical movement were rendering "great service" to multi-faith ecumenism in abandoning traditional Protestant vocabulary.[91] They were "watering down the Gospel with their introductions of the beat Gospel music . . . the Christian Rock groups . . . and relevant Christianity that played down the prophetic Word of God . . . [and] stressed only the need for social concern." For Kirban and his fellow fundamentalists, neo-evangelicals epitomized the dangers of worldly engagement. It was "all too clear now . . . too sickeningly clear! The apostasy of the early days . . . had borne its fruit."[92] Fundamentalists were being "sneered at, laughed at, and held in contempt," but their vindication was coming, Kirban reassured his readers, for one day the enemies of truth, and the neo-evangelicals among them, would realize that "all those odd Fundamental Christians" had suddenly disappeared.[93]

But Kirban's work admitted to its being culturally engaged. Like the neo-evangelicals defending "beat Gospel music," Kirban aimed to communicate in media relevant to his age. He wrote his novels with deliberately pragmatic intent. "While many people will not read the Scriptures or anything that has to do with church materials," he observed, "most will read a novel . . . a novel built with suspense, photographs, intrigue . . . and a novel that has to do with the FUTURE."[94] Kirban's 666 and 1000 made their evangelistic intentions clear. Both included a coupon entitled "My Personal Decision for CHRIST" that readers could sign, date, and return to the author for "a little booklet to help you start living your new life in Christ."[95] It was an urgent appeal, for those left behind could expect no safety—even in the "land of the free." Kirban instructed his readers in "responsible patriotism," but was certain that the ten kingdoms over which the Antichrist would rule would include the United States.[96]

The large sales of *666*—unprecedented in the history of the genre to that point—indicated the extent to which the prophecy novel was becoming a key component of fundamentalism's pop dispensational culture. Nevertheless, a great deal of this popular prophetic writing was being produced by a coterie of authors. Kirban had included in the acknowledgements to *666* a reference to Doctor Gary Cohen, who, he explained, had "carefully checked the final manuscript and supplied the Scripture references."[97] The acknowledgement was to be the beginning of a brief but fruitful writing partnership that produced, among other texts, *Revelation Visualized* (1971). Cohen followed Kirban's novels with an example of his own. This text, *Civilization's Last Hurrah: A Futuristic Novel about the End* (1974), was retitled and republished by Moody Press as *The Horsemen Are Coming* (1979). Cohen's retitled novel outlined an eschatological scenario that appeared somewhat chastened after the lurid prognostications of *The Late Great Planet Earth*. His preface emphasized speculative possibilities, rather than prophetic actualities: it claimed to "show in a fictional story just how the events prophesied for the end of this age may actually unfold. . . . Numerous details remain a mystery to us today. In this book the author has hazarded his own opinions—often guesses—as to how some of these details will actually occur," and, he admitted, "only time will tell how accurate or inaccurate these supplied details" might be.[98]

Cohen's modesty belied his long experience in teaching the dispensational faith. While Kirban was an Arab, Cohen was a messianic Jew who, by 1974, had become president of Graham Bible College, a lay-orientated institution in Bristol, Tennessee. He had already published *Understanding Revelation: A Chronology of the Apocalypse* (1968) and *Israel: Land of Prophecy, Land of Promise* (1974). His novel advanced a similarly conservative dispensational scheme. Unlike Kirban's writing, it included little in the way of evangelistic exhortation, lacked any citation of the Sinner's Prayer, a formulaic marker of spiritual commitment that grew in popularity throughout the twentieth century, and contained only muted descriptions of conversions to evangelical faith.[99] The novel appeared to be more interested in defending a beleaguered prophetic paradigm than in identifying itself as an evangelistic tool or pointing to dangerous trends in the contemporary world. Thus *The Horsemen Are Coming* insisted that "the rapture of the church is an *imminent* event which could happen at any moment—and no event in biblical prophecy need occur before it"—not even the establishment of the state of Israel.[100] It was hardly the argument that many readers might have expected of a messianic Jew who was also a persuaded dispensationalist. Cohen's novel was therefore an implicit critique of the *New Scofield Reference Bible, The Late Great Planet Earth,* and the prophetic revisions they represented. Although Cohen began his narrative "at a year not far from A.D. 2000," he was quick to point to the eschatological dangers of the contemporary cold war context.[101] *The Horsemen Are Coming* was terribly concerned by the expansionist goals of the Soviet bloc. The Soviet Union had "literally enslaved millions by a Communism which has stolen the freedom and religion of entire peoples."[102] It assumed that the threat of the Arab nations was linked to their left-leaning politics, rather than to their religious or economic threat. It imagined that the American Communist Party intended to "paralyze" the nation by a "general work-stopping strike" and that it was "crusading to eliminate marriage."[103] And, like the other cold war novels, it assumed that Communists would dominate Europe and spread their influence through such nefarious organizations as the Eurovision Song Contest.[104]

But Cohen's novel was aware of its genre context. The plot of *The Horsemen Are Coming*, like that of *666*, begins on an airplane. Alfred W. Tensing, the chief U.S. delegate to the United Nations, is returning from discussions designed to defuse the nuclear confrontation between the "United Arab Republic" and Israel.[105] In 1974, at the height of the oil crisis, the novel represented the Americans as favoring Israel. While refusing to identify the prophetic significance of the state, Cohen certainly insisted on its political significance, describing it as a "democratic island" amid the tyrannical states of the Middle East.[106] American support for Israel contrasts with the European and Russian plans to invade.[107] International organizations could offer no hope for the future—not when violent anti-Semitism was being embraced as "the solution which our world has sought after for thousands of years."[108] Cohen's novel involved itself in a large-scale reimagination of international geopolitics. It imagined the weakness of the United Nations, which, as an "amalgam of both peace-seeking and bandit nations, can hardly bring an enduring peace to a world whose problems are daily mushrooming with its burgeoning population."[109] In any case, the novel argued, the United Nations' cooperation with the Soviet bloc rendered the organization impotent. But this critique of the United Nations was pragmatic, not prophetic, for the weakness of the United Nations is accentuated in the novel by the growing power of Europe, which reconstitutes itself as the European United Republic (EUR) and locates its capital in Rome.[110] The novel imagines that that a series of Communist revolutions in the late 1980s would rob Europe of "its free speech, its free press, its free enterprise, and its freedom of religion."[111] As the EUR changes its name to ROME—the Republic of Mediterranean Europe—so it announces that it is "committed unswervingly to the cause of the people and to the Marxist-Leninist class struggle."[112] Echoing Tatford's fears about the combination of European Catholics and Communists, *The Horsemen Are Coming* was driven by a fear that the institutions of the end-time were firmly set in place.

Cohen's novel reiterated the genre's hostility to Modernism—though, by the 1970s, this specifically theological term was being less frequently applied as evangelicals identified a new enemy in a more pervasive "secular humanism." Nevertheless, the opposition to liberal theology remained: "When the modern theologians rejected the Bible in the nineteenth and twentieth centuries," one character explained, "they opened the doors for this flood of humanistic theories which is now removing all moral constraints."[113] During the tribulation, for example, "both men and women" would be "ordained as equals."[114] This shocking skepticism would reach its logical end in the United World Church, which, in the novel, combines theological liberality with a strident postmillennial hope. Church representatives hope to enter the "millennial kingdom of peace on earth through the narrow gate of human cooperation."[115] But this optimistic and egalitarian ecumenism sweeps almost everything before it. Persecution is so intense that there are only "thousands" of believers left for the rapture.[116] The small number of those removed means that normal life goes on without much notice of or concern about the disappeared.[117] Characters offer alternative theories to explain the disappearances—and an "interplanetary invasion" makes the first of its many appearances in the genre.[118] But Cohen's rapture makes some important exceptions that confirmed the old Protestant reading of Scripture: "Neither His Holiness, Leo XIV, nor any of the leaders of the United World Church are missing."[119] It was a conclusion that Myers, Tatford, Kirban, and Cohen could all share: Roman Catholicism was nothing less than an attack on America.

III

But later novels, anticipating the cultural reengagement of leading fundamentalists, grew more ambiguous in their references to the Roman Catholic Church. Carol Balizet's *The Seven Last Years* (1978) imagined a series of theological revolutions within the denomination—changes that made it plausible for the novel to suggest that the pope and "many of the cardinals" could be included in the rapture.[120] The novel frequently asserted the positive value of Roman Catholic belief: "'Why don't you like him, Craig? Is it because he's a Catholic priest?' 'Gosh, no, Hastings. I don't have anything against Catholics.'"[121] But it is not clear whether Balizet's novel shares its character's opinion. In *The Seven Last Years,* the Church is in disarray. One character, "like many American Catholics in the late 1980s," was in a state of spiritual confusion: "the catechism he had learned as a child had been watered down until almost nothing was left but for the individual to try to live a decent life. Nothing was clearly defined as either good or evil."[122] Some resisted the new ways. Many of those priests who sought the spiritual renewal of their parishioners began to "say Mass in the old unenlightened way."[123] But the Church's moral and theological failure also provided an opportunity for her enemies to act. When an

American bishop, the radical theologian Uriah Leonard, sets up an international food distribution program called "Feed my Lambs," it quickly acquires enormous influence and wealth. After the rapture, it takes on the role of the Federal Emergency Management Agency, or FEMA, in providing the infrastructure for the rebuilding of America. But with enormous power comes enormous temptation. Leonard achieves his goal of becoming the first American pontiff, but sees this as just one step on the way to his becoming the political leader of the world. Leonard—now His Holiness Sixtus VI, the 265th pope—is eventually unveiled as the Antichrist.[124] But worse horrors follow: he turns out to be a Satanist and a Jew.[125] For all its hinting as to the potential value of Catholic belief, therefore, *The Seven Last Years* reinscribed the historic Protestant convictions that nineteenth-century dispensational theorists had done so much to overturn. While in many other prophecy novels the pope is identified as the false prophet, in *The Seven Last Years* he is the Antichrist himself.

The conservatism of this assertion contrasted sharply with the novel's revisionist exegetical basis. In a rare gesture among more recent authors, Balizet advertised the exegetical basis of her fiction, including in her acknowledgements a reference to "Hal Lindsey, whose book started it all."[126] But *The Late Great Planet Earth*, to which Balizet owed so much, had reached markedly different conclusions about the eschatological dangers of the Roman Catholic Church. Thus Balizet's publisher included an explanatory preface, which referred to another influence, a supernatural "revelation" which the author had experienced. Balizet's "revelation" should not be disregarded, the publisher claimed, for she was "not only a Bible teacher but a registered nurse working night duty in a Tampa hospital, a mother of four daughters, a person passionately involved in Christian causes"; in other words, despite her "revelation," Balizet was someone her readers ought to take seriously.

But her wider debt to Lindsey was quite clear. Without any hesitation, Balizet located the rapture squarely in the summer of 1988.[127] *The Seven Last Years* was also emphatically nonpolitical, believing that the duty of Christians was to "to pattern ourselves after the New Testament church. The early Christians didn't try to change the political system which condoned slavery and dictatorships and injustice almost as bad as what we have now. They didn't try to change the social order; they tried to bring salvation to the people."[128] In any case, with such little time left and with the future already known, there was no point in changing the social order. Echoing the famous words of D. L. Moody—which the novel did not attribute—one character explained that "this world is a sinking ship. Our job is not to try to patch up the leaks but to get the crew off safely."[129] That "Survival Program" involved a return to the lifestyle of the premodern world, "gardening . . . raising chickens and fishing in the nearby bay."[130] Adopting a posture of principled nonviolence, believers are "specifically told" to avoid physical confrontation and call for spiritual aid to combat the Antichrist.[131] Believers go into hiding as opposition against their faith increases. Of course, fundamentalists had regularly argued for separation from "the world." In earlier days, as in the Angley's *Raptured,* that separation was entirely moral in orientation. By the later 1970s, believers were beginning to imagine that they should also be geographically separate as "the world" grew "meaner and more evil"—and gardening would be a crucial part of realizing that goal.[132]

Balizet invested in her separatism a strongly supernatural hope. Her publisher, Victor Books, was well-known for its support of the charismatic movement, the innovative and ecstatic mode of piety and worship that, by the late 1970s, had begun to make significant inroads into mainstream evangelical culture.[133] The charismatic agenda was certainly advanced in *The Seven Last Years.* Communities of tribulation saints would survive, Balizet argued, by realizing their possession of incredible supernatural powers. In her depiction of the tribulation period, occult powers and divine enabling seem stronger than ever before. Believers are threatened by demon-possessed vermin and domestic animals.[134] Unbelievers are frightened by levitating tables, disembodied voices, and mysterious apparitions.[135] And again and again, angels appear to direct the resources of the believers they help to survive.[136] Believers grow increasingly confident in their supernatural authority. Several young men witness a miraculous healing based on the theology of the "prayer of faith."[137] Another character prepares to "claim that garden for the Lord and rebuke anything that might be trying to take food away from His children"— and is astonished to discover that the strategy works.[138]

These claims for spiritual authority over animals and disease were an early indication of the "word of faith" theology that would make Balizet such a controversial figure in the later 1990s. Balizet went on to publish *Born in Zion* (1996), which argued that Christian families should have their children at home, as any dependence on medical care would intrude on the provision of God and would constitute an act of unbelief. Balizet was developing the anti-elitist medical themes that Salem Kirban had earlier articulated, but her convictions became tragic when they were adopted by the "Attleboro cult," a new religious movement in Massachusetts that was later investigated in connection with the deaths of several of its children.[139] Balizet had advised cultural withdrawal, but her ideas were developed in a context quite different from that of the charismatic fundamentalists she had earlier described. The cult may have been the ultimate expression of suspicion of the mainstream that Balizet had encouraged, but her reputation was one of the victims of the kind of separatist thinking her novel had expounded.

IV

Throughout the cold war period, therefore, while many fundamentalist leaders decried the threat of Communism, the prophecy novels their followers produced and consumed continued to focus on the enemy within. Prophecy novels could not point to the eschatological dangers of Communism while the European Union, the United Nations, and the Roman Catholic Church were revealing themselves as America's true enemies. Even Dan Betzer's *Beast: A Novel of the Future World Dictator* (1985) refused to refer to the cold war threats of the Communist bloc. It pointed to a new enemy, noting that ten nations now made up the membership of the European Economic Community, and imagined that the chairman of the EEC would one day be revealed as a bisexual, a reincarnation of Hitler, and as the Antichrist himself.[140]

By the mid-1980s, of course, many readers of pop dispensational literature were expecting to witness the imminent beginning of the end. Balizet's calling attention to the prophetic significance of the latter part of the decade—and specifically to 1988, the year that Lindsey had strongly implied would herald the rapture—pointed only to the failure of this revision of the dispensational faith. Many readers invested a great deal of hope in the eschatological potential of 1988, especially when Lindsey's ambiguous speculations were confirmed by the precise calculations of Edgar Whisenant, a former NASA engineer. Whisenant has been dismissed as a fringe figure, but the size of the fringe to which he appealed must be calculated from the fact that his *88 Reasons Why the Rapture Will Be in 1988* sold an estimated two million copies.[141] Whisenant revised his calculations in subsequent editions and rescheduled the rapture for each succeeding year until 1993.[142] But, as his expectations failed, it became clear to observers that the later decades of the twentieth century were years in which prophetic claims could be annulled as well as years in which prophetic claims could be confirmed. It is hardly surprising that many of the prophecy novels published after the apparent disconfirmation of Lindsey's suggestion seemed to prefer domestic themes and political quietude. Irene Martin's *Emerald Thorn* (1991) brought this stage of the tradition to its logical conclusion: its heroes escape from a tyrannical America for freedom in post-Communist Russia.[143] The fall of the Berlin Wall in 1989 and the subsequent collapse of European Communism were calling for a significant revision of the established apocalyptic narrative. Everything had changed: America was no longer the nation of the faithful, and old enemies had become new friends. But before these wider changes could be addressed, American evangelicals had to rethink their relationship to the nation that they had once understood to be their home.

5

Prophecy Fiction and Evangelical Political Reengagement

Looks like the persecution's started, folks.
— Frank Peretti, *Piercing the Darkness* (1990)

As the cold war drew to an end, evangelical authors in America were reimagining their relationship to prevailing trends in government. After the collapse of European Communism, that effort at prophetic revision seemed more urgent than ever. The end of the cold war "removed suddenly from mental maps a defining element of the post-1945 period: the figure of an adversary."[1] New adversaries had to be identified if the dichotomous imagination that underlay prophecy believers' conspiratorial worldview were to be sustained. But the new enemies were being found inside America—and, in the later 1980s, were being increasingly identified as New World Order conspirators and pedophilic satanic cults.[2] The new dangers they represented—internal to the once "redeemer nation"—called for a thoroughgoing reconsideration of the relationship between evangelicals and the American political mainstream.

The eventual decision by many conservative evangelicals to reengage with the secular political world ran counter to the political apathy that had characterized the piety of earlier fundamentalists. Throughout the middle decades of the twentieth century, fundamentalists and the prophecy novels they produced had displayed a strong preference for cultural and political retreat, both in the face of American secularity and the Communist threat that loomed on the horizon. The "Gospel Group" in John Myers's *The Trumpet Sounds* (1965) had hoped for nothing more than mere survival in the face of the Antichrist's all-consuming power. The theme still resonated three decades later, when the remnant in Jean Grant's *The Revelation* (1992) retreated to an isolated but self-sufficient California ranch. By the end of the 1980s, however, the mood of writers of prophecy fiction had clearly begun to change. America no longer felt safe for conservative evangelicals. Martin's *Emerald Thorn* (1991), as we have seen, advanced the ultimate subversion of cold war political binaries, suggesting that post-Communist Russia could provide an end-time haven for a beleaguered remnant of American tribulation saints.[3] Other evangelical writers were preparing fictions that were to suggest an alternative response to the hegemony of evil in the period that Tim LaHaye was beginning to describe as "the pretribulation tribulation."[4] These writers reversed the older fundamentalist notions of separatism. They insisted that that the Christian's duty was not to seek escape from the evil agencies of the persecuting world, but rather to resist them. If America was no longer safe for evangelicals, then America should be changed.

A trend toward political reengagement had existed since the early 1970s, when *The Late Great Planet Earth* admitted "the importance of electing honest, intelligent men to positions of leadership."[5] The idea was advanced with a degree of hesitation until the early 1980s. In 1982, Francis Schaeffer's *A Christian Manifesto,* which called for civil disobedience to protest against the legality of abortion, sold twice as many copies as *Jane Fonda's Workout Book.*[6] By the mid-1990s, the need for political reengagement was being widely disseminated.[7] The new mood demonstrated a substantial rethinking of the dispensational tradition's preference for cultural inaction and political despair at the same time as it represented a growing sense of alarm at the development of a spiritual "fifth column" within the United States. Throughout the cold war, the threat to believers had been successfully externalized beyond the boundaries of the nation. America had been imagined as a fundamentally Christian republic, however aberrant certain aspects of its contemporary culture might appear and despite occasional fears of Communist infiltration. In fact, by the late 1970s, the traditional ascendancy of the evangelical classes appeared to be confirmed. *Newsweek* proclaimed 1976, the year in which Chuck Colson's *Born Again* exposed a network of believers in leading White House positions, "the year of the evangelical," and, in the immediate aftermath of the first appearance of the "emerging Republican majority," victory for Jimmy Carter in the 1977 presidential election, and the consolidation and increasing influence of the Moral Majority, founded by Jerry Falwell in 1979, it was still possible to imagine some kind of public commitment to the ideal of a "Christian America."[8] Balizet's *The Seven Last Years* (1978) was markedly hopeful of American political life. Its rapture did not involve the president, but it did include the vice president, his wife, and many members of the Cabinet and Congress.[9] But by the mid-1980s, despite the leadership of a

Republican president whose public rhetoric resonated with dispensational themes and ideas, a new mood had gripped large sections of the evangelical public.[10] The faith of the nation they supported no longer seemed assured. Evangelical writers were increasingly alarmed by the spiritual condition of America. As the arms race escalated, and Ronald Reagan opted to bankrupt the Soviet Union through a policy of "peace through strength," evangelicals grew fearful of the subversion of civic religion. In schools and universities, in businesses and health agencies, institutional Christianity was being displaced by a series of spiritual alternatives whose plausibility obscured their "hidden dangers." Constance E. Cumbey's discussion of *The Hidden Dangers of the Rainbow: The New Age Movement and Our Coming Age of Barbarism* (1985) was among the first to delineate the eschatological potential of the new popularity of Eastern philosophies. Her conclusions were echoed and confirmed in a spate of succeeding publications.[11] Evangelical writers were articulating a suspicious withdrawal from mainstream culture at the same time as they advanced an increasingly ambitious attempt to appropriate its power.

This program of political reengagement took place in the context of a rapidly expanding market for evangelical fiction. The 1980s saw some of the movement's earliest best-sellers—the prairie romances of Janette Oke, for example, which were initially marketed through home parties, but which sold some eight million copies in the ten years after 1979.[12] Oke's novels offered a nostalgic and romanticized description of frontier life, and their popularity soared as evangelicals turned to reassuring fictions after the first flush of their political success. That demand for cultural reassurance was rapidly eclipsed as evangelicals began to recognize that the moral dichotomy of the cold war period could no longer be externalized. In the late 1980s, evangelicals understood themselves as a besieged minority, though this time their enemies were new religious faiths. At their most benign, these new faiths offered a pathway to enlightenment through a range of alternative spiritualities; at their least benign, they offered a gateway to witchcraft and even demonic possession. Some of these themes had surfaced in the paranoia of the later cold war fiction. *The Seven Last Years* (1978) had described a conspiracy of high-ranking Satanists, for example, which included the owner of the largest media conglomerate in America.[13] A similar occult conspiracy was reproduced in Dan Betzer's *Beast: A Novel of the Future World Dictator* (1985), and Satanist violence against Christians again appeared in Jean Grant's *The Revelation* (1992).[14] These novels agreed that a false religion presented a far more immediate danger than a false political hope. Older prophecy novelists also recognized the changing identity of their enemy. In 1979, thirty years after *They That Remain*, Dayton Manker was prepared to admit that his earlier thesis had been significantly revised. It was no longer clear to him that Communism represented the most serious danger facing the church. Latter-day "Babylonianism" would certainly include Communism, he believed, but could not be restricted to it. The end-time danger was religious in tone, and its sinister danger was entirely occluded by the benignity of its title. One prophecy novel identified the new philosophy as a "tangled web of death."[15] By the end of the 1980s evangelical writers had agreed on a consensus: strange and terrible things would come of the "New Age" movement.

Evangelical responses to the New Age movement conformed to the paradigms of a classic moral panic. The New Age scare identified a vehicle through which a particular social group could attempt to popularize their cultural and political goals.[16] Evangelical leaders began to link ostensibly harmless philosophies to tabloid ideas of a nationwide satanic attack. The urgent tone of their publications was justified by one of the most shocking of the period's media trials—the claims of ritual abuse in the McMartin preschool case in southern California in 1984, which alleged that members of the McMartin family had recruited children from their preschool into illegal sexual and occult activities.[17] Significantly, the panic was developed at the height of the "culture wars," when evangelical leaders were embattled and when they could best utilize the ultimate weaponry of fear by invoking the paranoid style in American cultural politics.[18] It was a moment in which leaders of the religious right were encouraging their followers to abandon the separatism of an earlier fundamentalism to embrace the alternative identity of "conservative Christians," an identity that would allow them to fight "worldly battles" and to seek "worldly power and influence in the name of 'Christian values.'"[19] This new cultural engagement developed in parallel with a new evangelical politics. But evangelical leaders were concerned by much more than merely the occult. As the panic developed, devil worship became "an all-embracing label with which to stigmatize any aspect of modern society with which the conservative religious leadership did not agree."[20] And their claims were widely disseminated—not least through popular print media, whose sudden experience of increasing competition and economic challenge drove it toward a tabloid style. Within evangelicalism, there was an explosion of books on New Age or occult subjects in the years after 1988.[21] Nevertheless, despite the strong media profile of several "occult cops," whose claims invested the satanic abuse allegations with a significant degree of credibility, early investigators concluded that the panic drew on political roots that could be "easily traced to the fundamentalist religious Right." The issue was "devised and defined in such a way that reflected the concerns and ambitions of Christian fundamentalists at a time when this movement was undergoing rapid expansion."[22] These were fears that some prophecy believers needed to project: an "upsurge in diabolism" was, after all, expected as the second coming approached.[23] But the new enemy required new reflection on the political identity of evangelicals themselves. In the long cold war they had hoped to face off the apocalyptic threat of Communism through school prayer and military strength. The New Age danger—with its eschatological potential and internalized threat—demanded an alternative solution.

This "upsurge in diabolism" was the context for the reception of the prophecy novels produced by Frank Peretti (b. 1951) and Pat Robertson (b. 1930).[24] Peretti was a thirtysomething Assemblies of God pastor-turned-carpenter before the success of his first publications—which seemed, to some readers, like "*The Invasion of the Body Snatchers* with a few themes from *The Exorcist* and Bram Stoker's *Dracula* thrown in"—earned him a reputation as "the Stephen King of evangelical culture."[25] At first, *This Present Darkness* (1986), a fantasy novel describing the conflict of angels and demons over small-town America, appeared to sell slowly, but word-of-mouth advertising drove spiralling sales which kept the novel and its sequel, *Piercing the Darkness* (1989), in the ten top-selling Christian novels from 1989 to 1994.[26] Their success allowed Peretti to position himself as a leading spokesman on the subject of "spiritual warfare."[27] Like other evangelical writers in the period, Peretti was fascinated by the evil potential of the New Age movement. His title quoted Ephesians 6:12 (ironically, from the Revised Standard Version that earlier evangelicals had abominated) and argued for the minority status of the believing remnant and the demonic character of the present age—and this despite the conservative advances represented by the recent election of President Ronald Reagan. Peretti's novels appropriated for evangelical purposes the tropes of the supernatural thriller.[28] By focusing on allegations of child abuse, both novels located that concern within the "real world" context of the McMartin preschool scandal. But Peretti's New Age villains did not represent an entirely domestic foe. While they certainly existed as a dangerous fifth column within the United States, they had links to many of the groups and institutions most commonly cited in evangelical conspiracy theories. But greater danger came from the fact that the New Age movement was itself a "conspiracy of spirit entities," the novels argued, and their narratives' assumptions turned on readers' expectations of the wickedness of university life and of the maverick religious philosophies that campus life embraced.[29] Therefore, as they reconfigured evangelical modernity, Peretti's themes became apocalyptic and politically confrontational without ever broaching the dispensational suggestion of escape by rapture. His novels were the very antithesis of the prairie romances that had sold so well in the earlier part of the decade. They were among the first to suggest that evangelicals should unite to actively—even violently—resist the values of the secular mainstream. And they were phenomenally popular. Though his plots were rather more Manichean than orthodox, Peretti's novels were among the earliest best-sellers in evangelical literary history. His novels figured evangelical characters in an open-ended struggle against demonic forces. But in their implicit resistance to dispensational escapism, and in their insistence that the future was open and that the spiritual condition of America could be changed, Peretti's novels offered an implicit critique of the determining assumptions of the prophecy fiction genre they would so profoundly influence.

Peretti's novels seemed to anticipate one evangelical leader's attempt at the ultimate act of cultural and political resistance—Pat Robertson's unsuccessful bid to become the president of the United States. Robertson's subsequent turn to prophetic fiction would, like Peretti's work, critique the dispensational theology then prevailing in the American evangelical world. Robertson's work seemed to draw on Peretti's readiness to engage—sometimes violently—with the physical manifestations of forces that were ultimately demonic in character. Robertson's contribution to the changing title of the tribulation saints indicated his increasing sense of the need for physical resistance to mainstream culture, and even for the militarization of prophecy believers. The separatist "Gospel Group" in Myers's *The Trumpet Sounds* becomes "The Remnant" in Peretti's *This Present Darkness;* but in Pat Robertson's *The End of the Age,* they are the "Christian Resistance," armed with nuclear weapons.

Neither Peretti nor Robertson were authors of rapture novels, strictly defined. Though they did not attack premillennialism, their novels opposed the fundamental assumptions of the dispensational faith. Peretti's novels ignore the rapture as a means of escape from a hostile world and describe their characters' attempts to delay, rather than promote or finally escape, the apocalypse. In *This Present Darkness,* the Antichrist figure is ultimately defeated in his bid to establish a series of one-world institutions, and the tribulation he desires never begins. In Pat Robertson's *The End of the Age,* by contrast, the tribulation begins long before the rapture, and believers resist the Antichrist's machinations by regrouping in New Mexico and by threatening his regime. Peretti's novels are ultimately supportive of evangelical agency, imagining that believers can successfully forestall the finale of world history; Robertson's novels, on the other hand, describe a successful revival and the construction of an evangelical enclave as the wider world rushes toward its end. Holed up in their Albuquerque ranch for the seven years of tribulation, Robertson's characters establish schools and hospitals as the world—quite literally—goes to hell. Peretti and Robertson therefore represented an entirely new mood in evangelical prophetic writing, developing a spirituality of resistance on a critique of dispensational faith. Nevertheless, both writers were to shape the prophecy fiction that presupposed that system's truth. In their imaginative resistance to secular humanism, Peretti and Robertson would reinvent the evangelical imagination.

But there ended their similarities. *The End of the Age* insisted on a tragic vision of history, and argued that near-future events could be readily anticipated—to the extent of setting dates for the eschaton. By contrast, Peretti's novels were entirely open-ended, and, in a narrative world where everything was contingent, refused to speculate on events in the near future. It was a vision of political possibility that even Hal Lindsey was beginning to share. In *The 1980's: Countdown to Armageddon* (1981), for example, he outlined his sense of latter-day political opportunity as the world rushed toward 1988, the year he had suggested would be of critical eschatological significance.[30] Even in that final decade of human history, Lindsey anticipated expanding opportunities for evangelical America and suggested that apocalyptic catastrophes could be avoided. Of course, in *The Late Great Planet Earth,* Lindsey had already encouraged his readers to vote for responsible leaders, but he could never have anticipated the surge of evangelical politics at the end of that decade.[31] Neither could he have anticipated that politics' sudden demise with the collapse of the Moral Majority, the scandals associated with Oral Roberts, the Bakkers and Jimmy Swaggart, and the end of Pat Robertson's political dream in the late 1980s.[32] But the legacy of that politics continued. The shift from tragic to comic, pioneered by Peretti and interrogated by Robertson, had "crucial consequences" for the reconstruction of the evangelical political imagination.[33]

I

Frank Peretti's *This Present Darkness* is a novel against America. Its evangelical heroes are led by the pastor of Ashton Community Church, Hank Busche, and a former *New York Times* journalist, Marshall Hogan, "a strong, big-framed bustler hustler" who becomes editor of the small town's newspaper.[34] As in earlier prophecy novels, the function of the journalist character is to put the case together, to order disparate facts into a coherent background narrative. And in a conspiracy thriller as wide-ranging as *This Present Darkness,* Hogan performs a critical role. He and Busche discover that a dangerous and violent group of New Age adherents are attempting to take over their local college. They are astonished to discover the spiritual power their enemies are able to wield. But that astonishment reached out from the pages of the novel into its readers' world: *This Present Darkness* confirmed the direst fears of American evangelicals when it presented apparently benign New Age ideas and philosophies within a context that confirmed their influence on a wide range of their socio-phobias. In the novel, the New Age group is led by Alexander Kaseph, a "real wheeler-dealer" from "back east, maybe New York," who was "loaded and . . . liked everybody to know it."[35] Kaseph is "a warlock and a gangster rolled into one," the ultimate embodiment of evangelical fears of the city and high finance.[36] His adherents are equally frightening, and in a catalogue of the fears haunting American dispensationalists throughout the mid-1980s, are influential in "Arab oil, the [European] Common Market, the World Bank, [and] international terrorism."[37] The group is intent on controlling America, owning law firms and lobbying groups that pushed for "special interest legislation" that was "usually anti-Jewish and anti-Christian" in tone.[38] But the public fronts for this panoply of preternatural power were apparently harmless spiritualities. Peretti's novels expose the baneful agenda of "all the usual 'isms.'"[39] "It's all a con game," his narrative explains; "Eastern meditation, witchcraft, divination, Science of Mind, psychic healing, holistic education—oh, the list goes on and on—it's all the same thing, nothing but a ruse to take over people's minds and spirits, even their bodies."[40] And that snatching of minds and bodies, *This Present Darkness* insisted, was all in preparation for the final manifestation of eschatological evil in small-town America.

Peretti's conspiracies were grounded in readers' assumptions of the malevolent intentions of astonishing unearthly powers. Both *This Present Darkness* and *Piercing the Darkness* premised the existence of "territorial spirits"—demons who effectively controlled particular geographical locations.[41] The idea had a disputed basis in Old Testament literature, but, as Peretti was writing, its peculiar emphases were evolving into a distinctive doctrine and were being promoted by significant charismatic leaders. The novels represented a very specific—but, internationally, an increasingly influential—style of evangelical belief.[42] It was a style of faith entirely alien to the traditional dispensational worldview; *Bibliotheca Sacra*, the theological journal published by Dallas Theological Seminary, was one of many conservative-minded publications to publish a robust critique of the new idea.[43] Nevertheless, Peretti's novels—and others like them—created and sustained a series of entirely new ideas about the unseen world.[44] Their approach seemed to resonate with that of a number of literary classics, but Peretti disclaimed the most obvious external influences and located the source of the idea in a moment of divine inspiration: "The Lord God provides the inspiration for my novels," he explained; "I write from whatever God has placed upon my heart."[45]

Wherever the idea originated, Peretti's novels provided it with massive exposure. Its impact has been gauged in a sociological study of the cosmologies of members of an evangelical student group at McMaster University in Canada. This study, documented in Paul A. Bramadat's *The Church on the World's Turf* (2000), discovered that Peretti's fiction, and especially *This Present Darkness*, was the most common influence on or reflection of the cosmologies of his subjects.[46] In fact, Bramadat claimed, when his student interviewees discussed the spirit world, they were "more likely to cite Peretti than the Bible."[47] Bramadat argued that the "unprecedented prominence" of spiritual warfare in "evangelical popular culture since the mid-1980s" was entirely due to Peretti.[48] In fact, he claimed, the influence of *This Present Darkness* has been so extensive that it has come to be known as the "Bible of spiritual warfare."[49] Though these claims may need to be qualified, there can be little doubt that Peretti's work has set an agenda. His writing has had a huge impact on the apocalyptic imagination of evangelicals, spawning "a minor industry of fiction and nonfiction titles on the techniques and nature" of demonic combat.[50] David E. Stevens, surveying the emergence and development of the idea, cited ten texts proposing and opposing it—all of them published after *This Present Darkness*.[51] Peretti's novels, which went on to sell some three and a half million copies, demonstrated that prophecy fiction could profoundly shape—and even, perhaps, invent—significant systems of belief.[52]

But *This Present Darkness* and *Piercing the Darkness* appeared to have a wider agenda than the construction of a new theory of the dynamics of the spirit world. Peretti's novels provided their readers with a deeply political meditation on the increasing marginalization of evangelicals. They considered the rights and wrongs of several kinds of strategies of resistance, from prayer and public protest to direct and confrontational action. The novels provided this exposition of evangelical agency in their extended descriptions of the invisible enemies threatening small-town America. Peretti's good characters are a species of evangelical Everyman, and his unspecified locations are purposefully archetypal. Ashton, in *This Present Darkness*, looked "typically American—small, innocent, and harmless, like the background for every Norman Rockwell painting."[53] Bacon's Corner, in *Piercing the Darkness*, appeared similarly innocuous, "nothing special, just one of those little farming towns far from the motorway, nothing more than a small hollow dot on the map."[54] Peretti's novels are not set in any particular state. They provide a myth for an American everywhere: "It could have begun in any town."[55]

Yet extraordinary demonic trouble is brewing behind these very ordinary façades. Ashton is under siege by a malevolent spirit known as the Prince of Babylon.[56] In Bacon's Corner, in the second novel, the Strongman is attempting to revenge the Prince of Babylon's earlier defeat. These demonic powers are shown to wield enormous influence. Ashton, in *This Present Darkness*, had never been so full of "rumors, scandals, and malicious gossip."[57] The town's most influential congregation, Ashton United Christian Church, had slipped from being a center of doctrinal precision to becoming an organization that only "endorses religious tolerance and condemns cruelty to animals."[58] The minister of the United Church, Oliver Young, is defined in terms of respectability and social influence, and his alignment with media-savvy evangelicals operates as a condemnation of both liberal and neo-evangelical constituencies: Young's office is dotted with "photographs of him posing with the governor, a few popular evangelists, some authors, and a senator."[59] His character enables the novel to position the variety of fundamentalism it supports in direct opposition to less dogmatic, media-friendly versions of neo-evangelical faith. But, whatever the suggestions of Peretti's conspiratorial theme, Young's relativistic theology would find few echoes among the big-name evangelicals of the middle of that decade. In contrast to their much-criticized exclusivism, Young's theology emphasizes that "each person must find his own way, his own truth."[60] The approach was affirmed by the courses taught in the college that dominated life in the town. Its curriculum included course titles like "Introduction to God and

Goddess Consciousness," "Pathways to Your Inner Light," and "How to Enjoy the Present by Experiencing Past and Future Lives."[61] Campus life is dominated by an influential New Age elite led by Professor Juleen Langstrat, a UCLA graduate with a "strong interest" in "some kind of neo-pagan religious group in California" and an unhealthy relationship with leading officers of law enforcement.[62] In the novel, as this relationship suggests, the most important American institutions have been subverted by New Age conspirators.[63] Their subversion leads the conspirators to attack the Constitution. As the novel progresses, there is less and less of an America to defend. As the influence of the conspiracy steadily extends, believers move from private prayer to public protest and find their meetings broken up by police who defend their actions by citing the distinction between church and state.[64] Ashton becomes "a police state," and the evangelicals it imprisons are denied any communication with "families, friends, lawyers, or anyone."[65] As Manker had earlier discovered, the "constitutional rights" of evangelical believers could come to mean nothing at all.[66]

But Peretti parallels his characters' political powerlessness with astonishing spiritual agency. That agency develops alongside the novels' theological innovations in an insistence that warrior angels owe their power to Christians' prayers. Prayers motivate God to action, and he empowers angels to answer the prayers of the saints. Angels, in other words, are entirely powerless unless Christians are consciously praying for their victory and "binding" the demonic forces arraigned against them.[67] It is a theme to which the angelic characters return. Experiencing weakness, they complain that "something had happened to their prayer cover";[68] experiencing strength, they observe that "the power of God was increasing now . . . the saints must be praying somewhere."[69] There is very little about divine sovereignty or omnipotence in this novel—the action is maintained by angels whose power is derived from human protagonists.

Nevertheless, this theology of spiritual power, emphasizing human prayer above divine initiative, is indicative of Peretti's wider purpose to provoke evangelicals into action. That purpose explains why the novels do so little to instruct their readers in the basics of evangelical belief. *This Present Darkness* gives an extended exposition of New Age thinking long before its rather briefer introduction to the Christian gospel.[70] In both novels, but particularly in *This Present Darkness*, the evangelistic theme is minor. The novel appears more concerned to activate evangelical readers than to recruit others to the fold. Its activists, "the Remnant," are led by Hank Busche, a "fundamentalist minister" who attended Bible school and seminary rather than the kind of secular college that the novel showed to be dangerously responsive to New Age control.[71] The novel describes the Remnant's progression from prayer and physical passivity to "prayer walks" designed to combat the territorial spirits that seemed to control life in the town.[72] The Remnant move from prayer walks to protest, and only finally to direct—and violent—action, converging on the college building in which their enemies had concentrated their strength.[73] It is this movement toward violence that brings about the Remnant's salvation. The police are called in response to the "religious fanatics" on the campus, but they are overruled by federal officers who demand that police protect the evangelicals and arrest the criminals inside.[74] Thus the novel's conclusion identifies its confidence in American institutions. Though open to corrupt influence, these institutions are basically sound, and their subversion can eventually be overturned. But America will be rescued—and true believers will be redeemed—only through the threat of evangelical violence.

The novel's conclusion was, therefore, almost apocalyptic. *This Present Darkness*, which reinvented prophetic agency and insisted that the combination of prayer, public protest, and direct action was necessary to prevent the forces of evil seizing the prophetic initiative and establishing their timetable of victory, was imbued with eschatological references. These motifs were invoked—though not developed—to provide the narrative with a profound sense of urgency. The novel listed the dangers facing America. The New World Order would bring an Antichrist, "the New Age Christ," whose followers would accept his status as "the Messiah, the answer for all mankind, a true prophet of peace and universal brotherhood."[75] The novel imagined that the final conflict in the spiritual realm would begin with the sound of a trumpet—a last trumpet, and one that would call angels to the defense of beleaguered Christian believers.[76] But the novel's most obvious apocalyptic reference was its repeated invocation of the fall of Babylon.[77] Tal, the captain of the angels, and Ba'al Rafar, the captain of the demons, had last met at the city's collapse.[78] When their forces gather over Ashton, many centuries later, their conflict is renewed. The New Age society harassing Ashton's Christians is therefore identified as a manifestation of Babylon the Great, the end-time enemy of the people of God, the description of which resonates with allusions to Revelation 18. The Christian characters in the novel have no doubt about the eschatological significance of the New Age phenomenon. Their enemy is nothing less than "Babylon revived right before the end of the age."[79] *This Present Darkness* identifies the New Age movement as Christianity's final danger.

These extended allusions establish the novel as an apocalyptic thriller. But, like many prophecy fiction novels, it is a thriller that points to the eschatological potential of the present. The New Age movement is far more dangerous than Kaseph's juxtaposition of education, seduction, and international terror. It represents the final, one-world religion that evangelical writers had long feared. But the conclusion to the novel undermines the finality of its eschatological motif. Babylon was being revived, but its eventual dominance could be forestalled. *This Present Darkness* was not a prophecy of the incontestable rise of evil, but an argument that its final manifestation—even its final victory—could be deferred by the prayer-ful activism of a believing remnant. Babylon the Great would certainly fall—but its prophesied rise to power could also be delayed. "Just remember, brothers and sisters," one character exhorts, "we are not contending against flesh and blood, but against the principalities, against the powers, against the world rulers of this pres-ent darkness, against the spiritual hosts of wickedness in the heavenly places"—and, in that conflict, he was arguing, believers could prevail.[80]

This Present Darkness presented a powerful argument against prophetic pessi-mism and the political passivity it so often seemed to generate. But it also opened up possibilities for Christian fiction. Peretti's novel provided future prophecy novels with a distinctive supernaturalism. Characters in Mel Odom's Apocalypse Dawn series have repeated encounters with demons, and the back cover of Jonathan R. Cash's *The Age of the Antichrist* (1999) insisted that no other novel "since Frank Peretti's *This Present Darkness* has . . . opened a window into the unseen world of spiritual warfare." But *This Present Darkness* also became "an important milestone in the history of evangelical publishing," and the catalyst for Crossway's decision to develop a line in Christian fiction.[81] The millions of copies it sold returned repeat-edly to the theme: the American future is open.

II

These conclusions reflected the cultural environment out of which evangelicalism's political renaissance emerged. Like characters in Peretti's novels, many American evangelicals rallied to the flag as they grew in suspicion of powerful and wicked elites. But some evangelicals attempted to capture the flag itself. It was a theme at the core of Pat Robertson's attempt to "help America"—his attempt to become the president of the United States.[82]

Robertson's good intentions placed him among the "capable hands" that Per-etti imagined might one day control America.[83] It was a career for which he had enjoyed extended training. His father, a socially conservative Democrat, had served in the House of Representatives from 1933 to 1946 and in the Senate from 1946 to 1966. Robertson himself was educated in history at Washington and Lee College (graduating in 1950) before completing legal studies at Yale (graduating in 1955) and ministerial preparation at New York Theological Seminary (graduating in 1959). In 1960, he established the Christian Broadcasting Network in Virginia.[84] One year later, he was ordained as a clergyman in the Southern Baptist Convention, a status which seemed inconsistent with his increasingly charismatic spirituality but which he only resigned in the late 1980s with the beginning of his political career.[85] His media empire expanded exponentially in subsequent decades, and Robertson was able to position himself as a significant evangelical leader. Laying to one side his long-standing hesitations about political involvement, he ran a brief campaign to be nominated as the Republican candidate for what he would later describe in typically superlative terms as "the highest office in the greatest nation."[86]

Robertson's campaign had unlikely beginnings. He could hardly have a chosen a less auspicious moment to enter the political arena as an evangelical broadcaster. In the late 1980s, "televangelists" had become objects of public scorn as, one by one, their empires had begun to topple. In March 1987 Oral Roberts informed his substantial television audience that God would kill him unless he raised $8 million within two weeks. The funds that saved his life turned out to have been donated by a businessman who had built his own fortune in gambling. Later that year, Jim and Tammy Faye Bakker, who operated the Praise the Lord television ministry, were accused of a series of financial and sexual irregularities. The accusations, which continued for months, exposed an empire of opulence and bad taste. Then, early in 1988, Jimmy Swaggart was discovered in a tryst with a prostitute in New Orleans. His confession of sin, which was nationally broadcast, was followed a few months later by his being caught with another prostitute in the same city.[87] Robertson's announcement that he would run for the presidential nomination of the Republican Party therefore generated huge media interest, and his background was scoured for any hint of irregularity.

Robertson's campaign nevertheless got off to a promising start.[88] In January 1988, Robertson beat the most likely nominee—Vice President George G. W. Bush—in the Iowa caucus, but lost momentum in the New Hampshire primaries shortly thereafter, and eventually finished third, before withdrawing from the contest. His campaign had been unsuccessful in achieving its ultimate goals, but its infrastructure provided for the consolidation of Robertson's agenda in the subsequent development of the Christian Coalition. The Coalition confirmed Robertson's standing as the public voice of evangelical conservatives and as a leading strategist in their project to "help America."[89] The campaign and the organization it spawned were signs of changing times. Frank Peretti's novels were gaining in popularity even as the evangelicals who consumed them were embracing an increasingly strident political tone. Evangelicals were taking advantage of an open future by resisting the political and spiritual powers behind "this present darkness." Robertson's bid to become the chief executive of the world's most powerful nation was the ultimate form of direct action against the vaunting ambitions of his enemy—the secular humanist elite.

This political reengagement called for a substantial reconfiguration of evangelical eschatological thought. Robertson's campaign for the presidency seemed to challenge his earlier preference for apocalyptic despair.[90] He had, for example, predicted a nuclear war for late 1982; it had been a signal of his expectations as to

the future of Western civilization.[91] But it is also clear that he had begun to distance himself from the dispensationalism he had once endorsed.[92] Many observers noted that the political campaign had made a significant impact on the tone
of his rhetoric. Robertson's public statements appeared more optimistic and his
commitment to the social pessimism so common in the dispensational tradition
had clearly begun to unravel. Some fellow prophecy believers were shocked by the
turn of events. One premillennial commentator suggested that Robertson could
yet turn out to be the Antichrist, deceiving even the elect.[93] Some of his rivals in
the bid to shape the evangelical imagination "outed" him as a postmillennialist.
Those who actually were postmillennialists knew better: Gary North has described
Robertson's revised eschatology as occupying the "halfway house" of "socially
activist dispensationalism."[94] But there was enough obscurity in his campaign's
approach to justify one observer's noting that Robertson's premillennial followers
were "acting increasingly like postmillennialists."[95] The ambiguity was politically
productive. The "convergence of the premillennial and post-millennial perspectives" developed a system of eschatological ethics that was "neither pessimistic nor
pietistic."[96] It certainly suited the aims of some of Robertson's opponents, such as
Charles Pack and even Constance Cumbey, to identify this new optimism as a variant of socially liberal postmillennialism.[97] But Robertson had made his premillennial commitments clear: as recently as 1984, he had stated clearly that the rapture
would occur "before the thousand-year reign of Christ on earth called the Millennium."[98] Robertson may have abandoned dispensationalism, but he retained the
premillennialism on which it was based.

The confusion of Robertson's critics was generated in part by his welding his
premillennial convictions to an expectation of "a great revival of faith in Jesus
Christ."[99] This expectation of "latter rain" had been widely shared by earlier generations of Pentecostals.[100] The "latter rain" doctrine implied that widespread social
transformation could occur in the last years before the end of the age. In Robertson's mind it included an "explosion of Christian evangelism that by the end of
the 1990s may result in a 'spiritual harvest' of between 500 million and a billion
people." Evangelism was therefore "not only a religious responsibility, required
under Christ's commission to his followers to preach the gospel to all the world,
but . . . an eschatological duty, a necessary precursor to the millennium," and a
duty with overtly political implications.[101] After all, these new believers would have
votes. Robertson's political interventions were much less ambitious than those of
the theocrats who appeared to be influencing his direction. His ambition was not
to advance the social conditions that would inaugurate the millennium, as Gary
North and some other proponents of Christian Reconstruction had averred, but
was ultimately defensive, hoping to prevent any further erosion of a socially conservative, broadly Christian society.[102] It was designed as an antidote to "the religion of secular humanism."[103]

"Secular humanism" combined many invisible threats. Robertson's exposé of *The New World Order* (1991), published three years after the end of his presidential campaign, provided his supporters with a rationale for his failure that, some critics claimed, drew heavily on established tropes in anti-Semitic polemic.[104] The title of the book was itself an indicator of its appeal. Although the expression "new world order" had been in common use since the beginning of the twentieth century, it had been provided with new significance after President George G. W. Bush's address to a joint session of Congress on September 11, 1990. Bush's speech described in glowing terms the new themes influencing government in the aftermath of the cold war. Robertson, by contrast, found the new world order entirely sinister. He used the term to describe the new society that was being promoted by powerful and often invisible forces, including Masons and the Illuminati.

This was a conspiracy far grander in scope than the small-town constitutional infringements described in Peretti's novels. Robertson's rhetoric—especially in the aftermath of his political defeat—provided ample evidence that religious and secular conspiracies had begun to cross over.[105] One leading historian of conspiracy has described Robertson as "the first modern religious and political figure of national stature to embrace a belief in an Illuminatist conspiracy."[106] But Robertson's conspiracist notions only came to widespread public attention four years after the publication of *The New World Order* (1991), the book in which they were most clearly described. In 1995, two articles in *The New York Review of Books* argued that *The New World Order* had drawn on earlier anti-Semitic publications.[107] Robertson's prophetic novel, published four years after *The New World Order* and in the same year as the controversy about his alleged anti-Semitism, evidenced similar varieties of the "paranoid style." In fact, its conspiratorial motifs were made all the more powerful by the narrative's almost exclusively American concerns.[108] Robertson—the failed presidential candidate—invited his readers to believe that the nation's most senior political appointments were being made through "manipulation and extortion."[109] In the late 1980s, *Piercing the Darkness* had imagined that a cultic conspiracy could one day involve a distinguished member of the Supreme Court. Less than a decade later, Robertson was prepared to consider that a cultic conspiracy could engulf the presidency itself. His political failure had confirmed his most terrible fears: powerful forces were arraigned against America.

The End of the Age (1995), Robertson's only work of fiction, appeared to be taking revenge on the office its author had failed to win. The novel's first president commits suicide, and his replacement, a "borderline alcoholic" with a bisexual wife, is murdered within days of taking office.[110] By contrast, Mark Beaulieu, the third president within one week of a cataclysmic meteor impact, is a perfectly blue-blooded American. But appearances can be deceiving: the new president turns out to be possessed by the spirit of Shiva and is finally revealed to be the Antichrist.[111] Beaulieu's characterization provided a major development of Robertson's critique of the presidential office. The Antichrist was no longer an ethnic or political "other." Now, possessing "remarkable charisma and brilliance," being "charismatic, compelling, magnetic, and electric . . . [the] one natural leader for the world," the Antichrist is the very quintessence of the American elite.[112] Like many writers of prophecy fiction, Beaulieu is disappointed by the United Nations, which had "failed time and time again to deliver the unity it has so often promised."[113] He aims to replace its "outmoded nationalism . . . outmoded traditions [and] unrealistic secularism" with a "new order of unity and cooperation."[114] This political renaissance is rooted in the re-enchantment of the West, a new world order of New Age proportions. *The End of the Age* presented an explicit critique of the danger of this political-religious movement, even as it pulled apart the rhetoric that underpinned it. The critique was designedly political in tone, and its target was the man who had beaten Robertson in the Republican primaries to assume "the highest office in the greatest nation."[115] Robertson insisted that those who promised access to "the New Age, the New World Order, the Age of Aquarius, or whatever else they decide to call it"—people, in other words, like President Bush—were nothing less than "psychics and gurus who take direction from demons."[116]

In *The End of the Age,* the associations between the "new world order" and cultic conspiracy were made explicit in the program for social revolution developed by President Beaulieu and his "false prophet," Tauriq Haddad, a New Age gangster with an Islamic name.[117] Together they develop an agenda to undermine American democracy, to replace the Christian religion and to destroy the American family.[118] As in Peretti's work, the novel's concern focuses on the spiritual and sexual exploitation of children. The educational initiatives developed by Beaulieu and Haddad require children to pray to Shiva—and many of them become demon possessed as a result.[119] This new educational agenda promotes a rapid deterioration in public morality as Congress grants "privileged status" to "those who engaged in even the most bizarre sex acts—pedophilia, incest, and bestiality. All forms of pornography are legalized—including the sexual exploitation of children."[120] Suddenly, in *The End of the Age,* it becomes clear to Christian characters that "the land that once was theirs had been taken away."[121] America was no longer theirs.

This realization epitomized the concerns about loss of control that resonated with the rhetoric of leaders of the Christian Right. That political danger is powerfully illustrated in Beaulieu's construction of the Union for Peace. The Union for Peace is designed to replace the United Nations, and Beaulieu decides to erect the center for world government in Babylon.[122] It is when he attempts to put the American military under international control that his identity as the Antichrist is confirmed. But, as the Christian Resistance, Robertson's tribulation saints do not meekly acquiesce. Indeed, the structure of the Christian Resistance is deliberately designed to forestall this new wave of government persecution. Its leaders model an activist spirituality, calling attention to the need for practical action in advance of the coming terror. One character collects "enough supplies and extra cash to help a lot of God's people."[123] Others invest in gold and prepare "a center to encourage resistance of the evil that is coming."[124] The "millions" of members of the Christian Resistance are organized into "thousands of cell groups" which communicate with each other through the Internet.[125] As in a number of other prophecy novels, they establish an alternative underground economy that is based on barter.[126] That economy moves toward collectivity when ten thousand of its members congregate on a ranch in New Mexico. The ranch belongs to Pastor Jack Edwards, a thinly disguised though somewhat idealized version of Pat Robertson himself.[127]

Jack Edwards's character resonates with Robertson's sense of his own end-time importance. The parallels between the character and author are obvious. Pastor Jack recalls standing in front of "five hundred thousand evangelicals and Roman Catholics from all over America" on April 29, 1980. "It was the largest Christian gathering in the history of America," he explained, called together by "a committee organized by a Puerto Rican pastor who had once been jailed as a heroin addict."[128] Pastor Jack's reference is clearly to the first "Washington for Jesus" event, held on April 29, 1980, which was organized by Robertson, Jerry Falwell, and John Gimenez in an effort to oust the Democratic president Jimmy Carter in favor of his Republican opponent, Ronald Reagan. Furthermore, Pastor Jack is described as "a descendent of Jonathan Edwards . . . one of the great early preachers, back in the middle 1700s. He's really proud of that heritage. Three hundred years later, Pastor Jack's still carrying on the tradition."[129] As this reference to "tradition" suggests, Pastor Jack becomes an archetypal figure. His ranch has the atmosphere of an authentic America, "a frontier town, with a thriving and bustling community doing business and carrying on their lives."[130] The image resonates within the prophecy fiction tradition. Characters in Don Thompson's *Prodigal Planet* (1983), one of the most widely seen prophecy movies, had taken refuge in an American heritage theme park on their way to rendezvous with tribulation saints holed up in Albuquerque. In *The End of the Age,* by contrast, Albuquerque becomes the site of the heritage community that will provide for the safety of believers.

Jack Edwards's character therefore conflates an idealized colonial individualism with the legacy of a formerly godly nation—and it does so as Robertson identifies himself with the most significant of the colonial preachers. But the character of Pastor Jack points as much to the difference between Jonathan Edwards and Pat Robertson as it does to the similarities between them. Despite the extended reference, *The End of the Age* made no other mention of Jonathan Edwards or to the content of the "tradition" that it claims the preachers share. Perhaps that is not surprising: historical facts challenge the idea of any significant theological continuity. Pastor Jack inculcates a firm premillennialism from which Jonathan Edwards's

postmillennialism can be easily distinguished, and Pastor Jack's sympathetic cooperation with Roman Catholics is clearly counter to Jonathan Edwards's declama-
tions against them.[131] Therefore, in *The End of the Age,* the link between Jonathan
Edwards and Pastor Jack is political rather than theological; Robertson appropri-
ates for political purposes the cultural and spiritual heritage of early Americans.
The character of Pastor Jack is thus most significant as evidence for Robertson's
imagining of himself.

But Pastor Jack also points to the significance of Robertson's career. In *The End
of the Age,* the Washington protest is described as possessing unique eschatological significance, the beginning of the end-time "sealing" of true believers described
in Revelation 7. This "sealing" precipitated the revival of evangelicalism which
then swept across the United States leaving "millions of Americans . . . energized
with faith. Huge churches sprang up all over the country . . . In the 1980s, the air-
waves in the United States were filled with church services, evangelistic meetings,
Christian teachings, Christian testimonies, and prayer for the sick. The nation had
never known anything like it."[132] Thus, at the end of the decade, as Communism
fell across eastern Europe, American Christians were well-prepared to address the
"spiritual vacuum that developed all over the world."[133] Their efforts would coincide
with "three years of concentrated prayer and evangelistic effort" sponsored by the
Roman Catholic Church. This unparalleled cooperation in evangelistic effort would
lead to a "tremendous harvest" in the 1990s when "over one billion people" would
"accept Jesus Christ as their Savior."[134] This "sealing time" pointed to the prophetic
significance of recent conservative advances even as it confirmed the utility of the
ecumenical ambition. "There has never been anything like it in the history of the
world . . . a worldwide spiritual harvest."[135] American conservatives were once again
finding their history in the Bible—and it all began with Pat Robertson's political
rally.

Nevertheless, despite its identification with American Protestant history, *The
End of the Age* made some significant ecumenical overtures. Peretti's world had
been entirely Protestant but Robertson's project was clearly broader in ambition.
Despite his earlier ministerial standing in the Southern Baptist Convention, Robertson wrote sympathetically of Roman Catholic piety and faith and refused to
imply that his Roman Catholic characters were doing anything other than confirming their faith when they were "born again."[136] The narrative strategy matched
the political strategy that lay behind the success of the Christian Coalition, but
there was no mistaking that *The End of the Age* was offering a significant rewriting of the traditional apocalyptic status of the Roman Catholic Church. This was
being developed at the same time as a number of dispensational writers—especially
those who shared Robertson's political concerns—began to redefine the relationship between evangelicals and Roman Catholics. Left Behind would include the

pope among those taken in the rapture, for example, and even such a mainstay of popular dispensationalism as Hal Lindsey would maintain in his prophecy novel, published one year after *The End of the Age*, that Pope John Paul II was "probably a true believer."[137] These comments represented a major shift in views of the apocalyptic potential of the Roman Catholic Church. Robertson refused to point to its danger. His novel concentrated on the beastly potential of state, not church, and the false religion in *The End of the Age* is Asian in its origin.

Nevertheless, the evangelical-Roman Catholic coalition provides for the military defense of the believers. The Christian Resistance—modeled on Robertson's Christian Coalition—is assisted by the one part of the U.S. military that adheres to the idea of national sovereignty and refuses to enter the Union for Peace. This military remnant, the Western Defense Zone, is led by a former secretary of defense. Combining their spiritual and military powers, the leaders of the Resistance identify themselves as a "military and a spiritual rallying point."[138] They represent themselves as "determined to fight and to win."[139] It is to that end that this faithful remnant of the American army aims its nuclear arsenal at "the heart of Babylon."[140] And, in a gesture that locates the influence of Peretti's recent publications, their community is protected by "unusual luminous columns in the sky" that turn out to be "clouds of angels" which are prepared to fight alongside their forces.[141] But it is only when the Christian Resistance decides to use the nuclear missiles that these angelic hosts engage in combat.[142] *The End of the Age* assured its readers that American evangelicals could never possess too much power. And if they expected any heavenly assistance, they must be prepared to go to extremes.

Still, as its title suggested, *The End of the Age* did have a strong focus on prophecy. Large sections of the novel contain lengthy passages of biblical exposition, though its conclusions are not typical of the dispensational tradition and the narrative frequently adopts a defensive tone.[143] One character explains that "evangelical Christians" had "always known" the content of Robertson's preferred eschatology, although another admits that they "haven't always understood what [Revelation] means, and there has been a lot of debate."[144] The novel certainly alludes to a number of otherwise competing positions. It attempted to mediate interpretive principles by balancing preterist and futurist hermeneutics. The novel admits that "the apostle John may very well have used a Roman emperor as a model" of the final incarnation of human wickedness, and, elsewhere, traditional urban myths of dispensationalism, such as the cashless society whose central computer is named "the Beast" and based in Brussels, are cited without ever being developed in the fictional narrative.[145] Historicist approaches were also being developed. The narrative imagined the prophecy of the Four Horsemen of the Apocalypse to have been fulfilled during the twentieth century, which had also witnessed many of the signs of the times.[146] The first major sign had been the Jewish recapturing of Jerusalem in 1967. This event restarted the prophetic time clock and guaranteed that events of eschatological importance could be expected within forty years—one biblical generation—of that event. The second major sign had been the increasing frequency of wars. This sign had been followed by the increasing frequency of earthquakes, and the spread of ravaging diseases, including Ebola and AIDS. The fifth major sign had been increasing apathy toward wickedness, including the toleration of "aberrant sex acts" and the "butchering of forty million innocent unborn children." The sixth major sign had been increasing worries about the sea.[147] In *The End of the Age,* therefore, Robertson appeared to be rethinking the classical form of the prophecy novel to appeal to a broader cultural and theological base. But the most significant difference between the eschatology of *The End of the Age* and that advanced by the more strictly dispensational prophecy novels is that Robertson's novel did not predict the rapture as an imminent event. Even as the tribulation begins, characters are advised that Jesus will return "after the next few years are over."[148] The novel rejects date-setting, but confidently defends its speculation: the forty years after 1967 would of course be fulfilled in 2007. Thus the novel suggested that the end of the Gentile age would come "around 2007"—in fact, around April 29 of that year.[149]

The date was loaded with significant themes. Its calculation was based on its importance in the Jewish repossession of Jerusalem, but also in its echoes in American history. A "prayer of dedication . . . by the first English settlers" at Cape Henry had been offered on April 29, 1607, Robertson argued, and was the moment in which America was properly constituted as a nation.[150] Robertson had noticed the event in *America's Dates with Destiny* (1986), but he had grown increasingly confident that it had unusual historical importance. *The New Millennium* (1990) and *The Secret Kingdom* (1992) developed the idea, noting that that April 29, 2007 marked "four hundred years from the beginning of America—ten full biblical generations." In other words, Robertson argued, "by some amazing coincidence—or might we say foresight of God—the four hundredth anniversary of the greatest Gentile power that the world has ever known coincides precisely with the fortieth year conclusion of the generation of the 'end of the Gentile power.'"[151] Of course, Robertson admitted, his claims were no more than "speculation," and he was not actually making any predictions.[152] Nevertheless, while "none of us knows the times and seasons which God has reserved for Himself . . . this scenario is fascinating to contemplate."[153]

The point, of course, was clear. Robertson was turning prophetic fiction into prophetic claims. At the same time, he was identifying the eschatological significance of his own career, for the "Washington for Jesus" events, which had also been scheduled for April 29, anticipated the date that would close "the end of forty decades of U.S. existence and the end of the Gentile age . . . in 2007."[154] Robertson had initiated the apocalyptic "sealing time" and had calculated the moment of America's demise. *The End of the Age,* therefore, was ultimately a novel of self-representation, and its contents allowed Robertson to invest his own career with a studied apocalyptic significance. Robertson was writing about the end of America—but also about his own importance.

III

As the cold war drew toward its conclusion, therefore, both Frank Peretti and Pat Robertson were exercising huge influence on the reshaping of the evangelical political imagination. Peretti's novels were best-sellers by the end of the 1980s, and Robertson's political maneuverings, for which Peretti's novels provided one important context, confirmed the argument in favor of greater cultural agency. As evangelicals moved into the 1990s, the attractions of apocalyptic speculation evidently continued: John Walvoord's updated edition of *Armageddon, Oil, and the Middle East Crisis,* republished to capitalize on concerns associated with the First Gulf War, sold more copies in ten weeks in 1991 than it did in the ten years since its first publication in 1974, with sales figures totaling 600,000 copies in its first year. The First Gulf War was frequently represented as a significant eschatological event. But, in its aftermath, "the prophecy movement became a causality of its own extravagance, unable to satisfy the expectations of supernatural deliverance which doomsday scenarios in the Gulf had raised." As "the prospect of Armageddon receded," prophecy writers "moved on to other subjects—the threat of homosexuality, the AIDS virus, radical feminism . . . Millennial idealism among church congregations and prophecy writers changed with the times and the quest to discover the false and the demonic assumed new forms."[155] But in the writings of Frank Peretti and Pat Robertson, the pattern of cultural engagement was established.

It is difficult to assess the influence of these books. *The End of the Age* certainly cannot be compared to Peretti's work in terms of units sold, but Peretti's fiction and Robertson's wider political agenda certainly set the terms for the re-energizing, and even the remilitarization, of evangelicalism. These works—and others like them—"altered what it meant to be a fundamentalist and reconfigured the larger fellowship of born-again Christians, the rules of national public discourse, and the meaning of modernity." These books helped transform a "marginal, antiworldly, separatist people" into "a visible and vocal public force."[156] They "rearranged the boundary between fundamentalism and postwar evangelicalism, fashioning a new constituency composed of newly engaged fundamentalists . . . and conservative evangelicals." And in doing so, they "changed the meaning of 'modern America.' "[157]

Peretti's novels appear ambivalent about the ethics of direct action but took their place in the cultural landscape that Robertson and his political allies were doing so much to reshape—and, as characters discovered in *The End of the Age*, "the world as they knew it would never be the same again."[158] Of course, some voices continued to prefer the older separatist option. Judith Gale's *A Promise of Forever* (1997) described believers retreating to a series of secluded hideaways, including an old church camp with a hidden underground level, in which the colony of tribulation saints would need to be "totally self-sufficient . . . for three-and-a-half years."[159] The trope is a Gentile equivalent for the Jewish remnant's retreat to Petra, but even in 1997 Gale was emphasizing withdrawal, not resistance, as the Christian code of conduct during the most evil period in the history of the world.[160] Other novels suggested that evangelicals could learn methods of resistance from other violent millennial movements.[161]

Above all else, evangelical fictions of the late 1980s and early 1990s were pondering the spiritual climate of post–cold war America: "Can our nation survive?"[162] But they were defiantly arguing in favor of increasing resistance to the secular mainstream. Later novels would be ambivalent about the Peretti and Robertson contributions, and Left Behind would include Robertson's Christian Broadcasting Network in its list of media corporations that the Antichrist would come to control.[163] Nevertheless, whatever their reluctance to admit it, Peretti and Robertson primed evangelical audiences for Left Behind. Both Peretti and Robertson made a seminal contribution to the reshaping of the evangelical political imagination. It was a conclusion their characters shared. Robertson's characters argued, in the early 1990s, that it was time to "break out of here and attack the system."[164] The immediate future was open—and America was there to be won.

6

The Left Behind Phenomenon

Like it or not, this is an epic struggle for the future.
—Pat Robertson, as quoted in Lienesch,
Redeeming America (1993)

The new ambition to reshape the social and political center was made immanent in the best-selling fiction series of the 1990s. Its success called for a significant reconsideration of the social significance of evangelical prophecy belief. In the years after 1995, a new wave of prophecy fiction emerged to demonstrate that the United States of America might actually be much more of a Christian nation than its intelligentsia had believed or its evangelicals could ever have expected.

The Left Behind novels, created by "prophecy scholar" Tim LaHaye and ghostwriter Jerry B. Jenkins, became a publishing sensation. The series' debut, *Left Behind* (1995), was given a muted reception. Two years after its publication, the series and the genre it represented were still sufficiently insignificant to be entirely overlooked by Jan Blodgett's groundbreaking study of *Protestant Evangelical Literary Culture and Contemporary Society* (1997).[1] But word-of-mouth advertising drove increasing sales. After 1998, every new installment in the series topped the *New York Times* best-seller list.[2] By the end of 1999, the series had sold twenty million copies, and its seventh book, *The Indwelling* (2000), reached number one in the best-seller lists of the *New York Times, Publishers Weekly,* the *Wall Street Journal,* and *USA Today*—all lists which do not include sales figures from exclusively Christian bookshops.[3]

In 2000, the first novel was dramatized in a $17.4 million movie production. Its production came one year after the mainstream success of *The Omega Code* (1999), a surprise crossover success for its dispensational makers.[4] The *Left Behind* movie aimed to consolidate its achievement. Its producers—the Lalonde brothers, themselves the authors of a number of prophecy novels—drew on their many contacts within the dispensational movement to include John Hagee, Jack and Rexella Van Impe, and John Walvoord in cameo roles in the opening scenes.[5] The decision to release the movie straight to video disappointed the series' authors, but it ensured that the movie outsold every other title in America in the first week of its release, selling three million copies in its first year.[6] After the terror attacks on the Pentagon and World Trade Center in September 2001, sales of the novels soared by sixty percent, and *Desecration,* released in October 2001, ousted John Grisham from the number one rank in *Publishers Weekly,* a position he had maintained for seven years, by becoming the best-selling work of hardback adult fiction in the world.[7] By the beginning of 2002, readers had purchased some thirty-two million copies of the novels and eighteen million associated products, including comic books, children's stories, and board games.[8] Simultaneously, the authors of the series discovered that they had become prominent media figures. In July 2002, Jenkins and LaHaye were featured on the front cover of *TIME,* and in May 2004 they appeared on the front cover of *Newsweek.*[9] In the same year, it was estimated, twenty-four percent of the American public had heard of the series, and nine percent had read at least one of its installments, including three million readers who did not identify themselves as "born again."[10] By 2006, the original franchise had been hived off into a board game, a music CD, a Web site, a series of graphic novels, an additional two movies, around forty children's titles, and a controversial video game.[11]

With this kind of sales success, and a product range to match, there is no doubt that the authors have made fortunes for themselves and for their publisher. Tyndale House had enjoyed long-standing success in marketing their books outside the evangelical subculture.[12] But that degree of success was transformed with the publication of Left Behind: the annual income of Tyndale House quadrupled to $160 million in the three years to 2001.[13] This success has been achieved as the sector itself has grown: Christian fiction sales quadrupled between 1995 and 2005, while the number of Christian novels being published doubled in the same period.[14] And the stock of the series' authors continues to rise. Four additional series have been developed, including two published by mainstream publishers Hodder and Stoughton and Bantam, from whom, it has been reported, LaHaye received a $45 million advance for Babylon Rising.[15] Whatever its critics' claims, therefore, Left Behind has become a cultural phenomenon. The statistics hardly require comment. After the end of the 1970s, Hal Lindsey had been "the most widely read interpreter of prophecy in history."[16] By the beginning of the twenty-first century, LaHaye bypassed Lindsey's massive contribution to the mainstreaming of popular dispensationalism in his claim that the Left Behind novels had made the rapture "almost a household word among vast numbers of people across America."[17] By April 2007, when the sixteenth and final installment of the original series was published, Left Behind had sold sixty-five million copies in over thirty languages.[18] Tim LaHaye and Jerry B. Jenkins had become some of the best-selling authors in the history of American literature, and evangelical prophecy fiction had become some of its most successful products.

Despite this success, the significance of Left Behind should not be overstated. As the franchise has expanded, its theological core has begun to fragment.[19] The authors have admitted differences in their own theological perspectives. In reported interviews, they have recorded differing opinions on the age of accountability, the survival or non-survival of the 144,000 Jewish witnesses, the identity of the two witnesses, and whether we are in fact living in the end times.[20] Jenkins has also admitted to differences between the reprints of individual novels in the series.[21] An early edition of Left Behind, for example, included Mother Teresa in the rapture, but this passage was dropped from later editions.[22] Jenkins has insisted that he and LaHaye resisted the commercialization of the brand: "one of the things that Dr. LaHaye and I have been very firm about is that we don't want products to come from Left Behind that are just there for the sake of sales . . . We want to make sure that each derivative from the original has ministry value intrinsic to it."[23] But, as the expanding product range suggests, it is not clear that this requirement has been followed. Left Behind products are now marketed by different companies with increasingly incompatible aims. The series' three movies have been produced by the Lalonde brothers' Cloud Ten Productions and distributed by Sony, but LaHaye has reportedly been concerned by their lack of exhortatory purpose and launched an unsuccessful legal attempt to recover the rights.[24] The fragmentation of the brand goes beyond the specifics of LaHaye's preferred theology. In 2006, the franchise's video game, Left Behind: Eternal Forces, was released to huge public controversy on both sides of the Atlantic when commentators suggested that players would be rewarded for executing Jews, Muslims, and other enemies of the Christian faith.[25] This kind of religious genocide was certainly not the game's purpose, but its supposition that spiritual warfare could become edifying entertainment, or that consumers could benefit by playing as the Antichrist, took the Left Behind franchise a substantial distance from the novels' original didactic intent.[26] Other novels in the wider franchise have also moved a significant distance from evangelical orthodoxy. The Apocalypse Dawn series, written by Mel Odom, teaches a species of baptismal regeneration.[27] Odom himself is certainly not a dispensationalist and may not even be an evangelical: in a reported interview, he explained his belief that "if you've lived a good life, and you've believed in something beyond yourself . . . there's still room for everybody to live in heaven. It's not like there's limited space."[28] Odom also explained that he had not met LaHaye and certainly distanced himself from any dispensational vision of the end times: "I have no idea of how the end times are going to work out," he admitted, arguing that his books are more about the conflict between good and evil than eschatological specifics.[29] The fragmentation of brand coherence is evident even within the culture of Tyndale House itself. Some commentators were surprised by the publisher's decision to release one of the novels on 6/6/6—an unexpectedly ironic gesture by an evangelical publisher that had previously treated eschatological themes with deference and respect. The Left Behind brand has exploded, therefore, and some products now appear to be competing with others in the wider franchise. Left Behind products cannot be understood in totalizing terms. Little more than a decade after its beginning, the brand is losing its coherence and is spiraling out of its creators' control.

Nevertheless, Left Behind products have generated intense public controversy. The novels, in particular, have attracted a wide range of critical comment, some of it from liberal intellectuals concerned by their commitment to social and political conservatism, some of it from liberal theologians appalled by their lack of scholarly gravitas, and some of it from evangelicals worried by their deviation from traditional patterns of orthodoxy or their preference for social and political inaction.[30] The series has been roundly dismissed by its most vocal critics. Its alleged combination of right-wing conspiracy theories with conservative social mores and its demonizing of Jews, Muslims, and Roman Catholics have generated fierce opposition from across the social and political spectrum. In popular media, that hostility has been intense. In the United Kingdom, the *Times* described the series as "the oddest literary phenomenon in the English-speaking world," as "Nostradamus rewritten by Jeffrey Archer."[31] *The Independent on Sunday* suggested that the series' appeal is "clearly bound up in class. Nobody with an educated view of either religion or literature would give it the time of day."[32] As if to prove the point, the *Times Literary Supplement* noted the "awkwardness" with which Jenkins and LaHaye blended "folksy humour, treacly sentiment and religiously justified bloodbaths."[33] Nevertheless, the *TLS* continued, the novels offered "very precise implications" for public policy, for "the God worshipped by LaHaye and Jenkins considers abortion to be wrong, has it in for gay people and feminists, and opposes most forms of government regulation, especially gun control."[34] In the United States, the *New York Times* described the series as an exercise in "brand management" rather than religion: "Being wrong has rarely been so lucrative."[35] Critics have returned to the novels' place among LaHaye's wider financial interests. Michael Standaert's *Skipping towards Armageddon: The Politics and Propaganda of the Left Behind Novels and the LaHaye Empire* (2006) is a spirited, if not always accurate, description of the network of business and personal interests that surround the series, and Nicholas Guyatt's *Have a Nice Doomsday* (2007) offers a range of critical perspectives on the series it deplores.

Academic criticism has been slower to emerge. In 2000, Gershom Gorenberg noted the general failure of academics to engage with the Left Behind phenomenon.[36] Until very recently, the series had been discussed by only a handful of journal articles and chapters in books, two monographs, and an introductory collection of essays. Most scholars who have written on the subject have made clear their hostility to the series' worldview. Amy Frykholm's brief chapter in the collection of essays edited by Forbes and Kilde is the most sustained historical discussion of these texts.[37] While her *Rapture Culture: Left Behind in Evangelical America* (2004) shows good awareness of the genre's history, making a number of important points about the series' predecessors and noting their details in its bibliography, its focus is firmly on questions of readership. Almost every other publication represents Left Behind as something new—even the only book-length study of the novels themselves, Glenn Shuck's *Marks of the Beast: The Left Behind Novels and the Struggle for Evangelical Identity* (2004).

But this academic hostility has provoked as much high-minded rhetoric as close textual analysis. Shuck makes a rare gesture toward the novels' ambiguity in his identifying their articulation of a "continuum of possibilities within the evangelical subculture"; his analysis suggests the existence of a "fainter, but nevertheless significant voice" in the novels, questioning the construction of community and warning against the strict delineation of evangelical boundaries.[38] Other critics see the novels as representing a more robust cultural politics. Frykholm noted that the novels can be seen to lend themselves to a "conservative, patriarchal, even racist agenda," or as combining a "hostile antifeminist perspective, hints of anti-Semitism, and . . . overt homophobia"; she quoted another reviewer's description of the series as "hard-core right-wing paranoid anti-Semitic homophobic misogynistic propaganda."[39] Darryl Jones has described LaHaye's rhetoric as "the unhinged right-wing ranting of a crazy old coot," but, he added, readers of the novels should never forget their importance to his wider project, which Jones described as "a more general ideological attempt to theocratize modernity by imposing a right-wing Christian agenda upon its polity."[40] LeAnn Snow Flesher similarly complained that the novels "smack of ethnocentrism . . . The authors' attitude that their own race, nation, culture, and even gender is superior to all others is prevalent in their novels."[41] Other critics have merely scoffed at the series' earnest tone. Earl Lee's *Kiss My Left Behind* (2003) and its sequel, *Raptured: The Final Daze of the Late, Great Planet Earth* (2007), provided a heavily sexualized parody of the series based around the character of "Ramrod Steele."

But secular and mainstream commentators are mistaken if they think that the series lacks its critics within Christendom. Left Behind has generated an impressive number of theological exposés. Paul Thigpen wrote *The Rapture Trap: A Catholic Response to "End Times" Fever* (2001), while Carl Olson—a former dispensationalist—posed the question, *Will Catholics Be "Left Behind"?* (2003), and answered firmly in the negative. David B. Currie—another former dispensationalist—provided a critique of the series in *Rapture: The End-times Error That Leaves the Bible Behind* (2003). He recognized that "rapturist theology" had been "the most effective means of pulling Roman Catholics out of the Church and into Protestantism," but insisted that dispensational theology provided an uncertain foundation for any kind of faith as it failed to center on the crucifixion of Jesus Christ.[42] Barbara R. Rossing, a Lutheran biblical scholar, made similar claims in *The Rapture Exposed: The Message of Hope in the Book of Revelation* (2004). Within the Reformed tradition, Gary DeMar's *End Times Fiction* (2001) interrogated the novels' exegetical assumptions and Tim Kirk's *I Want to Be "Left Behind"* (2002) advanced its critique of the series on the back of extensive quotations from the church fathers.[43] Daniel Hertzler, an Anabaptist commentator, described the series' theology as "a dramatic expression of . . . foolishness," while Steve Wohlberg, a Seventh-day Adventist, illustrated the differences between the eschatology of Left Behind and that of his own denomination in *The Left Behind Deception* (2001) and a series of other works.[44] Within evangelicalism, Dave Bussard has questioned *Who Will Be Left Behind and When?* (2002) and the present author has analyzed the series in his wider account of *Rapture Fiction and the Evangelical Crisis* (2006). But the novels have also attracted critics within dispensationalism itself. Stephen Spencer, formerly a professor at Dallas Theological Seminary, the intellectual headquarters of the dispensational movement, has described the books as providing a speculative socio-cultural commentary rather than a carefully-constructed theology, and other dispensationalists have argued that the series is not at all representative of the tradition from which it has emerged.[45]

Some of this criticism from within evangelicalism has resulted in the publication of fictional alternatives. Left Behind was parodied in Nathan D. Wilson's *Right Behind: A Parody of Last Days Goofiness* (2001) and its sequel *Supergeddon: A Really Big Geddon* (2003).[46] With more seriousness, *Survivors* (2002), by "Zion Ben Judah," was an interrogation of the series from the point of view of an anti-capitalist and very controversial new religious movement, the "Jesus Christians." Representing a more respectable tradition within the evangelical mainstream, Hank Hanegraaff and Sigmund Brouwer developed an alternative to rapture fiction that reflected quite different exegetical preferences. Their novels, *The Last Disciple* (2004) and *The Last Sacrifice* (2006), argued that "the plain and proper reading of a biblical passage must always take precedence over a particular eschatological presupposition or paradigm," and claimed that Left Behind's failure to adopt this interpretive method had ultimately driven it to undermine "the deity and resurrection of Christ."[47] Hanegraaff and Brouwer may have described the debate as "collegial," but *The Last Disciple* was released into virulent controversy when LaHaye protested that his publisher—Tyndale House—should spend the earnings of Left Behind on a series that advanced an eschatology it diametrically opposed.[48] LaHaye has since responded to Hanegraaff and Brouwer by describing them as false teachers.[49] But he has also provided an alternative to their claims. His most recent fiction series, the Jesus Chronicles, includes an account of the life of the "last disciple" that directly counters the Hanegraaff and Brouwer approach, and even alludes to their series in its title, *John's Story: The Last Eyewitness* (2006).

Other evangelicals have rushed to the defense of the Left Behind series. Todd Strandberg and Terry James used excerpts from the novels to illustrate *Are You Rapture Ready? Signs, Prophecies, Warnings, Threats, and Suspicions That the Endtime Is Now* (2003). One year later, LaHaye addressed his critics in the foreword to *The Truth behind Left Behind* (2004), an extended defense of the series by two authors involved in writing nonfictional supporting material, Mark Hitchcock and Thomas Ice. LaHaye's comments in the book's foreword blurred the traditional boundaries of the evangelical movement when he appealed to his "Christian" critics not to undermine the series' evangelistic aspirations. "Seventh-day Adventists, Catholic scholars, and particularly Reformed theologians" should be "thrilled," he thought, "that multitudes of people worldwide are coming to Christ through these books. You would think they would be pleased that thousands more are being motivated to holy living, evangelism, and a renewed missionary vision. Why would any Christian object to these outcomes?"[50] It was a point repeated by Hitchcock and Ice in the main body of the text: the "over-riding message" of the Left Behind series was not the truth of dispensational premillennialism but an emphasis on "the need to receive Jesus Christ by faith as your Savior from sin before it's too late." The series' critics, Hitchcock and Ice complained, "could even cause many who have believed the gospel from reading these books to entertain serious doubts."[51]

Not everyone has been convinced of the danger. Left Behind has redefined the American mainstream and propelled a series of evangelical social concerns to the center of public consciousness. But it has left a large part of its audience unsettled. Its success has made it possible to believe that Christians could be raptured at the height of their cultural influence: LaHaye has suggested that "from one half to a billion people could suddenly go up in the Rapture."[52] The figure is as high as it appears anywhere in the prophecy fiction genre, and an indication of his investment in the kind of rhetoric that defies the marginality the novels attempt to recreate. Nevertheless, while many secular-minded critics regard Left Behind as a dangerous assertion of the polemics of the Christian Right, many of its most sympathetic readers believe it is neither evangelical nor dispensational enough.

I

It was in the mid-1980s that Tim LaHaye first developed the idea of Left Behind.[53] He was, he has recalled, "on the way to speak at a prophecy conference" when he witnessed "the captain of the plane come out of his cabin and begin flirting with the head flight attendant. I noticed he had a wedding ring on and she didn't. As the sparks flew between them, I thought of a remark by one of my lifetime friends to the effect, 'Wouldn't it be interesting if the Rapture occurred and the pilot recognized that the hundred people that suddenly were missing from his aircraft meant that his Christian wife and son would be missing when he got home?'"[54]

The scenario was already familiar within the popular culture of American dispensationalism. The opening scene of Salem Kirban's *666* had likewise recorded the impact of the rapture on an intercontinental airplane. Twenty-five years later, William T. James, another popular prophecy expositor, returned to the image: "Half a world away, the captain of a 747, having just received permission to take off, will push the throttles fully forward and the gigantic bird will begin its roll between the runway lights that appear to come together in a sharp point in the distant darkness . . . Then, in a mind-confounding split-second, it will happen!"[55] The scenario is significant—the rapture is depicted as occurring at a moment of departure, as a nation is left behind and believers and fellow travelers find themselves in the liminal space between Earth and heaven, America and the beyond. The image resonates with the nostalgia for the American past that haunts the literary culture of dispensationalism, for the period in which, as LaHaye has put it, "America was . . . the freest, safest, most honorable, moral, and happiest nation of people on earth. That was when it was the most God-fearing country in the world, because that is how it was founded. That was also when the conscience of the nation was set by its churches. Not one, but hundreds of churches and denominations, most of whom took the Bible seriously and believed the Ten Commandments were the best civic code every existed."[56] This nostalgia for a golden age reflects the central themes of LaHaye's career, as well as major texts in the tradition of evangelical prophecy fiction.

Tim LaHaye (b. 1926) is one of America's veteran culture warriors and a founder of the Christian Coalition. He spent his formative years at Bob Jones University, after which he took on a pastorate in El Cajon, California, developing an early interest in social issues, writing a series of texts on psychology, marriage guidance, and dispensationalism and founding Family Life Seminars in 1972. *The Battle for the Mind* (1980) reflected his newly political aspirations. Together with his wife, Beverly, he identified and sought to counter the influence of "secular humanism" in the National Organization for Women, the American Civil Liberties Union, the National Association for Education, and the United Nations.[57] His eschatological writing has consistently returned to themes of their threat to America.

Left Behind was designed to combine these various interests. LaHaye initially developed the idea as a trilogy that he hoped might reach half a million readers.[58] His agent put him in touch with Jerry B. Jenkins, a writer of children's fiction and ghostwriter of sporting and spiritual autobiographies. LaHaye provided Jenkins with the outlines of each of the books, highlighting their biblical basis, and Jenkins fleshed out the plot. The trilogy grew to a dozen titles before the authors decided to add four volumes of prequel and sequel narrative. And their efforts have not ended there. Both writers have gone on to produce other apocalyptic tales—all of them politically encoded with the themes that have developed throughout LaHaye's career.

It is not hard to see why the secular-minded should be alarmed. *Left Behind* (1995) is a prophecy fiction *tour de force*. Taut and frantic, it documents the initial impact of the rapture and introduces central characters as they respond to the sudden disappearance of one-third of the passengers on their aircraft. Despite its apparent novelty, the first of the series' novels was profoundly conscious of its genre and nonfiction contexts. The novels took no pains to conceal the dispensational meta-narrative—*Assassins* (1999) was dedicated to John F. Walvoord, whose lifelong commitment to the movement "has helped keep the torch of prophecy burning." As this dedication suggests, the novels had a clearly polemical role, endorsing a particular variant of classical dispensationalism while combining the genre's standard narrative tropes with contemporary political and cultural concerns.[59] Its debt to the work of Sydney Watson was particularly obvious. Watson's novels constituted the first series in the prophecy novel genre. But, beyond this, they offered characters and incidents that Left Behind adopted. One of the main characters in the series is Cameron "Buck" Williams, for example, a thirty-year-old bachelor journalist who finds love, loses his job, and gets the opportunity to start his own Web-based news portal, which quickly achieves international success. In Watson's series, almost ninety years before, as we have noticed, Tom Hammond is likewise a thirty-year-old bachelor journalist who finds love, loses his job, and gets the opportunity to start his own newspaper, which quickly achieves international success.[60] Similarly, Cameron "Buck" Williams, like the protagonist of Kirban's *666*, witnesses the rapture while traveling on a plane. Left Behind's political interests also betray its context in evangelical prophetic literature. Cold war suspicion of Eastern Europe is echoed in the fact that the rising Antichrist—Nicolae Carpathia—is a Romanian who hijacks the ambitions of the United Nations. In the threat they represent, conspiring Eastern Europeans are the new international Jewish cabal.

It would be unfair, however, to dismiss the series as entirely derivative. The novels display surprising negotiation with the prophecy fiction tradition. It is important to note that the rapture imagined by Jenkins and LaHaye is quite different from that represented in the mainstream dispensational tradition. Earlier writers, not taking at face value the opinion poll calculations of those Americans claiming to be "born again," would have regarded the huge numbers of those involved in this rapture as hopelessly optimistic. Equally innovative is this rapture's inclusion of the unborn and all pre-teenage children. Don Thompson's films—the most widely distributed prophecy fictions before the success of Left Behind—had included only the children of believers in the rapture.[61] Left Behind's decision to include all unborn and prepubescent children demonstrated the impact of the antiabortion movement on the increasingly politicized American evangelical community, as "right to life" rhetoric identified human personhood from the moment of conception.

But perhaps the most significant aspect of Left Behind's rapture is that it includes the pope. The novels' presentation of Roman Catholicism has often been criticized, but observers have consistently failed to appreciate the watershed in evangelical opinion that these novels represent. Historically, as we have seen, evangelical exegetes and prophecy fiction authors had either identified the pope as the Antichrist or had predicted the centrality of Roman Catholicism to the Antichrist's project of demonic control. Left Behind challenges these assumptions, echoing a major rethinking of evangelical attitudes to Roman Catholicism, and the hugely influential rapprochement represented by the project of Charles Colson and R. J. Neuhaus's *Evangelicals and Catholics Together: The Christian Mission in the Third Millennium* (1994). In one novel, an entire congregation of Roman Catholics is represented as among the raptured, with no hint or suggestion that they had become closet evangelicals.[62] The situation is more ambivalent with Pope John XXIV, who is included in the rapture because of his interest in promoting Lutheran reform.[63] His name and interests invite comparison with the reforming and ecumenical interests of Pope John XXIII (1958–63), who called the Second Vatican Council and received Geoffrey Fisher on the first visit of an Archbishop of Canterbury to the Vatican.[64] The name of John XXIV also performs the vital rhetorical task of claiming the imminence of the rapture while indefinitely delaying it: the next Pope John would indeed be the twenty-fourth, but the reader has no knowledge of when the next Pope John may appear.

But the novels seem to want to have their cake and eat it, too. Despite this attempt at conciliation, the novels endorse the traditional evangelical reading of the Vatican's role in the prophetic future. John XXIV's replacement is identified as the eschatological enemy of the truth and the new one-world religion that the Antichrist sponsors is centered, initially, on the Vatican.[65] LaHaye, nevertheless, has downplayed the series' apparent opposition to Roman Catholicism: "every church has some renegade people in it, and we just picked one of theirs," he has explained.[66] He has also downplayed Roman Catholic critiques of the series, reporting that he received fewer complaints from Roman Catholic readers than he expected: "We went out of our way to show that the Rapture is not limited to

Protestants, but as we believe, many Catholics have accepted Christ by faith as the only means of salvation. There are some Catholic purists who refuse to think any ill of their church or their popes. We have tried to point out to them that Peter Mathews was a renegade priest—and history shows there have been many . . . just as there have been many renegade Protestant ministers."[67] And there is evidence that some readers have been convinced: Tyndale House has estimated that eleven percent of the series' readers are Roman Catholics.[68]

The advent of one-world systems illustrates the extent to which the Left Behind novels reinforce the standard paradigms of cultural fear exploited by the American prophetic tradition. In the aftermath of cold war dichotomy, the novels reinvent dispensational pessimism by citing the effect of the meltdown of the superpowers.[69] The well-being of established nation states is contrasted with the acquisitive ambition of the United Nations, which, in response to the global catastrophe of the rapture, begins to build the one-world government that dispensational exponents have historically feared. Combining administrative prowess with entrepreneurial wizardry, the United Nations oversees the introduction of a single world currency, taking a 0.1 percent tax on every dollar spent.[70] The administrative infrastructure required to make this possible is the stuff of urban legends. The novels reach into the world of their readers when they refer to a supercomputer called "the Beast"; since 1983, evangelical prophecy "experts" have repeatedly claimed that a machine with this name actually exists at the heart of the European administration in Brussels.[71] Similar appeals to current prophetic speculation lend weight to the novels' claim that bar code and biochip technology make possible the electronic mark of the beast.[72] The novels put a spin on contemporary advances in veterinary science by linking the Antichrist's ability to implant the electronic mark into humans to the existing method of injecting electronic tags into pets.[73] With technology thereby providing the means of electronic commerce and population control, the foundations are laid for the Antichrist's centralized bureaucracy: "one economy highlighted by one currency, no need for passports, one government, eventually one language, one system of measurement, and one religion."[74] The new world government, in other words, is the European dream writ large: "Today is the first day of the rest of utopia."[75] Critics of the series have often fastened on its antagonism to one-world institutions, but it is important to record Jenkins's explanation for the series' focus on the United Nations. He has downplayed the political significance of his anti–United Nations polemic in a move that makes the novels much less geopolitical than earlier examples in the genre—and much less geopolitical than they might at first appear: "Of course, we don't know that the biblically predicted seat of world government will be the United Nations . . . that was strictly a vehicle for me as a novelist . . . I suppose there are things to criticize about the U.N., but in these books I use it strictly as a literary device."[76]

There is much less ambiguity about the authors' cultural politics. With his control of the population largely established, Carpathia wages his own "culture war," aiming to overturn traditional aesthetics by targeting the classic and the beautiful, destroying valued art treasures, and seizing control of crucial media.[77] Believers will find themselves increasingly alienated from the cultural mainstream. The Antichrist, in other words, will consolidate the existing marginalization of the American evangelical community. With broadcasting and publishing in his power, only the Internet is free from his spin.[78] This control of minds is linked to his attempt to control bodies; his ethical policies, peppered with the demands of contemporary liberals, descend to the fascist, idealizing "proper legislation concerning abortion, assisted suicide, and the reduction of expensive care for the defective and handicapped."[79] Neither does "the most technologically advanced regime in history" accommodate dissent.[80] Carpathia's administration creates "the most powerful enforcement juggernaut the world has ever seen."[81] In the face of this hegemony, the series' evangelicals epitomize American individualism as they mobilize to resist: "the very idea of a one-world government, or currency, or especially faith . . . is from the pit of hell."[82]

Their resistance is significant, in that it negotiates the problematic silence of the prophetic Scriptures: what happens to America? The novels affirm the dispensational tradition that the United States has no role in biblical prophecy and that, they conclude, must mean that America is going to be destroyed.[83] The events preceding that destruction are startling to anyone who reads these novels as a barometer of contemporary evangelical opinion. America fails when the world needs it most. Opposition to the United Nations' new one-world regime comes, significantly, from the American president, Gerald Fitzhugh, who is described as "a younger version of Lyndon Johnson" and "the greatest friend Israel ever had."[84] But the president is out of step with his military. When his top brass promise support for Carpathia's program, the president finds his only allies in the right-wing militias.[85] These "patriotic militia forces" are "surprisingly organized," the novels note, but despite their support by Egypt and "England" (rather than the United Kingdom), their military resistance is futile.[86] British and American cities are destroyed in a brief nuclear war.[87]

Resistance to the Antichrist is therefore focused on the surviving evangelical communities—the self-styled and neo-survivalist "Tribulation Force." The novels' description of social norms among these post-rapture evangelicals is fascinating. Conversion and church fellowship are alike figured with tactility: Buck, who "had already fallen in love with God," noted lots of hugging in church services, "especially among men."[88] As in other examples of the genre, scenes in the local fellowship are the means of disseminating dispensationalism's central hermeneutic: "Rayford was more than fascinated . . . Not long ago he would have scoffed at such teaching, at such a literal take on so clearly a poetic and metaphorical passage. But what Bruce said made sense."[89] Simultaneously, these discussions of the "literal hermeneutic"—now confirmed by recent fulfillments of erstwhile expectations— defend the assumptions of the novels' implied audience against contemporary derision that "right-wing, fanatical, fundamentalist factions . . . have always taken the Bible literally."[90] So, the novels argue, does God.

This foregrounding of the prophetic meta-narrative complicates the novels' discursive technique. The discovery and articulation of a dispensational paradigm works to dissolve any sense of mystery at how the story will end. Close adherence to a well-established prophetic scheme presents a challenge to the writers when the basic chronological framework of the projected twelve novels is already well known to the reader the novels expect. One character "felt helpless. No one"—not even Jenkins and LaHaye—"could stem the tide of history."[91] Interestingly, however, the authors try to take advantage of this problem, attempting to turn narrative determinism into narrative possibility. Plot and prophecy interact in tension, and questions of ethics, timing, and agency are central to the books. "What kind of a God would he be if he felt compelled to act on your timetable?" one character asks.[92] Elsewhere, Rayford wonders whether he would ever be justified in murdering the Antichrist, and the Tribulation Force are warned against prophetic presumption. Although "this script has already been written," they are admonished to "guard against trying to help God . . . fulfill his promises."[93] But the narrative possibilities in this tension between prophecy and agency remain largely unexplored, and the providential theory that the prophetic discourse sponsors increasingly counteracts the successful development of character and plot. As the series progresses, its limited version of naturalistic realism gives way, and episodes of obviously divine intervention become increasingly implausible and routine: "Another day, another deliverance."[94] The prophetic and interventionist mode provides the material for this fiction, but is increasingly handled in such a way as to counter its successful development. What happens to narrative tension when the authors continue to conjure up miracles to solve intractable difficulties in the plot?

Nevertheless, the narratives do take unexpected turns, and the tribulation offers unexpected promise. When secure communication is possible only through the Internet, Chloe begins her resistance to the Antichrist's global hegemony by establishing an alternative economy, based on resistance to the mark of the beast, by developing an international Co-op.[95] Building a worldwide business empire is a peculiarly American method of combating the tyranny and evil of the Antichrist. Her Tribulation Force partner, Ben-Judah, likewise disseminates his prophetic teaching through "the most popular Web site in history."[96] The regime bans all access to the site, but their attempt at Internet regulation proves impossible to monitor, and Ben-Judah's "Internet church" explodes in its numbers of adherents.[97] Fortunes and reputations can be established in the tribulation, when faith, technology, and business become the new faith, hope, and love.

II

But faith, hope, and love are still important. The Left Behind novels, like the prophecy fiction genre from which they emerge, are a species of occasional fiction: they
do not attempt to outline a complete systematic theology, nor do they claim to
present a rounded, polished discussion of evangelical faith. This is in keeping with
their status in the wider literary culture of evangelicalism. In the United Kingdom,
particularly, figures from evangelical bookshops indicate a strong market preference for titles dealing with Bible study (fifty-eight percent of total sales), prayer
and devotion (forty percent), doctrine (thirty-five percent), music and worship
(thirty-five percent), and children's books (thirty-five percent). Fiction accounted
for only thirteen percent of titles sold in British Christian bookshops during the
period.[98] Figures from the United States—were they available—would probably
indicate a greater percentage of fiction sales within evangelical bookshops, though
it is important to remember that figures from these bookshops are not included in
the statistics that pushed the Left Behind novels into America's secular best-seller
lists. The point remains, however, that few evangelicals would consume only the
Left Behind novels. At the same time, however, the series offers a clear example
of conversionist writing. The novels frequently include exhortations for characters (and, implicitly, readers) to embrace salvation, and there is evidence that the
series has been successful in seeing these goals achieved. In 2002, the series' publishers had received letters from some three thousand readers, testifying that the
books had enabled them to "receive Christ."[99] In the same year, a survey of readers'
reviews on Amazon.com discovered that a number of respondents were attribut-
ing their conversions to their having read the novels while a further thirty percent
were claiming that the novels had "caused them to reflect on their own spiritual
convictions."[100] The series' authors have made similar claims. *Soul Harvest* (1998)
was dedicated to "our brand-new brothers and sisters"—evidently, those who had
become evangelicals as a consequence of reading books in the series. Several years
later, LaHaye and Jenkins published an anthology of readers' conversion narratives
entitled *These Will Not Be Left Behind: True Stories of Changed Lives* (2003). The
series' authors and publisher have therefore invited readers to consider the novels
as spiritually forming texts, as texts which develop or encourage the development
of specified options of response. Throughout the genre, several possible varieties
of that response have been illustrated in characters coming to faith for the first
time, in other characters moving from nonevangelical Christianities to embrace
the evangelical faith, and in evangelical characters moving toward the dispensational premillennialism that contours the genre's plots. In the Left Behind project,
more than any other prophecy fiction project before it, the novels' theology and
spirituality are made credible by the results they appear to have in the lives of

thousands of their readers. Published details of "changed lives" highlight the novels' status as spiritual texts and their formative influences on those who consume them. Jenkins has noted that "one of the things Dr. LaHaye wants in every book is what he calls a believable, reproducible conversion experience . . . We hear from people all the time who say they prayed the prayer of salvation right along with the character."[101] *The Authorized Left Behind Handbook* (2005) noted that the authors "get many letters every day from readers who have had their relationships with Christ strengthened through reading the books," and also claimed that the series' success has "driven the opportunity for an unprecedented harvest of souls."[102] The quotation revealed a moment of self-reflexive observation: the impact of the series was being explained in terms of the novels' own imaginative world, the "soul harvest" that provided the title to volume four.

Of course, as their critics complain, the novels have done much more than merely produce conversions. They have also called for a redefinition of the American cultural mainstream. The success of the ninth book in the series—*Desecration* (2001)—signaled the franchise's commercial power. Ousting John Grisham from the number one spot in *Publishers Weekly*, the novel took its place at the top of the best-seller lists alongside Bruce Wilkinson's *The Prayer of Jabez*, the number one nonfiction title. Jenkins has recorded his response to news of the sales statistics: "I was mentioning to Bruce [Wilkinson] on the phone that John Grisham is also a man of faith, and he had the number 2 novel for 2001. I said, 'Do we know who's number two on the nonfiction side? If it's a Christian, we'll have the top 4 spots.' He said, 'Well, actually I am, for *Secrets of the Vine*.' I don't know if that will ever be duplicated—4 books by believers on top of the best-seller charts."[103] *Desecration*—a novel of apocalyptic marginality—was being celebrated as marking a moment of evangelical dominance. It was symptomatic of the larger effect of Left Behind. Scholars have been compelled to propose new formulations of the relationship between evangelical and mainstream cultures. Before Left Behind, evangelical and mainstream cultures had often been considered to be dichotomous. In the aftermath of Left Behind, Melani McAlister has argued not only that the novels are in "the mainstream of postmodern American life," but also that the brand of fundamentalism they represent "might *be* the mainstream of American life."[104]

III

With the success of Left Behind, prophecy fiction—once a marginal component of a marginal subculture—has come to dominate the American imagination. The limited chronological scope of Left Behind focused the energies of Jenkins and LaHaye. The original twelve novels limited their plot to the seven years of tribulation and exploited the disaster themes by allowing the apocalyptic mode to continually eclipse the millennial. In the first ten of the series' twelve novels, for example, there are only a handful of references to the future thousand-year reign of Christ.[105] This concentration on apocalyptic rather than millennial themes is justified by a claim that more Scripture is devoted to the last three and a half years of the tribulation than to "any other period except the life of Christ."[106] But there can be little doubt that market forces also find that period more congenial. Dystopia and disaster always sell, and the reason they sell to evangelicals is because these kind of fictions emerge from their culture when the movement they address is in or anticipates being in periods of acute crisis. The content of these novels is marketable as apocalyptic because their function is to emphasize the dichotomy between faith communities and their hostile environments, as apocalyptic literature always has.[107]

Whatever their marketing success, then, it is in their negotiation with the commonplaces of their theological tradition that Left Behind novels are at their most interesting. Narrative contours, even stock characters, are shared across the genre, stifling the creative process: as one of Watson's characters admits, "nothing blinds and obstructs like a preconceived idea."[108] But the self-consciousness of the genre, as the same materials are reworked and reworked, provides for its very utility as a barometer of evangelical cultural fear. LaHaye and Jenkins issue a reprimand to their world's most successful journalist: "You have a creative mind, Buck. Paranoid too."[109] But from the evidence of Left Behind, it is the latter quality, rather than the former, that generates the series' phenomenal success as a barometer of the changing evangelical condition.

7

Prophecy Fiction after
Left Behind

Prophecy is hard to understand. You just can't pull out a calculator and figure out what a prophecy means.

—James BeauSeigneur, *In His Image* (1997)

But the evangelical condition has continued to evolve. Since the later 1990s, the success of Left Behind has driven the production and distribution of a huge range of alternative prophecy fiction novels. These alternatives aim to cash in on the market success of premillennial prognostication even as they challenge central components of the series that made possible their popularity. These texts have dissected Left Behind's exegetical assumptions by offering competing visions of what the end might bring. And a very large number of these novels have been produced. The bibliography at the end of this volume—which, admittedly, may not be complete—suggests that as many prophecy fictions have been published in the decade since the mid-1990s as were published in the century to that date. Their number includes several texts first published under evangelical imprints that were later picked up and republished by larger secular houses.[1] Published in the aftermath of its unparalleled success, recent novels appear increasingly aware of their dialogic relationship with Left Behind. As Left Behind came to define the contours of a new literary genre, so more recent texts could not help but engage with its assumptions. And, if the variety of these novels is anything to go by, prophecy must certainly be "hard to understand."

Debates between the most recent prophecy novels have ranged across the board. Some of these competing points of view have appeared within Left Behind's writing partnership itself. Jerry B. Jenkins has disputed themes that were central to the narrative of Left Behind when *Soon* (2003), the first volume of a later apocalyptic series, imagined that the rapture was much farther away than readers of Left Behind had been encouraged to expect. The novel investigated the condition of America in 2046, and, in its descriptions of spiritual dystopia, invited readers to imagine that evangelical prophecy belief had never entered the secular mainstream and that popular culture and political aspiration had never been influenced by dispensational ideas. But as an expression of the mood of many evangelicals in the opening years of the twenty-first century, *Soon* reflected the geopolitical confusion of the post–cold war world, returning to the older moral dualism while projecting it exclusively onto the United States. The latter-day enemies of the Christian faith are no longer external to the "redeemer nation": as in earlier conspiratorial prophecy novels, America contains its own latter-day enemies, but in *Soon* they are more obviously in power.

Other debates take place between products within the Left Behind franchise. *Apocalypse Dawn* (2003) bolted itself onto the narrative framework of Left Behind and assumed the rise of Nicolae Carpathia and the tyranny of the United Nations as a necessary background to its plot. Written by Mel Odom—who had gained fame as the writer of *Buffy the Vampire Slayer, Tomb Raider,* and *Blade* movie spin-offs—*Apocalypse Dawn* also mounted a sustained challenge to some of the most basic evangelical assumptions of the earlier series, most seriously in suggesting the possibility of salvation through water baptism.[2] No more foundational challenge to evangelical orthodoxy could have been attempted. Other debates between recent novels have taken place within a wider dispensational culture. Robert Van Kampen's *The Fourth Reich* (1997) argued against the pre-tribulation rapture, an expectation it described as "a false hope."[3] James BeauSeigneur's the Christ Clone Trilogy (1997–98) also advanced an innovative theory of the rapture, but argued that the resurrected Christians would leave their human bodies behind; this rapture would lead to the appearance of mass deaths rather than mass disappearances. Other of the novels' debates have been political in tone. Hal Lindsey's *Blood Moon* (1996), which reflected its author's increasing concern with political Islam, mounted a sustained attack on the "land for peace" deals of successive Israeli governments.[4] But these debates have been continued beyond the boundaries of the premillennial movement. Michael Hyatt and George Grant's anti-rapture novel, *Y2K: The Day the World Shut Down* (1998), argued that the pop dispensationalism of Hal Lindsey and his ilk had stymied evangelical cultural engagement and that evangelicals could achieve nothing of any significance while "apocalyptic reticence was chided as faithlessness, while practical intransigence was enshrined as faithfulness."[5] Hyatt and Grant attempted to prove their point by advancing a species of preterism, an exegetical method that argued that most New Testament prophecies had been fulfilled with the fall of Jerusalem in A.D. 70. This approach was most memorably developed in *The Last Disciple* (2004) and *The Last Sacrifice* (2006), by Hank Hanegraaff and Sigmund Brouwer, who, as we have seen, claimed that Left Behind's interpretive approach served ultimately to undermine "the deity and resurrection of Christ."[6] It was a startling conclusion. But just as the exegetical debate could not be confined to eschatology, neither could it be confined to evangelicalism. Other novels from outside the evangelical community were prepared to correct the specifics of Left Behind's prophetic scheme. Michael O'Brien's Children of the Last Days series (1996–), sharing many standard evangelical social concerns, advanced a Roman Catholic alternative to Left Behind's apocalyptic thought. Other writers, such as Mark E. Rogers, author of the zombie rapture thriller *The Dead* (1990, reissued 2000), and Brian Caldwell, author of *We All Fall Down* (2000, reissued 2006), adopted elements of the dispensational narrative to satirize its system of belief. As the debates continued, LaHaye and Jenkins set about providing prequels and sequels to their original twelve volumes. But the wider series of disputes were illustrating the self-consciousness of their exegetical decisions. The sheer variety of alternative approaches insisted upon the point they wanted to elide: whatever LaHaye and Jenkins might argue to the contrary, prophecy was "hard to understand."

Yet prophecy was more important than ever. As the skyline of Manhattan assumed the appearance of an end-time conflict, and a "war on terror" commenced with robustly eschatological intent, the clarity of prophecy belief became occluded by the rapidity of the changing world. Some novels appeared not just as fictional developments of prophecy, but as prophecy itself. The opening scene of Joel C. Rosenberg's *The Last Jihad* (2002)—written before 9/11, though published some months after the bombings—began with a hijacked jet *en route* to a suicide attack on the president of the United States and ended with the toppling of Saddam Hussein.[7] It was a chilling moment in a genre that had repeatedly advertised itself as anticipating future trends. And Rosenberg's prescience did not go unnoticed. Between 2002 and 2006, one million of his four prophetic novels were sold;[8] it has also been reported that he has become a consultant to senior staffers in the Bush administration.[9] Rosenberg's pro-government approach has certainly been developed. In a new surge of patriotic feeling other prophecy novels attempted to move away from the culture of conspiracy that threw in doubt the beneficence of American government. Neesa Hart's political thrillers rehabilitated FEMA from the worst fears of conspiracy theorists.[10] By contrast, a profound skepticism of American institutions has been reflected in Tim LaHaye's new adventure series. In its second installment, *The Secret on Ararat* (2004), the quest to discover the location of Noah's Ark is frustrated by the murderous activities of a CIA operative determined to preserve its secrets for the benefit of an intelligence elite.[11] In the aftermath of Left Behind, prophecy novels no longer agree on a basic American patriotism. Prophecy seems as hard to understand as the world it purports to represent.

I

Evangelical prophecy novels have been consistently political, but not all have endorsed the general support in dispensational culture for Israel and the United States. That critique of recent Israeli policy has been nowhere more surprising than in the work of Hal Lindsey. Lindsey had gained fame for his strong support for the Jewish state. The Late Great Planet Earth had described the "rebirth of Israel" as the "paramount prophetic sign" of the imminent end of the age.[12] Lindsey's celebration of Israel developed in a lavishly illustrated guidebook he prepared for tourists, as well as in his consultancy work for the Pentagon.[13] But Lindsey's rapture novel, Blood Moon (1996), was much less celebratory in tone.

Blood Moon was published shortly after the first installment of Left Behind.[14] While it could not take account of the sudden popularity of Left Behind, it was clearly articulating an alternative to its claims. The novel's focus was more political than spiritual and more obviously directed toward the present than the future: "I want this book to be a blessing for all who read it," Lindsey stated; "I hope it opens your eyes to the amazing truth of biblical prophecy and how it is being fulfilled all around us."[15] As this statement implied, Blood Moon was intended to reinforce the limited historicism that had become foundational to Lindsey's literary project, but, above all else, it was intended to consolidate his position as the high priest of "pop" dispensationalism. It was a necessary rehabilitation—but one that offered only a minor modification of his earlier views. On a number of occasions, characters in Blood Moon remembered that they had been exposed to Lindsey's prophetic teaching long before their conversion. As the world plunges into chaos, Jeremy Armstrong grows "curious about lessons his Mom had tried to teach him" when she sent him "books by some nut named Hal Lindsey."[16] After his conversion, Armstrong is no longer prepared to dismiss the "frayed old book . . . The Late Great Planet Earth," for its author no longer sounded like a "total nut case." Armstrong began to realize that "most of what [Lindsey] interpreted from the Hebrew prophets is now coming true."[17]

None of the novel's characters point to Lindsey's failed expectations as to the prophetic significance of 1988, but they did articulate one of Lindsey's most obvious admissions of error. His confession that only "most of what he interpreted . . . [was] coming true" conceded that his exegetical method—based on a literal hermeneutic, "the golden rule of interpretation"—was not as reliable a guide to the future as his earlier publications had maintained.[18] *The Late Great Planet Earth,* for example, had clearly aligned Lindsey's "interpretations" with the word of God itself: Lindsey's book had been designed to allow God to present "His views."[19] But much of the earlier certainty remained. The novel reiterated his claim that "this generation"—the generation that had lived through the "rebirth of Israel" in 1948—would witness the second coming.[20] This claim was maintained despite the failure of Lindsey's earlier hinting that "this generation" could probably expect the rapture to occur in 1988.[21] But, in the novel, Lindsey's limited historicism remained unshaken. *Blood Moon* focused on the prophetic significance of contemporary political events. It was more critical of Israeli government policy than any other prophecy novel and used both Jewish and Muslim characters to condemn the "land for peace" deals: even the apocalyptic enemies of the Jewish state could realize that its leaders were betraying the Zionist cause. In *Blood Moon,* therefore, dispensational piety was being subsumed into dispensational politics. Lindsey's prophecy novel was an implicit critique of the political apathy and chronological reserve of Left Behind.

That political criticism continued one year later, when Kim Young—then a student at Dallas Theological Seminary—published *The Last Hour* (1997). Its low production standards were clear. The text was littered with errors in grammar, punctuation, spelling, and fact, drew freely on the urban legends of earlier dispensational ephemera, and its plot bore marked similarities to events described in Left Behind, such as the "miracle" defeat of the Russian air force's attack on Israel, and events described in Robertson's *End of the Age,* such as the first lady's assumption of presidential power.[22] But Young's novel also challenged some of the central tenets of dispensational orthodoxy. Although she was writing in the intellectual headquarters of the dispensational movement, her novel indicated that she did not intend to be "dogmatic" about the details of her faith and hinted at her uncertainty as to whether the events of the tribulation would happen "before or after the rapture."[23] In her opening comments, Young even suggested that the rapture might come midway through the tribulation, though her narrative adopted the traditional view.[24] As in later Left Behind spin-offs, Young's rapture removes a bipartisan and ecumenical third of the global population, including "many" Catholics as well as many members of the House and Senate.[25] Even the president—a thinly disguised version of Bill Clinton—appears to have been numbered among the disappeared. It was a signal of the redemptive potential of the evangelical gospel: "The blood covered even him."[26]

Despite this nod toward bipartisan politics, *The Last Hour* mounted a robust attack on the Clinton administration. Set in the late 1990s, the novel depicted the fictional First Family of Bob and Emily Wells.[27] Their similarities to Bill and

Hillary Clinton went far beyond the assonance in their first names. Bob's early life clearly paralleled Bill's.[28] Both men are of similar age, and both men achieve political success while indulging as philanderers.[29] The novel begins with a nod toward a series of harassment charges made against the president by "Debra Thames"—a recognizable equivalent of Paula Jones.[30] After the disappearance of the president and the vice president's death, which Emily Wells blames on a Republican coup, the first lady assumes massive political power and appoints into her cabinet a circle of women "wrapped in a web of international secrecy, women who were members of either the Council on Foreign Relations, the Trilateral Commission, or the Bilderbergers—organizations whose goals included bringing an end to American dominance, and installing a global, One World Order."[31] The new appointments include "militant lesbians, feminist new-agers, anti-Christian activists, sex perverts, doctrinal Marxists, and global elitists."[32] Their attempt to effeminize the nation would be well represented in their decision to replace the greenback with a new dollar bill—issued only in pink.[33] At the lowest point of the tribulation, Emily nationalizes American industries, allows FEMA full control of the media, and inaugurates a massive surveillance of American citizens with the cooperation of the Masons and other secret societies.[34]

Young's deference to the conspiracy models of earlier dispensational writers is evident in her repeated references to an "inner circle" who "keep the masses in tow."[35] The conspiracy is disseminated through media, such as the Hollywood "trash" that flaunts its "new age overtones."[36] But the conservatism with which *The Last Hour* identifies is uniquely chauvinist in tone. The novel pits "heartland values" against those of the "blue" states, and its ethical struggle is ultimately violent in its manifestation: the Antichrist complains of "a growing faction, particularly in Texas," the home of Dallas Theological Seminary, which his forces find difficult to control.[37] But the novel demonstrates profound ignorance of the world beyond the Bible Belt, and, for example, identifies NATO as a "North American Treaty Organization," which exists to provide non-Americans with "the protection of the United States."[38]

More seriously, the novel borders on the anti-Semitic. While, during the years of the tribulation, "the world experienced the greatest evangelistic movement of all time," the only conversions we see in this novel are the conversions of Jews.[39] These conversions are hardly robust. One Jewish character is brought to "evangelical" faith through the exhortations of a messianic Rabbi in an account that contains no reference to Jesus Christ.[40] Neither are these conversions sufficient to safeguard Jews from "the coming holocaust"—even thought this is a holocaust engineered by their fellow religionists.[41] As in Left Behind, a good pope is raptured and is replaced by a bad pope, an American Jew whose spiritual authority is matched by the political authority the World President, a German Jew, who turns out to be the

Antichrist himself.[42] These conspiring Jews lead a revival of Marian devotion that unites the competing ideologies of the earth.[43] The narrative points to the guilt by association of two evangelical "others": while prominent Catholics can be saved, the Roman Catholic Church, in its latter-day manifestation, exists as the confidence trick of a manipulative Jewish cabal. No wonder, therefore, that the remnant of evangelicals moves en masse to a mountain retreat in Colorado.[44] In their bunker they are haunted by longing for the old political order. As the world plunges into chaos, the believers return to the old question of the accuracy of evangelical nostalgia: "This is still America, isn't it?"[45]

II

Other evangelical writers turned to fiction to warn dispensational readers of the dangers of exactly this kind of conspiratorial thinking. *Y2K: The Day the World Shut Down* (1998), by Michael Hyatt and George Grant, alluded to the conspiracy of the Elders of Zion, but only to dismiss it as a ridiculous (and—oddly—a liberal) point of view.[46] Like *The Last Hour*, *Y2K* evidenced profound nostalgia for the American past: "we're not the same country we were."[47] But this was a situation the novel believed it could change. *Y2K* prepared to combat premillennial hysteria among evangelicals in a period in which, the novel observed, "the speculations of men ran to the frantic and the frenetic. Ecstatic eschatological significance was read into every change of any consequence—be it of the weather or of the government. Apocalyptic reticence was chided as faithlessness, while practical intransigence was enshrined as faithfulness. Fantastic common wisdom replaced ordinary common sense, and plain selfish serenity replaced plain selfless civility."[48] It was, in a sense, an attack on exactly the mentality the rapture novels attempted to exploit. Hyatt and Grant were particularly concerned by believers' widespread speculation about dates. Never before had evangelicals been faced with such an unusual calendrical opportunity, and many evangelicals, the authors feared, had become dangerously preoccupied by fears that January 1, 2000, "may be the day the world shuts down."[49] Of course, the novel was prepared to recognize that this "pretty serious hooey" had some basis in fact, citing a real-life article in *Business Week* that promised to describe "how the year 2000 bug will hurt the economy."[50] But, the novel exhorted, Christians should be prepared not just for imminent technological disaster but also for the long-term reconstruction of a Christian civilization that the disaster would make possible. As in Left Behind, the protagonist, Bob Priam, is a less-than-godly husband and father in a family of genuine faith.[51] He loses his job, but sets up as an independent Y2K consultant and experiences spiritual renewal as he prepares his family for the impending crisis. His story opens and closes with a cautionary tale, with descriptions of the scene in St. Peter's Church, Rome, on the last day of 999, when, "weeping and wailing," Christian believers had "gathered . . . to await the end of the world."[52] But their expectations were denied, and the congregants left St. Peter's to rebuild the world they had imagined they would never see. *Y2K* called on its evangelical readers to go and do likewise.

Y2K was certainly oppositional: the novel attempted to associate Hal Lindsey with the "frantic and frenetic" spiritualities it opposed. The character in the novel that most closely represents the authorial point of view admitted that he was "not at all surprised that the year 2000 would attract the attentions of conspiracy theorists, prophetic doomsayers, eschatological seers, eternal pessimists, and various other worrywarts. The Y2K computer crisis had obviously become the latest Armageddon option: a convenient catastrophe for those who had alternately looked to killer bees, Beast-coded Social Security checks, hitchhiking angels, conflict in the Middle East, secret federal cover-ups, biological warfare, Area 51 alien invasions, botched genetic engineering, and black helicopter deployments to usher in the last days of this, the terminal generation."[53] The statement was a damning indictment of Lindsey and the pop dispensationalism he represented. It juxtaposed an allusion to the title of *The Terminal Generation* (1976), his "nonfiction" textbook, with the wacky and the weird. It was a telling dismissal of the self-proclaimed most influential of the premillennial writers. But the novel's attack on the conspiratorial culture of a large and panicking section of popular evangelicalism was equally striking.[54]

Like *The Last Hour*, *Y2K* advanced a searing critique of Clinton's America, lamenting the collapse of leadership in a society facing the "potential for a complete meltdown."[55] Political sentiment in the novel was deeply conservative, not least in its reactions to "new revelations about the President's sex life." Priam's condemnation of the president was not merely an articulation of prim piety: "The only thing that disappointed him more than the President's more recent escapades was the American public's response to it—or lack of response. No one seemed to care as long as the economy was healthy."[56] And yet the economy was much less robust than many people realized. The "veneer of prosperity" was "fragile" and Americans were "stretched to the limit by debt." People were "living beyond all reasonable means from paycheck to paycheck, and utterly dependent upon a continuing boom in the economy for even a semblance of their current standard of living." Middle-class prosperity, the novel concluded, "appeared all too . . . terribly vulnerable," and the social safety nets were not worthy of their trust.[57] The "lumbering bureaucracies" of Medicaid and Medicare were "rife with corruption and mismanagement."[58] Americans, in the final analysis, had no one to believe in but themselves.

It was in this context that *Y2K* proposed its radical alternative—an alternative that resonated throughout the prophecy fiction tradition and which the novel described as "the grandma strategy."[59] This strategy for survival encouraged evangelicals to live out their nostalgia for the American past, to return to a homesteading lifestyle, to live in community, "get out of debt, keep a productive garden, have some food on hand in case of a storm, learn how to tend sickness at home, be able to defend yourself, have some basic tools around and the skills to use them, have a good contingency plan if times get tough, save up for a rainy day, and simplify your needs."[60] Only this could allow believers to endure the social collapse the authors expected, as they depicted the imposition of martial law in the United States and witnessed Western Europe "teetering on the verge of social chaos."[61]

But the sheer practicality of this solution underplayed the novel's evangelistic intent. The conclusion of the novel was strangely lacking in evangelical zeal—or even any significant Christian reference. Exhortatory dialogue—so common in the prophecy fiction genre—was restricted to proposing business and technical solutions.[62] It was a theme emphasized on the novel's endpaper, which provided an advertisement for Hyatt's *New York Times* best-seller, *The Millennium Bug: How to Survive the Coming Chaos* (1998), which, in turn, was part of his wider interest in disaster preparation: his e-business was selling a year's supply of food for $3,395 plus shipping.[63] However, as the novel noted elsewhere, "preparing for the end, though perhaps dispiriting, was not nearly so difficult as preparing for what comes after the end"—especially if events were to undermine your direst predictions.[64] And they did. Y2K did not sufficiently forestall the impending apocalypse. There was to be no "coming crisis," and the world did not "shut down" in technological disaster in January 2000, but the challenge to the prophecy fiction consensus did continue.

The most significant challenge to the Left Behind consensus—in terms of sales and theology—was also the most inventive series in the genre. Like many of its peers, it advanced a politicized nostalgia: "Things had changed a lot . . . Most of the old taboos had disappeared, except among a few conservative religious groups. Public nudity, or partial nudity with a few skimpy accessories that hid nothing, was common in most of the world, and it was not unusual to find couples or even groups having sex on the beaches or in the parks."[65] But these novels, the Christ Clone Trilogy, were unusual in that they was written by a former politician, James BeauSeigneur, a military consultant and former Republican congressional candidate who had published two books related to national defense.[66] The publishing origins of BeauSeigneur's novels were somewhat less auspicious. *In His Image* (1997), *Birth of an Age* (1997) and *Acts of God* (1998) first appeared under the imprint of an insignificant evangelical firm. In an interview in March 2000, BeauSeigneur was modest about this achievement: Selective House, he explained, was "a small publishing company whose focus is books and videos which bring the Gospel to a secular audience." His interviewer asked whether the books were likely to be available in "an average chain secular bookstore": he thought they would be available, "but you'll probably have to ask." BeauSeigneur did not appear anxious to promote his own work: "If God chooses to use my writing . . . He knows where to find me. I am at a point in life that I am available to God if he's got something he wants me to do, but I no longer wrestle to be first in line to be hanged."[67] The need for modesty changed in 2003, when the trilogy, with their contents updated to refer to the war on terror, the brutal execution of Daniel Pearl, and the war in Iraq, was republished by Warner Books and distributed as mass market paperbacks "wherever books are sold."[68] By 2007, the series had been translated into Spanish, Italian, Portuguese, German, Croatian, Bulgarian, Hungarian, Korean, and Greek. Supported by a powerful Web site, and with widespread marketing support, the Christ Clone Trilogy was clearly expected to sell.

BeauSeigneur's work broke the trend that had seen prophecy novels be prepared by working theologians. Of course, his work had theological influences. He cited C. S. Lewis and prophecy writer Arnold Fruchtenbaum as two positive role models, but recorded his disappointment with previous publications in the field. Hal Lindsey's nonfiction books, he thought, "strain reality and common sense." BeauSeigneur had read Kirban's 666 with high hopes, having been "impressed" by his nonfiction, but he found the novel "dreadful, just plain silly." The limitations of Lindsey's interpretive fancies and Kirban's novels convinced BeauSeigneur of the need for "well-conceived and well-written" prophetic fiction, and he began work on the Christ Clone Trilogy in 1987.[69] His aim was clearly to succeed where Lindsey and Kirban had failed.

There is little doubt that BeauSeigneur's work is among the most accomplished in the genre. In an "Important Note from the Author," BeauSeigneur emphasized that his work would be much more concerned with voice and characterization and much less overtly didactic than many of the earlier texts. "Never assume that the characters—any of the characters—speak for the author," he insisted, and he reiterated the point in occasional footnotes when the going got theologically rough.[70] It was a point worth repeating, for BeauSeigneur's work toyed with some surprising theological conclusions.

The Christ Clone Trilogy was heavily influenced by science fiction texts.[71] Footnotes to authentic texts and scientific studies peppered the three novels. Similarly, in BeauSeigneur's account of the concealing of the Ark of the Covenant in southern France by the Knights Templar and the Priory of Sion, one might be forgiven for believing one were reading Dan Brown's *Da Vinci Code* (2003)—a supposition that would have been reinforced by a footnote citing the faux-historical *Holy Blood, Holy Grail* (1982).[72] But BeauSeigneur's point about the instability of the narrative voice was most useful in terms of the work's theological content. Most obviously, the rapture, in the Christ Clone Trilogy, is utterly unlike anything else in the genre. When believers are taken to heaven, their bodies are left behind in death. BeauSeigneur's novel doctrine was explained in the final installment: "The bodies of the people who were raptured were corruptible . . . Those bodies never would have been permitted in heaven and so were simply sloughed off, or shed like old clothes. When they were raptured, they were given new bodies: perfect, incorruptible, and without flaw."[73] The doctrine is provided with an uncharacteristically complex defense: "The Greek word in the passage [1 Corinthians 15:50–53] that is translated as *changed,* is elsewhere translated as *exchanged* . . . It is the term used when discussing changing clothes."[74] BeauSeigneur's rapture would make bodies die, not disappear, but it would still be extensive in its scope. The rapture involves one quarter of a million of inhabitants of France, half a million Saudi Arabians, one million Britons, three million Pakistanis, eight million Egyptians, twenty-five million Indians, and fifteen to twenty percent of the American population, including "twelve senators, sixty-odd congressmen, three Cabinet members, and the vice president."[75] The Christ Clone Trilogy is similarly innovative in its prophetic chronology. There are ten years between "the Disaster" and the beginning of the tribulation, and over twenty years between the rapture and the end of the age.[76] Nevertheless, the novels are certain, the enemies of truth are propounding the same old sinister agenda, working toward the "New World Order" which President Bush had predicted.[77]

Whatever the political similarities, the most significant difference between the Christ Clone Trilogy and earlier prophecy fictions is the entire absence of any tribulation saints. While other fictions focus on the efforts of those who attempt to survive or even resist the Antichristian regime, the Christ Clone Trilogy concentrates on Decker Hawthorne and the circle immediately surrounding the emerging Antichrist, and those tribulation saints who appear in the series appear only as incidental characters. In part this is linked to the series' downplaying of evangelistic exhortation. The novels never inform their readers how post-rapture characters come to faith in Jesus Christ. The series has no "Sinner's Prayer" moments, and its first example of evangelistic exhortation occurs midway through the trilogy's final installment.[78] Similarly, Hawthorne's "conversion" occurs at the end of the final novel, in the seconds after his decapitation and before the death of his brain—for, in evangelical prophecy novels, the guillotine can never be escaped. His conversion is that of an old man, almost in the series' final pages, and so the story is one of a spiritual quest leading up to a decisive spiritual moment. In Left Behind, by contrast, Rayford Steele's conversion occurs in the first of the series' installments, and his story through the next eleven volumes is one of survival against impossible odds.

In privileging this spiritual search over the realization of spiritual certainty, the Christ Clone Trilogy adopts a comic form. Its open-endedness is enhanced by a subtle exploitation of important themes in the theory of millennial studies. The series suggests that prophecy belief can be self-fulfilling and cites Charles Manson to prove the point.[79] Elsewhere, Hawthorne draws on a long scholarly tradition to attempt to engineer an example of cognitive dissonance, and other characters discuss reinterpretation theory, which is explained by reference to the history of the Jehovah's Witnesses.[80] The Christ Clone Trilogy therefore refuses to present in the defense of Scriptural authority a simple "argument from prophecy."[81] Prophecy, after all, is "hard to understand."[82] But, whatever its other uncertainties, the trilogy did not hesitate to identify its enemies. Reflecting the context of its early preparation, BeauSeigneur's fiction returned to the dangers of the New Age movement. Like Peretti, BeauSeigneur listed some of the groups and productions through which New Age ideas had been promulgated, including the Christian Science movement, *Star Wars,* and *Star Trek.*[83] The novels identified a huge range of evil influences. In fact, they argued, "it would be hard to find any area of life where the influence of the New Age has not reached."[84]

The ubiquity of New Age ideology points to the series' insistence on the common combination of religious and political ideals. In the Christ Clone Trilogy, the goal of the Antichrist figure is to secure the evolutionary leap in human consciousness that would herald the New Age. Christopher Goodman had been cloned from cells found on the Turin Shroud. After the death of his father-figure, he turns to Decker Hawthorne, who brings him up as his ward, and discovers that the good-natured and precocious teenager is "quite a big fan of the UN."[85] This reference to the United Nations demonstrates the constant evolution of evangelical prophetic concerns. When BeauSeigneur began work on the trilogy, in 1987, the European Union, not the United Nations, was the focus of most dispensational conspiratorial thinking. By 1997–98, when the novels were first published, the success of the Left Behind series indicated that the European Union had been eclipsed in the dispensational imagination. But, like Jerry B. Jenkins, BeauSeigneur has claimed that his position on the United Nations is actually ambiguous: he claims to portray it as "basically positive," but exploited for evil purposes.[86] That exploitation is eschatological, in its final takeover by the Antichrist, but it is also immanent, in its being currently dominated by dangerous New Age philosophies. The existence of this conspiracy explains why Goodman climbs so rapidly through the ranks of the organization, and why he, as its new leader, can move its headquarters to Babylon while motivating the World Health Organization to administer the innocuous vaccination that turns out to be the mark of the beast.[87] Goodman's plans were engineered in the context of widespread and long-standing international conspiracy that included "heads of state, members of the World Court, celebrities from television and movies, sports figures, labor leaders, the entire board of the World Council of Churches, several Roman Catholic and Orthodox bishops and cardinals, some high-profile Protestant ministers, and numerous other religious leaders."[88] The shared goals of this ecumenical cabal included the final extermina-tion of all religious dissent.

Perhaps this is why the dissenters turn to violence. Many of the series' believ-ing characters remain piously passive. The tribulation saints head for Petra, for example, and when they and the Jewish believers are threatened, the earth opens up and swallows their antagonists, just as it does in Left Behind.[89] But other believ-ers engage in more aggressive behavior. These "fundamentalists," as the novel describes them, begin with public protests on the first day of the distribution of the vaccination.[90] In "scenes reminiscent of the sit-ins of the 1960s or the . . . blockades of women's clinics in the 1990s," the series explained, "fundamentalists started the day in dozens of cities from Sydney to Beijing by attempting to block the entrance to communion clinics as they opened."[91] But the protests quickly spiraled out of control. A number of clinics are firebombed, and while fundamentalists deny responsibility, they are identified as being responsible for the outrage.[92] Other fun-damentalist "terrorists" engage in violent hijackings and get involved in drive-by shootings.[93] Some of these attacks are described as the work of a "lunatic fringe," and others were stage-managed by the Antichrist and the United Nations to dis-credit the true believers, but one attempted murder, at least, is represented as being biblically sanctioned.[94] While the Left Behind novels remained fundamentally ambivalent about the morality of assassinating the Antichrist, the Christ Clone Trilogy identifies certain circumstances in which his assassination can become a moral duty. One character, Tom Donafin, is identified as Jesus's official "Avenger of Blood."[95] He is the one individual with a divinely sanctioned right to pursue the Antichrist' death, and, in shooting Goodman, he is represented as "striking the head of Satan in accordance with the prophecy in Genesis."[96] In the context of this surge in sacred terror, it is hardly surprising that the media could make "funda-mentalists" sound "subhuman" while it pursued them in "a regular witch-hunt."[97] The End of the Age, by a former presidential hopeful, had extolled the virtue of evangelical nuclear blackmail. The Christ Clone Trilogy, written by a former con-gressional candidate and addressing an increasingly politicized evangelical move-ment, appeared to defend the potential legitimacy of violent public protest and political assassination.

III

The danger of this kind of political engagement was a theme that resonated through Jerry B. Jenkins's dystopian thriller, Soon (2003). This pre-rapture prophetic novel described the next step in the evolution of American society. In Soon, America becomes evangelicalism's apocalyptic other, and Jenkins imagines a future that had no recollection of the success of Left Behind. *Soon* is deeply ambivalent about the success of its authors' earlier series. Jenkins, like LaHaye, has responded with some hesitation to its success and the media profile it has generated. *Soon*, another *New York Times* best-seller, focuses on life before the rapture, but offers a more significant revision of the paradigm of Left Behind.

Soon suggests that Left Behind never happened. It is a futuristic thriller, which extrapolates its description of a humanistic totalitarianism from actual letters to *TIME* magazine that a frontispiece reproduces. The novel imagines what will happen if Left Behind is wrong and Christ does not come back in the immediate future. It ignores the current prophetic revival, evidenced in the millions of sales of prophecy novels, and describes a future for evangelicalism against the backdrop of a series of religious wars springing from the attacks on the World Trade Center in 2001 and the invasion of Iraq in 2003. From these incidents, the novel projects an escalation of the Israeli-Palestinian conflict and terrorist strikes throughout North America and Europe in 2008. These wars of religion intensify into "attacks, counterattacks, reprisals, and finally, an all-out nuclear war that most thought signaled the end of the world."[98] The war brings the United States to the verge of extinction: a coalition of Muslim nations destroys Washington, D.C., and a North Korean ballistic missile, "the largest warhead ever to land on American soil," obliterates the Pentagon.[99] Worldwide, bombs "snuffed out tens of millions of lives" and, by literally splitting China in two, generate a tidal wave "a million times more destructive" than the Hiroshima explosion, a tsunami that "engulfed all of Hong Kong Island, swamped Taiwan with hundreds of feet of water, raced to the Philippine Sea and the East China Sea, obliterated Japan and Indonesia, swept into the Northwest Pacific Basin and the Japan Trench," "swallowed" Hawaii, and killed "thousands more" in California.[100] The unprecedented scale of its devastation brings a sudden end to all religious wars, as the battling faithful realize that global destruction is no longer a divine monopoly. Extremists abandon the religious convictions that had almost destroyed humanity, and nations embrace the ideal of a world purged of sectarian terror. Under the shadow of the United Nations, the new world is represented as "an intellectual, humanistic society that eschewed both religion and war."[101] But in advancing that goal, the new American regime inaugurates "the most repressive time in human history," spying on every citizen and banning religious belief.[102]

Thirty-six years later, in 2046, Paul Stepola is given the responsibility of rooting out the menace of the American Christian underground. As a special agent with the National Peace Organization (the successor to the FBI and the CIA), Stepola capitalizes on the specialist knowledge he had gained during his doctoral studies in religion. Shocked by revelations that both his father and his former military commander were believers, Stepola embarks on a spiritual journey that leads him inexorably toward evangelical conversion. But the interests of the evangelicalism he investigates challenge his expectations just as much as they challenge the expectations of prophecy fiction readers. This novel's pre-tribulation saints—"the Watchmen"—are an underground militia, headquartered in "a city beneath a city" in a northern state, driven by their belief that the miracles tormenting the humanistic administration are signs of the second coming.[103] They are prepared, much more than the characters of Left Behind, to be subversives and to take lives in order to secure their own. Stepola's conversion develops his character, and he struggles on to "sense the mind of God," who provides him with a new mission, "to motivate every underground believer he could find to pray and plead with God to show Himself to the enemy."[104] His duty to suppress the Christian underground leads Stepola to its ultimate defense, but his initial preference for active physical resistance gives way to the quest for a miracle and an emphasis on prayer that seems fundamentally incompatible with the globe-trotting, empire-building economic and militaristic resistance of Left Behind's survivors, the Tribulation Force.[105]

Stepola's concentration on the fate of Christian America mirrors that of the novel as a whole. Soon's narrative is based on a fundamental rethinking of the relationship between evangelicals and the American establishment and assumes that, within forty years, the influence of evangelical prophecy in the Ronald Reagan and George W. Bush administrations will have reached its antithesis. In Soon, Americans are as patriotic as ever, but this new patriotism is stripped of its religious content.[106] In its depiction of America, Soon stands as the logical outcome of a longer trend in evangelical eschatology. Prophecy scholars have often attempted to discover America's role in prophecy.[107] Seventeenth- and eighteenth-century theologians attempted to identify the new world as possessing unique millennial agency; Jonathan Edwards wondered whether the "awakening" in which he participated might be heralding the millennium on American soil.[108] But, throughout the nineteenth and twentieth centuries, as dispensationalism began to dominate the evangelical imagination, America lost its prophetic identity, and its end-time role steadily diminished.[109] Left Behind, as we have noticed, worked on the assumption that the United States had no role in biblical prophecy.[110] But Soon marries this changing prophetic perspective with America's new geopolitical situation. Left Behind was criticized for its international naïveté (for example, in its treatment of the Palestinian problem), but Soon avoids this charge by neglecting international contexts entirely: there is no outside world to be concerned about.[111] Cold war prophecy writers had imagined a bipolar political world—East versus West—in a dualism that had mirrored the conflict's basic moral division.[112] But this tradition is completely upended in Soon. America has lost its sacred status, and the moral bipolarity of the cold war is projected onto a single nation. Soon is, in this sense, the ultimate post–cold war fiction. America has been stripped of its prophetic significance at the same time as it has lost its moral authority as the counterweight to atheistic communism. The moral dichotomy that characterized cold war geopolitics was being projected onto an exclusively American canvas. In stark contrast to the uncomplicated patriotism of a great deal of American dispensational writing, America itself was now being identified as evangelicalism's eschatological "other."

Evangelicals had to reimagine their relationship to the United States. *Soon* rewrites that relationship by drawing parallels with the old Communist bloc. One character remembers how Soviet Russia "closed almost all its churches and disposed of more than forty thousand clergy. They turned city churches into museums and country churches into barns or apartments . . . What happened in Russia and China and Romania decades ago could re-emerge here, right under our noses," in America.[113] But there are hints in the novel that the nation is still culturally divided. The population divides into the familiar contours of the "50:50 nation," with "half" the population prepared to consider the possibility that the strange events that so perplex the authorities are the miracles the Christians claim.[114] The moral polarity of America is highlighted by the geography of *Soon*'s plot. The action in *Soon* is almost entirely urban and is notably concentrated in Chicago, Washington, D.C., Las Vegas, several California cities, and a single Texan oil well. The novel's apocalyptic scenarios tend to avoid the Bible Belt and those Southern states where most readers of prophecy fictions live.[115] Undoubtedly, this largely urban focus reflects traditional evangelical suspicions of the city, but also provides a mechanism for prophecy believers to imagine the outpouring of divine judgments on those parts of America that are least receptive to their point of view.[116] Perhaps Jenkins is identifying the United States' traditional political divisions with the future prophetic dichotomy his dispensational readers expect. Whatever the significance of its geography, *Soon* represents the return of evangelicals to the social, cultural, and political margins. The novel is oblivious to the success of Left Behind, as it had to be, if Jenkins's writing were not to veer from dispensationalism's orthodox center. His commitment to dispensationalism's traditional narrative patterns—which consistently emphasize the increasing marginalization and eventual persecution of the faithful—demanded the deliberate elision of the earlier series' success. As *Soon* illustrates, dispensationalists need to be alienated because they expect to be alienated at the end of the age, and they must always believe they could be living in that period. *Soon* wrestled to reassert evangelical marginality.

Technological advances certainly made that marginality look possible. One of the most consistent fears in the prophecy novel genre, and the dispensationalism from which it emerged, has been the haunting fear of an aggressive modernity. Prophecy fictions have regularly worried about the technological invasion of the body, often by computer chips identifying the individual to the regime or by the individual's being branded with the mark of the beast. These worries play on fears of diminishing privacy, but move beyond that typically modern concern to the ultimate fear that the Antichrist will destabilize the last bastion of freedom—a coherent and independent subjectivity. For Kirban, for example, the tribulation would involve young people looking like "men from outer space with computers plugged into their heads."[117] Fortunately, for readers of rapture fiction, this invasion of individuality is regularly limited to the Antichrist's violent assumption of ultimate power during the tribulation.

In *Soon*, however, this autonomous subjectivity ends long before the tribulation—and long before the rapture. The regime the novel describes has its citizens wearing "ID biochips" beneath the skin.[118] These biochips are not, as in earlier prophecy novels, the mark of the beast, but like the mark of the beast they do serve the purposes of an apparently all-powerful totalitarian system. *Soon* echoes earlier fictions in describing the administration's technology, which allows the government to spy on every citizen.[119] Individuals are subject to such invasive security precautions as iris scans and locks coded to specific sequences of DNA.[120] Perhaps most significantly of all, individuals carry "molar receptors," which allow teeth to receive radio and TV signals directly into the head.[121]

In many ways, the technological world of *Soon* is more frightening than that of traditional prophecy fiction, for it extrapolates the technology of the tribulation into the pre-rapture age. Yet *Soon* is less ambivalent about technical modernity than is Left Behind. In the earlier series, believers took advantage of the Internet, as the only medium free from government control. In *Soon*, it offers similar possibilities, but believers also take advantage of their biometric implants.[122] However, realizing that "electronic equipment will become useless at some point," they also resort to the traditional methods of letter-press printing to begin their "mass-communications program."[123] Taking on the administration's oppressive media hegemony, believers use advanced technology, but prepare for its ultimate passing. The novel's dispensationalism is ultimately figured, like millennialism more generally, as a reaction against progress.[124]

This reaction against progress feeds into that other basic trope in evangelical writing—ecclesiastical primitivism. In *Soon*, persecution takes believers back to their original situation. Paul Stepola's readings in the Bible "told of constant persecution . . . Paul was amazed that he had totally forgotten that the early Christians were also persona non grata with the government and had to meet in secret and worship virtually underground."[125] Persecution was offering believers the chance of a new beginning, the chance to meet without denominational divisions. In *Soon*, as a consequence, evangelical attitudes to the Roman Catholic Church are further modified. No longer is the Vatican the focus of apocalyptic fear: along with other world landmarks, it, too, is destroyed by "extremists," and Roman Catholics, along with people of other faiths, become the victims of this new administration.[126] But this destruction of denominational boundaries raises the question of what kind of Christians the novel's evangelicals are. The issue was plausibly avoided in Left Behind: dispensational orthodoxy teaches that those who come to faith after the rapture are not, strictly speaking, part of the church, and should not, therefore, celebrate the sacraments, those monumental indicators of distinctive denominational affiliations.[127] For this reason, Left Behind understandably avoided any references to baptism or the Lord's Supper. But there is less excuse for this in *Soon:* its plot is set before the rapture, when the ordinances were still in force, but, like Left Behind, it shows underground fellowships enjoying Bible study, while avoiding the ordinances altogether. This extremely "low church" atmosphere allows the narrative to continue without pausing to explain or choose between the theologies of infant or adult baptism, for example, and therefore allows the narrative to carry the sympathies of a wide range of Christian readers. But in these novels, evangelicalism has been rewritten. Recent prophecy novels take evangelicals beyond their notoriously low views of ecclesiology into a situation where the church itself can hardly be said to exist.

Ironically, this modified evangelicalism has seemed to grow in its capacity for violence as it has lost its theological edge. Throughout their history, prophecy novels have been powerfully ambivalent about the morality—and practical implications—of violence. Left Behind played with this ambiguity for narrative effect. At times the novels appear to justify murder when it would further the determined ends of history.[128] Steele prayed for the "privilege" of torturing and killing the Antichrist, though he knew that his death would only make him stronger and more satanic.[129] Tsion Ben-Judah, normally the voice of reason and authority, believed "we are at war. In the heat of battle, killing the enemy has never been considered murder."[130] Little wonder that the Antichrist's elite, discussing Steele's ethic of murder, considered his grasp of situation ethics: "Maybe he convinces himself it's a holy war. Then I guess anything goes."[131] (Or, as the protagonist put it in Don Thompson's movie *Image of the Beast,* "What's your definition of morality? This is war!"). But the suggestion that a "holy war" means "anything goes" reinforces audience suspicions. Although Steele eventually seems to dismiss the idea, it does appear to underpin the remarkable movement in Jenkins's writing from his depiction of the rapture as exodus (Left Behind) to his depiction of the rapture as battle (*Soon*).[132] Despite debates about the relationship between millennialism and violence—and the relationship between prophetic beliefs and behavior has been described as "unfathomable"—scholars agree that dispensational groups have demonstrated "no proclivity" for violent action.[133] Significantly, however, characters in *Soon* remember the violence of Christian fundamentalists in the first decade of the new millennium, when "religious extremists . . . persecuted homosexuals, assassinated abortion doctors . . . and bombed stem-cell research labs . . . And after the terrorist attacks of '05, it was the extremists who defied the tolerance laws and rioted, killing Muslims."[134] They continue to worry about the possibility of an armed evangelical rising. And these fears appear to be confirmed in the novel's depiction of the Watchmen, those believers organizing "Operation Soon," a project designed to spread the illegal news that the events the government dismisses as terrorist attacks are actually divinely wrought miracles heralding the imminent return of Christ. The believers construct a massive underground complex in an abandoned mine and post armed guards to maintain security and, if necessary, kill intruders.[135] Paul Stepola was shocked by the revelation: "How do you justify that?" "We don't, Paul. We pray it never happens."[136] *Soon* appears to show believers in different states responding in different ways to the possibility of violence. The physical resistance of the Watchmen in the northeast is paralleled by the eventual pacifism of believers in the southwest. In Los Angeles, government military intervention meant that believers were dying on a scale elsewhere unseen.[137] Under Stepola's guidance, believers discuss the possibility of disrupting the city's water supply.[138] The idea is later abandoned, and the believers issue a brochure which "stated unequivocally that the underground Christians in Los Angeles were not armed and never planned to be."[139] Nevertheless, as the novel's closing pages describe a final miracle—evidently designed to lead readers into the next installment—the novel suggests that the event would be first of many that would be known, over ground, as the "Christian Guerrilla War."[140] Once again, *Soon* moves beyond the expectations of audiences familiar with the relative caution of Left Behind.

It is difficult to assess the significance of these depictions of evangelical violence. Scholars in millennial studies suggest that the violent outbreaks of millennial groups are linked to a complex of isolation, paranoia, aspirations for dominion, and crisis mismanagement on the part of those agencies that would seek to intervene.[141] These scholars also argue that a basic difference exists between those groups which are militarily organized and those which merely assume an occasionally violent posture.[142] Whatever their inherent proclivity to physical struggle, nevertheless, prophetic movements "pose a fundamental challenge to the established social order and . . . are in high tension with it," and are most dangerous when that resistance is made sacred.[143] Richard Landes has proposed a typology that explains millennial agency as a matter of timing.[144] He distinguishes "normal" time from "apocalyptic" time and argues that millennial groups tend to remain passive and quietist until their sense of apocalyptic time is triggered. In the case of dispensationalism, normal time continues until the rapture, at which point apocalyptic time commences and normal codes are suspended. But *Soon* overturns this dispensational tradition. It reverses the division between normal and apocalyptic times and suggests the sacral function of violence. Using Landes's typology, *Soon* shows Jenkins moving from a depiction of passive fundamentalism in this age, represented in Left Behind as normal life before the rapture, to a depiction of violent fundamentalism in this age, represented in *Soon* as believers arming themselves in response to mounting persecution before the rapture. The remarkable thing about this persecution is that it seems to mirror the totalitarianism that dispensationalists formerly expected of the Antichrist in the tribulation period. In other words, *Soon* reimagines normal time and imports into the age before the rapture the conditions and ethics that dispensationalists expected to be typical of the tribulation. It requires its characters to reorient themselves to an American establishment that bears in this age the characteristics of Antichristian tyranny. *Soon* shows evangelicals facing social conditions that dispensational theologians argued they would never see and developing their sense of responsibility accordingly. *Soon* dramatizes growing pessimism about the short-term future of evangelicals in the United States. This pessimism seems to draw on the recent experiences of other separatist religious minorities. Confirming dispensationalism's proclivity for conspiracy theories, *Soon* hints that the evangelical future could parallel the Branch Davidian past. Shadows of Waco engulf the novel's description of government forces besieging a religious community it suspects of being "heavily armed and dangerous," and engaged in "anti-American subversive activities."[145] But just as Jenkins's readers imagine the militarization of Christians in normal time, so their hesitancy about violence may be beginning to change.

Soon represents the cult-ing of dispensationalism. Painting a picture of paranoid social withdrawal, *Soon* represents evangelicals taking on the traditional stereotypes of new religious movements, engaging in illegal and underground activity and demonstrating an alarming propensity for violence. The novel abandons traditional dispensational expectations of this age as excessively optimistic, and imagines, in contrast to previous dispensational writers, that a nuclear war and unprecedented worldwide destruction could be entirely unpredicted by Scripture. *Soon* prizes the future free from biblical controls and opens up the possibility of the triumph of worldwide atheism under the government of the United Nations. *Soon* is a prophecy novel that breaks free from genre archetypes by exploring the eschatological significance of normal time. And in normal time, evangelicals have become a cult bent on violent struggle.

The novel's emphasis on normal time—the period before the rapture—perhaps challenges its description as "prophecy fiction." The novel's cover subtitles the book "the beginning of the end." But the novel begins with expectations of the second coming, announced in a letter that Stepola discovers was written by his father, and the rapture itself, first mentioned on page 201, is its expected conclusion.[146] *Soon*, as a title, is a reference to the imminence not just of the second coming of Christ, but also to the social conditions the novel describes. *Soon* is a powerful dramatization of one possible evangelical response to the cultural logic of late capitalism. The novel itself, as "a remarkable mainstreaming of evangelical pop culture," depends for its success upon the very conditions it disdains.[147]

But market forces are at play. Like the other spin-off products, *Soon* capitalizes on its audience's "ever-widening circles of consumption."[148] The novel's cover highlights Jenkins as the "best-selling author of the *Left Behind* series." Nevertheless, just as Left Behind reinvented the paradigms of earlier prophecy fictions, so Left Behind itself is reinvented by *Soon*. The novel's totalizing demands are evident. Jenkins does not lead a movement—he addresses a reading community which is free to negotiate its relationship to his novels as it follows his imagination into a world of increasing paranoia, increasing separation from the social mainstream, and increasing suspicion of national and international governments.[149] Nevertheless, like Left Behind, *Soon* demands total commitment. Jenkins's readers, like characters in his Christian underground, cannot be "fence straddlers."[150]

IV

This call to commitment resonates throughout the novels that have been published in the aftermath of Left Behind. They propose significant modifications of the earlier series' eschatology; but their proposals for the modification of its political engagement are almost inevitably more conservative in tone. This chapter has documented a range of evangelical responses to the sudden mainstreaming of prophecy culture in the aftermath of Left Behind. It has described some of the most important of these many texts—those sharing the series' branding and publisher, those prepared by the series' authors with a different branding and publisher, those by other authors taking advantage of the popularity of apocalyptic narratives, and those written to counter the series' claims. In particular, this chapter has focused on these novels' challenge to Left Behind's politics, and especially their representation of Israel and the Jews; their challenge to Left Behind's theology, including its exegesis and its description of the rapture; and their challenge to the cognitive dissonance of Left Behind's success, which represented the sudden mainstreaming of a system of belief that must retain its sense of marginality if it is to coherently survive. Most significantly of all, this chapter has demonstrated that contemporary prophecy novels are increasingly ambivalent about the propriety of violence in the period before the rapture. Reinscribing evangelical marginality, recent prophecy novels offer a sustained argument in favor of an aggressive and potentially dangerous evangelical cultural engagement. Prophecy novels after Left Behind have turned militantly marginal.

Conclusion

There is hope, there is reason to hope. Don't give up now.
—Ken Abraham and Daniel Hart,
The Prodigal Project (2003)

Writing the Rapture, as the introduction explained, is not a history of a discrete genre, but an account of the most important elements of contemporary evangelical prophecy belief and a description of an increasingly important element of the American cultural mainstream. The success of Left Behind and the recent enthusiasm for its alternatives and competitors suggests that a properly qualified analysis of this narrative mode should now be central to any attempt to depict the *mentalité* of evangelical prophecy believers.

Instead of providing a full history of the genre, *Writing the Rapture* has focused on the cultural ramifications of the evolution of this narrative form. There are, of course, many other ways of reading the genre's history. It reveals a variegated imagination and one could certainly make more of the novels' increasing literary value, their increasing female agency, their late development and rapid abandonment of anti-Catholic rhetoric, their early racism and repeatedly anti-Semitic concerns, and their sense that Communism represents a danger to America only because of its relationship with an international Jewish conspiracy. One could also make more of the novels' refraction of larger themes in millennial studies scholarship: their contribution to the final collapse of the myth of "manifest destiny," and, in their being massively consumed at a moment of evangelical cultural power, their substantial qualification of the increasing qualified deprivation thesis.[1] Nevertheless, no one studying the origins, impact, and aftermath of Left Behind could doubt the series' place in the "first outlines of a fully commercialized, fully mediatized Christian blockbuster culture," its status as a flagship of the "growing conservative culture industry," or the "conservative revolution" it represents and exploits.[2] Anyone doubting the cultural power of evangelicalism within the American mainstream should take account of the series' popularity and the media interest it has generated. Moving from the outer edges of fundamentalism to the center of the "secular" mainstream, evangelical prophecy fiction has dramatically challenged established notions of America. The form of prophecy fiction may resonate within wider contexts of consumption in popular culture and may echo themes in dystopian horror and science fiction, but there is no doubt that many readers of these novels take their narrative themes very seriously indeed. Their success has complicated the narrative of American modernity. Of course, it is possible that the mainstreaming of evangelicalism is much less recent than many observers believe: Randall Balmer, one of the most sensitive scholars of evangelicalism, has argued that the movement is the "most resilient and influential . . . in American history," and promotes a "quintessentially American" creed.[3] If that was not true in the past, it certainly is true now. Evangelicalism is no longer an easily identifiable "subculture."[4] At least, some of the movement's most significant voices no longer regard it as a subculture—and cannot do so when they are prepared to imagine that the rapture could include from one fifth to one third of the global population.[5]

Despite that nod towards social expansion, prophecy fiction has throughout its history represented the illusion of a monochrome culture. Its novels, after all, have most often been written by and for white American men—and often with distinctly racist overtones.[6] This consistent racial and gender specificity should not obscure the ideological variety that haunts the narrative form. Over the course of the twentieth century, prophecy fiction moved from reflecting the eclectic theology that was still permissible in the last days of Protestant America to reproducing the increasing marginalization of that culture in the self-fashioning of emerging fundamentalists. In the middle part of the twentieth century, prophecy fiction consolidated with the rise of dispensational scholasticism, but a new mood of cultural engagement and the end of the cold war called for a systematic rethinking of its narrative preferences as prophecy fiction was increasingly taken up by less specifically defined evangelicals like Pat Robertson and Tim LaHaye in the middle 1990s.[7] The commercial success of evangelical prophecy fiction drove its being suddenly fashionable at the beginning of the 2000s, when even nonevangelical publishers began to consider the revenues they could expect from the mode. In the aftermath of Left Behind, prophecy novels were published with increasing frequency as their narrative and theological core began to fragment and as the genre returned to the eclecticism from which it had emerged. This renewed eclecticism, accompanying vast commercial success, cannot simply be explained by the failure of secular publishers to properly police the boundaries of the evangelical faith. A wider range of authors—including many more evangelical women and nonevangelicals—have begun to appropriate the recognized modes of evangelical prophecy fiction to make specific interventions of their own. Evangelical prophecy fiction had, historically, reflected the theological culture of evangelical prophecy belief; by the beginning of the twenty-first century, prophecy fiction was increasingly attempting to reshape it. Earlier interventions—such as those of Angley's *Raptured* (1950)—had attempted to pull evangelical readers towards a greater sobriety in a "sanctified" lifestyle. Later interventions—such as the proposal in the Christ Clone Trilogy (1997–98) that the resurrection would leave bodies in their graves—were increasingly theological in tone. Throughout its history, prophecy fiction has constructed and deconstructed the movement of which it has been a part. Evangelical prophecy fiction emerged from the high point of Protestant America, witnessed to its defeat, and participated in its eventual reconstruction and return. *Writing the Rapture* is not the history of a genre. It is a record of prophecy authors' interventions in—and from—evangelical America.

But the prophecy fiction phenomenon also suggests the extent to which, as one novelist put it, the "word of prophecy" has "fallen upon evil days."[8] Dispensational theologians have repeatedly insisted that true believers ought to expect increasing marginalization as the end approaches, and recent authors of prophecy fiction—like Jerry B. Jenkins, in *Soon* (2003)—have worked hard to imagine the condition of an America that had never known the impact of Left Behind. Jenkins's return to the older narrative of marginality indicates that the market success of his own novels is the greatest disconfirmation of dispensational expectations of the near future. Characters in recent novels might struggle to understand the significance of the sudden disappearance of the entire evangelical population, but there must be few people in modern America who have no idea what that event might mean. Authors of prophecy fiction are increasingly alert to the fact that the success of Left Behind and other recent fictions demonstrates that American evangelicals are much farther from the cultural margins than they had imagined—and therefore much farther than they imagined from the second coming of Jesus Christ. Prophecy fiction—in imagining an America in which the central tenets of the evangelical faith are entirely unknown—no longer reflects the world its authors attempt to convert. *Writing the Rapture* is ultimately, therefore, a record of the ideological failure of the most significant product of the dispensational imagination. The evangelical imagination has entered the cultural mainstream, but that success has undermined the central tenets of dispensational cultural theory. The commercial success of prophecy fiction therefore argues for the failure of dispensational ideas. Hopes for the imminence of the rapture have been denied by the success of the fiction that sought to represent it.

More seriously, the prophecy fiction genre also reflects the increasing erosion of central evangelical ideas. Evangelicalism has historically been a movement that centered on the story of the Cross: this "crucicentrism" has even been identified as one of the movement's four distinctive features.[9] But, in the vast majority of evangelical prophecy fictions, the Cross is obvious only in its absence. While the Cross is invoked in the novels' content, it is often undermined in the novels' form. Evangelical prophecy fictions offer increasingly dichotomous views of church–society relations and are increasingly pessimistic about the potential to rescue individuals from the fallen world.[10] Unbelievers are there to be resisted, not served or saved: the Cross is no longer enough.

This is why the success of prophecy fiction has contributed to a wider crisis of belief and identity within the American evangelical movement.[11] The novels have redefined dispensationalism, but they have also redefined the evangelical understanding of the gospel and the lifestyle it demands. Evangelicalism's most successful cultural interventions fail to represent the theological core that has been maintained within the movement throughout most of its history, the message that, as my grandfather's *Scofield Reference Bible* put it, "all have sinned, and come short of the glory of God; being justified freely by his grace through the redemption that is in Christ Jesus" (Romans 3:23–24), and that believers should "do good unto all men, especially unto them who are of the household of faith" (Galatians 6:10). One may read prophecy fiction for a long time before the message or the ethics of the Cross are explained. Prophecy fiction now demonstrates the extent to which evangelicalism has lost its theological coherence, and its vast success suggests the internal corrosion of the evangelical imagination. Prophecy fiction reveals far more than it realizes about the evangelical future.

The evangelical future may be more open than many readers of prophecy fiction imagine. Even Tim LaHaye has admitted as much, though his rapture novels seemed to argue for the contrary. "There is still time to restore America's conscience," he has recently claimed. "God could still send our nation one last spiritual revival and moral reformation."[12] But LaHaye's optimism could become a victim of his popularity: Left Behind is now a vital component in the way in which evangelicals imagine their future. However we account for their popularity, therefore, prophecy fiction novels are much more than ephemeral entertainment consumed by marginal believers. They demonstrate the changing identity and increasing cultural power of evangelical America. Pat Robertson was right: "Like it or not, this is an epic struggle for the future."[13]

Glossary

This glossary is revised and expanded from an earlier version which I first published in Crawford Gribben and Andrew R. Holmes (eds.), Protestant Millennialism, Evangelicalism and Irish Society, 1790–2005 *(Basingstoke, UK: Palgrave, 2006), pp. x–xii.*

Amillennialism   The belief that the "thousand years" described in Revelation 20 does not refer to an end-time period and is instead a metaphor for all or a substantial part of the period between Christ's incarnation and second coming.

Antichrist   The church's theological enemies are described as "antichrist" in several New Testament passages (1 John 2:18, 22; 1 John 4:3; 2 John 7). In popular discourse, however, "the Antichrist" is a single figure who tends to combine elements of the various eschatological enemies described in Daniel and Revelation. Historically, Protestants have identified the Antichrist as the pope, though this gave way to a range of other opinions as futurist premillennialism gained influence.

Apocalyptic   A biblical genre, with disputed characteristics, that has given its name to a wider approach to the understanding of world affairs. Apocalyptic literature emphasizes the sudden (and often imminent) end of all things. In contrast to the millennium, the apocalyptic mode can seem dualistic (evil is in constant struggle with goodness), pessimistic (world conditions are not likely to improve), deterministic (the future has been planned by God), ethically passive (if conditions are not likely to improve, there is little that can be done to improve the world), and final.

Christian Reconstruction   The belief that the postmillennial coming of Christ will be preceded by the establishment of "godly rule" on Earth. This "godly rule" will be marked by an unprecedented revival of Christianity and civil societies' adoption of the Mosaic judicial and penal code.

Dispensationalism   A variety of *premillennialism* that argues for a radical disjunction between Israel and the Church and teaches that the "secret rapture" will precede the *tribulation*. Dispensationalists commonly mark seven distinct stages in the development of the history of redemption, which may or may not have different conditions of salvation. Dispensationalism has developed through three major stages: classical dispensationalism, which is best represented by the *Scofield Reference Bible* (1909; second edition 1917) and the writings of L. S. Chafer and J. Dwight Pentecost; revised dispensationalism, which is best represented by the *New Scofield Bible* (1967); and progressive dispensationalism, which is best represented by the writings of Craig Blaising and Darrell Bock.

Eschatology   Classically, the study of the "four last things"—death, judgment, heaven, and hell—but the term has been expanded in use to refer to other aspects of end-of-the-world belief. Evangelical eschatology can be either pessimistic, in its expectation of apocalyptic events, or optimistic, in its expectation of the millennium.

Futurism   A system of hermeneutics that understands New Testament prophecies to be chiefly concerned with the last few years before the second coming of Christ. Futurists tend to argue that the Antichrist will not be a pope. Futurism is common among amillennialists and premillennialists, and is a basic feature of dispensationalism.

Historicism   A system of hermeneutics that understands New Testament prophecies to detail all or much of the course of church history. The identification of the pope as Antichrist is common in Protestant historicist interpretation. "Historicist" premillennialism, one variant of which is represented in the writings of Hal Lindsey, should be distinguished from "historic" (i.e., nondispensational) premillennialism, which may or may not be historicist, and which Lindsey would certainly oppose.

Millenarian/millennialist   Conventionally, scholars working in millennial studies have followed Ernest L. Tuveson in distinguishing "millennialists" (believers who adopt postmillennial, optimistic, and gradualist theologies) from "millenarians" (believers who adopt premillennial, pessimistic, and radical theologies). Ernest R. Sandeen has noted, however, that the terms are interchangeable in the literature of the emerging fundamentalist movement and a strict distinction should probably not therefore be imposed.*

Millennium   A utopian period whose general characteristics are based on the description of the binding of Satan in Revelation 20 and the prophecies of the renewal of the natural world in the Hebrew prophets. Its specific characteristics vary according to the interpreter, and the millennium can be used as a trope for a wide and sometimes contradictory range of political, cultural, and religious presuppositions. The three most common of evangelical millennial schemes, a-, pre-, and postmillennialism, should not be anachronistically read into older material. Not every exegete would share the basic assumption of these schemes, the idea that Revelation 20 refers to only one thousand-year period. The *Oxford English Dictionary* dates the development of the pre- and postmillennial terms to the mid-nineteenth century, though the interpretive paradigms they represent can be traced to the late Reformation; it does not provide any information on the development of "amillennial."

National election   The idea, popular in ancient Israel, Reformation Britain, and modern America, that God has chosen a nation, invested its progress with the earthly display of his glory, and will therefore make certain its dominance. This is not necessarily an uncritical nationalism, however; national election points to the responsibilities as much as the privileges of being God's chosen people, and can often lead to a jeremiad on the decay of truth among the chosen. It is based on a providential worldview that recognizes the hand of God in the drama of human history, and lies behind some forms of the American "redeemer nation" myth.

Postmillennialism   The belief that Christ will return after the millennium has substantially reformed life on Earth. Postmillennialists can be either apocalyptic or gradualist, and vary in the extent to which they believe the millennium can be expedited by their own effort. Postmillennialism has been revived among some conservative Presbyterians, particularly those with interests in Christian Reconstruction, but, among evangelicals more generally, remains much less popular than premillennialism.

---

* Ernest L. Tuveson, *Redeemer Nation: The Idea of America's Millennial Role* (Chicago: University of Chicago Press, 1968), pp. 33–34; Ernest R. Sandeen, *The Roots of Fundamentalism: British and American Millenarianism 1800–1930* (Chicago: University of Chicago Press, 1970), p. 5 n. 3.

Premillennialism   The belief that the second coming of Christ will take place before the millennium. Historic premillennialism believes that Christ will return after the tribulation ("post-tribulational"); this was the view of, for example, C. H. Spurgeon and G. E. Ladd. Dispensational premillennialism, developed from the works of J. N. Darby, argues that Christ will return for the "secret rapture" before the tribulation ("pre-tribulational"). This rapture will "catch up" believers in order to take them into heaven while the Antichrist rages on Earth. The second coming proper will take place at the end of the tribulation, and Christ will then usher in the millennium and reign over the world for one thousand years. Premillennialists debate whether believers will live on Earth during the millennium and debate the specific roles of Israel and a range of other powers in this end-time scenario.

Preterism   A system of hermeneutics that understands New Testament prophecies to be chiefly concerned with the Roman sacking of Jerusalem and the end of Temple worship in A.D. 70. Preterism has influenced a number of recent evangelical pre- and postmillennial Bible commentaries.

Sinner's Prayer   A conversion technique that grew in popularity in mid-twentieth-century evangelicalism. It assumes that the repetition of a formulaic prayer, which confesses sin and asks for God's forgiveness, will guarantee salvation.

Tribulation   The belief (shared by many premillennialists) that the Bible predicts a final seven-year period of terrible suffering during which the Antichrist persecutes believers and God pours judgment on the world.

Notes

INTRODUCTION

1. This claim is made in Tristan Sturm, "Prophetic Eyes: The Theatricality of Mark Hitchcock's Premillennial Geopolitics," *Geopolitics* 11 (2006), p. 250 n. 14.

2. Recent literature that identifies a loosely defined genre of prophecy fiction includes Crawford Gribben, "Rapture Fictions and the Changing Evangelical Condition," *Literature and Theology* 18:1 (2004), pp. 77–94; Bruce David Forbes and Jeanne Halgren Kilde (eds.), *Rapture, Revelation, and the End Times: Exploring the Left Behind Series* (New York: Palgrave Macmillan, 2004); Amy Johnson Frykholm, *Rapture Culture: Left Behind in Evangelical America* (Oxford: Oxford University Press, 2004); Sherryll Mleynek, "The Rhetoric of the 'Jewish Problem' in the *Left Behind* Novels," *Literature and Theology* 19:4 (2005), pp. 1–17; Glenn W. Shuck, *Marks of the Beast: The Left Behind Novels and the Struggle for Evangelical Identity* (New York: New York University Press, 2005); and Klaus J. Milich, "Fundamentalism Hot and Cold: George W. Bush and the 'Return of the Sacred,'" *Cultural Critique* 62 (2006), pp. 108–13.

3. Melani McAlister, "Prophecy, Politics and the Popular: The *Left Behind* Series and Christian Fundamentalism's New World Order," *South Atlantic Quarterly* 102:4 (2003), p. 782.

4. See, for example, Darryl Jones, "The Liberal Antichrist: *Left Behind* in America," in Kenneth G. C. Newport and Crawford Gribben (eds.), *Expecting the End: Contemporary Millennialism in Social and Historical Context* (Baylor, TX: Baylor University Press, 2006), pp. 97–112.

5. See the discussion in Amy Johnson Frykholm, "What Social Messages Appear in the *Left Behind* Books? A Literary Discussion of Millenarian Fiction," in Bruce David Forbes and Jeanne Halgren Kilde (eds.),

Rapture, Revelation, and the End Times: Exploring the Left Behind Series (New York: Palgrave Macmillan, 2004), p. 169.

6. Frykholm, "What Social and Political Messages Appear in the Left Behind Books?" p. 174.

7. David W. Bebbington, "Evangelical Theology in the English-speaking World during the Nineteenth Century," *Scottish Bulletin of Evangelical Theology* 22:2 (2004), p. 133.

8. The links between evangelicalism and popular culture have been surveyed in David Bebbington, *Evangelicalism in Modern Britain: A History from the 1730s to the 1980s* (London: Routledge, 1989); Paul Boyer, *When Time Shall Be No More: Prophecy Belief in Modern American Culture* (Cambridge, MA: Belknap Press of Harvard University Press, 1992); David F. Wells, *No Place for Truth, or Whatever Happened to Evangelical Theology?* (Grand Rapids, MI: Eerdmans, 1993); and Mark A. Noll, *The Scandal of the Evangelical Mind* (Leicester, UK: IVP, 1994).

9. Bebbington, "Evangelical Theology in the English-speaking World," p. 138.

10. For tensions between theological and sociological definitions of evangelicalism, compare the approach of Bebbington's *Evangelicalism in Modern Britain* with that of George Marsden in the introduction to George Marsden (ed.), *Evangelicalism and Modern America* (Grand Rapids, MI: Eerdmans, 1984), and George Marsden, *Reforming Fundamentalism: Fuller Seminary and the New Evangelicalism* (Grand Rapids, MI: Eerdmans, 1987; 1995), pp. vii–xvi; and see Donald Dayton, "'The Search for the Historical Evangelicalism': George Marsden's History of Fuller Seminary as a Case Study," *Christian Scholar's Review* 33 (1993), p. 18.

11. For a useful summary of this approach to the argument, see D. W. Bebbington, "The Place of the Brethren Movement in International Evangelicalism," in Neil T. R. Dickson and Tim Grass (eds.), *The Growth of the Brethren Movement: National and International Experiences,* Studies in Evangelical History and Thought (Milton Keynes, UK: Paternoster, 2006), pp. 241–60.

12. This is the argument of Bebbington, *Evangelicalism in Modern Britain.* A number of important qualifications of the Bebbington thesis are made in W. R. Ward, *Early Evangelicalism: A Global Intellectual History, 1670–1789* (Cambridge: Cambridge University Press, 2006), and Michael Haykin and Kenneth Stewart (eds.), *The Emergence of Evangelicalism: Exploring Historical Continuities* (Leicester, UK: Apollos, 2008).

13. Philip Jenkins, *Mystics and Messiahs: Cults and New Religions in American History* (Oxford: Oxford University Press, 2000), p. 5. Bozeman disputes the idea that the "errand into the wilderness" was eschatologically driven; Theodore Dwight Bozeman, *To Live Ancient Lives: The Primitivist Dimension in Puritanism* (Chapel Hill, NC: University of North Carolina Press, 1988), pp. 193–94.

14. Harvey Cox, *Fire from Heaven: The Rise of Pentecostal Spirituality and the Reshaping of Religion in the Twenty-first Century* (London: Cassell, 1996), p. 21.

15. Crawford Gribben, "Evangelical Eschatology and 'the Puritan Hope,'" in Michael Haykin and Kenneth Stewart (eds.), *The Emergence of Evangelicalism: Exploring Historical Continuities* (Leicester, UK: Apollos, 2008), pp. 375–93.

16. The range of early modern millennial opinion is described in Crawford Gribben, *The Puritan Millennium: Literature and Theology, 1550–1682* (Dublin: Four Courts, 2000).

17. See the relevant chapters in Crawford Gribben and Timothy C. F. Stunt (eds.), *Prisoners of Hope? Aspects of Evangelical Millennialism in Britain and Ireland, 1800–1880,* Studies in Evangelical History and Thought (Milton Keynes, UK: Paternoster, 2004), and Crawford Gribben and Andrew R. Holmes (eds.), *Protestant Millennialism, Evangelicalism, and Irish Society, 1790–2005* (Basingstoke, UK: Palgrave, 2006).

18. On the impact of Brethren eschatology in Ireland and Scotland, see Crawford Gribben, "'The Worst Sect That a Christian Man Can Meet': Opposition to the Plymouth Brethren in Ireland and Scotland, 1859–1900," *Scottish Studies Review* 3:2 (2002), pp. 34–53.

19. Stephen R. Sizer, *Christian Zionism: Road-map to Armageddon?* (Leicester, UK: IVP, 2004), p. 66. For a useful corrective to Sizer's analysis of Darby, see Paul Wilkinson, *For Zion's Sake: Christian Zionism and the Role of John Nelson Darby,* Studies in Evangelical History and Thought (Milton Keynes, UK: Paternoster, 2007).

20. For the early growth of dispensationalism, see Ernest R. Sandeen, *The Roots of Fundamentalism: British and American Millenarianism, 1800–1930* (Chicago: University of Chicago Press, 1970); F. Roy Coad, *A History of the Brethren Movement* (Exeter, UK: Paternoster, 1968); C. Norman Kraus, *Dispensationalism in America: Its Rise and Development* (Richmond, VA: John Knox, 1958); Bebbington, *Evangelicalism in Modern Britain,* pp. 75–86.

21. Ronald Lora and William Henry Longton (eds.), *The Conservative Press in Twentieth-century America* (Westport, CT: Greenwood, 1999), p. 89.

22. The text of Harry Emerson Fosdick's sermon, "Shall the Fundamentalists Win?" (1922) can be found in Paul H. Sherry (ed.), *The Riverside Preachers* (New York: Pilgrim, 1978), pp. 27–38. On the history and development of fundamentalism, see Robert C. Fuller, *Naming the Antichrist: The History of an American Obsession* (Oxford: Oxford University Press, 1995), pp. 120–33; Harriet A. Harris, *Fundamentalism and Evangelicals* (Oxford, UK: Clarendon Press, 1998), pp. 19–56; George M. Marsden, *Fundamentalism and American Culture: The Shaping of Twentieth-century Evangelicalism, 1870–1925* (Oxford: Oxford University Press, 1980; new edition, 2006), pp. 231–57.

23. David J. MacLeod, "Walter Scott, a Link in Dispensationalism between Darby and Scofield?" *Bibliotheca Sacra* 153:610 (1996), pp. 155–76.

24. Boyer, *When Time Shall Be No More,* pp. 97–98. Up to fifty million copies of the *Scofield Reference Bible* were sold between 1909 and 1989; 4.2 million were sold between 1967 and 1989, eighty-six percent of which were in leather-bound editions; Randall Balmer, *Mine Eyes Have Seen the Glory: A Journey into the Evangelical Subculture in America* (1989; fourth edition, Oxford: Oxford University Press, 2006), p. 46 n. 5. For a brief history of twentieth-century fundamentalism, see Steve Brouwer, Paul Gifford, and Susan D. Rose, *Exporting the American Gospel: Global Christian Fundamentalism* (New York: Routledge, 1996), pp. 33–46.

25. This context is explained in R. Todd Mangum, *The Dispensational-Covenantal Rift: The Fissuring of American Evangelical Theology from 1936 to 1944,* Studies in Evangelical History and Thought (Milton Keynes, UK: Paternoster, 2007). Mangum's work is especially useful for its sociological insights.

26. "Scopes Trial," in Randall Balmer, *Encyclopedia of Evangelicalism* (Louisville, KY: Westminster John Knox, 2002), pp. 511–12. Susan Friend Harding, *The Book of Jerry Falwell: Fundamentalist Language and Politics* (Princeton, NJ: Princeton University Press, 2000), p. 62. On the Scopes trial, see Harding, *The Book of Jerry Falwell,* pp. 61–82. On the construction of a fundamentalist infrastructure, see Joel A. Carpenter, *Revive Us Again: The Reawakening of American Fundamentalism* (Oxford: Oxford University Press, 1997).

27. Brouwer, Gifford, and Rose, *Exporting the American Gospel,* pp. 16–17.

28. "Neo-evangelicalism," in Randall Balmer, *Encyclopedia of Evangelicalism* (Louisville, KY: Westminster John Knox, 2002), p. 404. The emergence of "neo-evangelicalism" is fully described in Marsden, *Reforming Fundamentalism.*

29. This was the perspective adopted, for example, in the *Scofield Reference Bible* and in Lewis Sperry Chafer, *Systematic Theology,* vol. 4 (1948; repr. Dallas, TX: Dallas Theological Seminary, 1975). On the latter text, see Jeffery John Richards, "The Eschatology of Lewis Sperry Chafer: His Contribution to a Systematization of Dispensational Premillennialism" (Ph.D. dissertation, Drew University, 1985).

30. For the range of evangelical readings of the Jewish future, see Wilkinson, *For Zion's Sake.*

31. Boyer, *When Time Shall Be No More,* p. 5.

32. *New York Times Book Review,* April 6, 1980, p. 27.

33. *Los Angeles Times,* February 23, 1991, p. F16; Daniel Wojcik, "Embracing Doomsday: Faith, Fatalism and Apocalyptic Beliefs in the Nuclear Age," *Western Folklore* 55:4 (1996), p. 305. See also Jonathan Kirsch, "Hal Lindsey," *Publishers Weekly,* March 14, 1977, pp. 30–32.

34. Hal Lindsey, *The Late Great Planet Earth* (1970; repr. London: Marshall Pickering, 1971), pp. 59, 135.

35. Thomas Ice and Randall Price, *Ready to Rebuild: The Imminent Plan to Rebuild the Last Days Temple* (Eugene, OR: Harvest House, 1992); see also Mark Sweetnam, "Tensions in Dispensational Eschatology," in Kenneth G. C. Newport and Crawford Gribben (eds.), *Expecting the End: Millennialism in Social and Historical Context* (Baylor, TX: Baylor University Press, 2006), pp. 173–92.

36. The term was coined by Gary North in his "Publisher's Preface" to Dwight Wilson's *Armageddon Now! The Premillenarian Response to Russia and Israel since 1917* (1977; repr. Tyler, TX: Institute for Christian Economics, 1991), p. x.

37. This controversial redaction of dispensational theory is explored in Craig A. Blaising and Darrell L. Bock, *Progressive Dispensationalism* (Wheaton, IL: Victor, 1993).

38. John F. Walvoord, *The Return of the Lord* (1955; Grand Rapids, MI: Zondervan, 1980), p. 45.

39. Jan Blodgett, *Protestant Evangelical Literary Culture and Contemporary Society* (Westport, CT: Greenwood, 1997), p. 34.

40. Note Graham's movement away from a strongly fundamentalist dispensationalism to a less immediately apocalyptic and more liberal evangelicalism.

41. Wilson, *Armageddon Now!* p. 12.

42. Sizer, *Christian Zionism,* p. 23.

43. Stephen D. O'Leary, *Arguing the Apocalypse: A Theory of Millennial Rhetoric* (Oxford: Oxford University Press, 1994), p. 182.

44. Boyer, *When Time Shall Be No More,* p. 141; George M. Marsden, "Fundamentalism as an American Phenomenon," in D. G. Hart (ed.), *Reckoning with the Past* (Grand Rapids, MI: Baker, 1995), p. 319; James Mills, "The Serious Implications of a 1971 Conversation with Ronald Reagan: A Footnote to Current History," *San Diego Magazine* (August 1985), p. 141.

45. Ronald Reagan, "Address to the National Association of Evangelicals, March 8, 1983," in Paul Boyer (ed.), *Reagan as President: Contemporary Views of the Man, His Politics, and His Policies* (Chicago: Ivan R. Dee, 1990), pp. 165–69.

46. Boyer, *When Time Shall Be No More,* p. 175.

47. I borrow the expression "America's sacred lexicon" from Peter J. Thuesen, *In Discordance with the Scriptures: American Protestant Battles over Translating the Bible* (New York: Oxford University Press, 1999), p. 30.

48. Sydney Watson, *Brighter Years: The Second Part of the Autobiography of Sydney Watson* (London: Hodder and Stoughton, 1898), p. 277.

49. Even David R. Beaucage's *The Shiloh Project* (Tulsa, OK: Virgil W. Hensley, 1993), an evangelical prophecy novel which makes no reference to the rapture, assumes the standard dispensational chronology and points to the eschatological significance of the founding of Israel in 1948.

50. There is some debate among dispensational writers as to whether these "tribulation saints" should be described as Christians.

51. *Left Behind*'s insistence that more than 144,000 Jews will enter the millennial kingdom distinguishes its eschatology from the dispensationalism of J. N. Darby; LeAnn Snow Flesher, *Left Behind? The Facts behind the Fiction* (Valley Forge, PA: Judson, 2006), p. 36.

52. This standard outline of dispensationalism is provided in J. Dwight Pentecost, *Things to Come: A Study in Biblical Eschatology* (Grand Rapids, MI: Zondervan, 1958) and Chafer, *Systematic Theology,* vol. 4.

53. BeauSeigneur is the obvious exception to this rule of thumb, as will be explained in the final chapter.

54. "Cerullo, Morris," in Randall Balmer, *Encyclopedia of Evangelicalism* (Louisville, KY: Westminster John Knox, 2002), p. 120.

55. Morris Cerullo, *The Omega Project* (San Diego, CA: World Evangelism, 1981), p. 11. The theme was repeated in Beaucage, *Shiloh Project,* p. 146.

56. Peter and Paul Lalonde, *Apocalypse* (Niagara Falls, NY: This Week in Bible Prophecy, 1998), p. 210.

57. Jean Grant, *The Revelation: A Novel* (Nashville, TN: Word, 1992), p. 77.

58. Ken Wade, *The Orion Conspiracy: A Story of the End* (Boise, ID: Pacific Press, 1994), p. 256.

59. Robert D. Van Kampen, *The Fourth Reich* (Grand Rapids, MI: Baker Book House, 1997; New York: Dell, 2000), p. 81.

60. Kim Young, *The Last Hour* (Phoenix, AZ: ACW, 1997), p. 9.

61. David Dolan, *The End of Days* (1995; second edition, Springfield, MO: 21st Century Press, 2003), pp. 5–6.

62. Joseph Birkbeck Burroughs, *Titan, Son of Saturn: The Coming World Emperor: A Story of the Other Christ* (Oberlin, OH: Emeth, 1905), p. 14.

63. Peter and Patti Lalonde, *Left Behind* (Eugene, OR: Harvest House, n.d.), p. 134.

64. Todd Strandberg and Terry James, *Are You Rapture Ready? Signs, Prophecies, Warnings, Threats, and Suspicions That the Endtime Is Now* (New York: Dutton, 2003), p. 232.

65. *Scofield Reference Bible*, pp. 3–5; Hal Lindsey, *Blood Moon* (Palos Verdes, CA: Western Front, 1996), p. 156. See also Milton H. Stine, *Ancient Cities and Civilizations Modernized* (Harrisburg, PA: Evangelical Press, 1931), p. 272.

66. Stine, *Ancient Cities and Civilizations Modernized*, p. 114; Sydney Watson, *The New Europe* (London: William Nicholson and Sons, [1918]), p. 72. On the significance of Petra, see H. L. Wilmington, *The King Is Coming* (Wheaton, IL: Tyndale House, 1973), 147–48.

67. Pat Robertson, *The Secret Kingdom* (Nashville, TN: Thomas Nelson, 1984), p. 45.

68. See, for example, Mel Odom, *Apocalypse Dawn* (Wheaton, IL: Tyndale House, 2003), pp. 342, 363, 398; Neesa Hart, *End of State* (Wheaton, IL: Tyndale House, 2003), pp. 256–58; Neesa Hart, *Impeachable Offense* (Wheaton, IL: Tyndale House, 2004), p. 178.

69. Burroughs, *Titan*, p. 73.

70. Lindsey, *Blood Moon*, p. 73.

71. Tim LaHaye and Bob Phillips, *The Secret on Ararat* (New York: Bantam, 2004), p. 199. See also one character's statement that "God took on the form of the Son—Jesus[o]"; p. 201.

72. D. A. Manker, *Youth's Dream Time* (Frankfort, MI: Victor, n.d.), p. 6.

73. Lindsey, *Blood Moon*, p. 213.

74. Lalonde, *Apocalypse*, pp. 128, 135, 139, 147, 150, 170, 240. In *Left Behind*, one airplane passenger who disappears in the rapture leaves his clothes in a "neat pile" on his seat; Tim LaHaye and Jerry B. Jenkins, *Left Behind* (Wheaton, IL: Tyndale House, 1995), p. 16.

75. Blodgett, *Protestant Evangelical Literary Culture and Contemporary Society*, p. 2.

76. Ibid., p. ix.

77. O'Leary, *Arguing the Apocalypse*, p. 6; Heather Hendershot, *Shaking the World for Jesus: Media and Conservative Evangelical Culture* (Chicago: University of Chicago Press, 2004), pp. 178–80.

78. Blodgett, *Protestant Evangelical Literary Culture and Contemporary Society*, p. 1.

79. This is described in O'Leary, *Arguing the Apocalypse*, pp. 147–54.

80. James BeauSeigneur, "Important Note from the Author," in *In His Image*, The Christ Clone Trilogy (1997; reissued New York: Warner, 2003), p. 217, n. 31; p. 462 n. 64; James BeauSeigneur, *Birth of an Age*, The Christ Clone Trilogy (Rockville, MD: SelectiveHouse, 1997; reissued New York: Warner, 2003), p. 246.

81. A variety of reading responses to Left Behind are described in Frykholm, *Rapture Culture*, passim.

82. The theology of the Roman Catholic Church is decidedly antimillennial, as the recently issued *Catechism of the Catholic Church* (ET 1994) makes clear, but the long tradition of Catholic apocalyptic devotion has revived in the aftermath of the Second Vatican Council; Amy Luebbers, "The Remnant Faithful: A Case Study of Contemporary Apocalyptic Catholicism," *Sociology of Religion* 62:2 (2001), p. 230.

83. "S. M. C.", *As the Clock Struck Twenty* (Notre Dame, IN: Ave Maria, 1953), p. 16.

84. Dodie Smith, *The Starlight Barking* (1967; repr. London: Puffin, 1970), pp. 42, 122. I owe this reference to Sarah Wareham. See also Smith's *It Ends with Revelations* (London: Heinemann, 1967).

85. I am grateful to Geoff Ryman for supplying this reference.

86. Frederic Baumgartner, *Longing for the End: A History of Millennialism in Western Civilization* (New York: Palgrave, 1999), p. 220.

87. Nevertheless, as the latter observation indicates, the significance of these allusions in mainstream popular culture should not be exaggerated. They do not necessarily indicate a large reading public with deep sympathies for the evangelical cause. Indeed, if sales figures are anything to go by, readers of "spiritual" fiction have very eclectic tastes. James Redfield's *The Celestine Prophecy* (New York: Bantam, 1994) was the best-selling novel of 1995–96, selling twenty million copies in its first decade. Its success has been followed by that of Dan Brown's *The Da Vinci Code* (New York: Doubleday, 2003), which sold sixty million copies in the three years to 2006, and that of the several volumes describing the career of the trainee wizard Harry Potter (1997–2007), which together have sold 325 million copies. While each of these texts could be described as being interested in "the spiritual," they could certainly not be described as defenses of the kind of evangelical faith dramatized in Left Behind. Rapture fictions may not reflect a stable popular mainstream, but they are certainly consumed by a wide range of readers, both inside and outside the traditional boundaries of the evangelical movement.

88. Gary G. Cohen, *The Horsemen Are Coming* (Chicago: Moody, 1979), back cover.

89. LaHaye and Jenkins, *Left Behind,* back cover.

90. I owe this point to David Matthews.

91. Balmer, *Mine Eyes Have Seen the Glory,* pp. 61–62; Bruce David Forbes, "How Popular are the Left Behind Books . . . and Why? A Discussion of Popular Culture," in Bruce David Forbes and Jeanne Halgren Kilde (eds.), *Rapture, Revelation, and the End Times: Exploring the Left Behind Series* (New York: Palgrave Macmillan, 2004), p. 11.

92. See Tim LaHaye, Jerry B. Jenkins, and Norman B. Rohrer, *These Will Not Be Left Behind* (Wheaton, IL: Tyndale House, 2003). For Thompson, see Balmer, *Mine Eyes Have Seen the Glory,* pp. 48–70, and Hendershot, *Shaking the World for Jesus,* pp. 182–89.

93. John M. Myers, *The Trumpet Sounds* (New York: Pageant, 1965), n.p.

94. Carol Balizet, *The Seven Last Years* (Lincoln, VA: Chosen Books, 1978), pp. 369–76.

95. The chart was not included in my copy of the text.

96. This text has not yet been published.

97. Gary DeMar incorrectly notes that the book first quotes from LaHaye in chapter 11; "The Fiction behind Left Behind," *Biblical Worldview* (July 2004), p. 3.

98. See, for example, Christian Thorne, "The Revolutionary Energy of the Outmoded," *October* 104 (2003), p. 98.

99. Paul C. Gutjahr, "No Longer Left Behind: Amazon.com, Reader-response, and the Changing Fortunes of the Christian Novel in America," *Book History* 5 (2002), p. 215; Shuck, *Marks of the Beast,* pp. 1, 5; Baumgartner, *Longing for the End,* p. 240; Boyer, *When Time Shall Be No More,* p. 106; Frykholm, *Rapture Culture,* pp. 205–7.

100. One of the most significant projects in recent millennial studies has been Bernard McGinn (ed.), *Encyclopedia of Apocalypticism,* three vols. (New York: Continuum, 1998). Scholarship in millennial studies has been surveyed in Leonard I. Sweet, "Millennialism in America: Recent Studies," *Theological Studies* 40 (1979), pp. 510–31; Hillel Schwartz, "The End of the Beginning: Millenarian Studies, 1969–1975," *Religious Studies Review* 2 (1976), pp. 1–15; and, most recently, Douglas Shantz, "Millennialism and Apocalypticism in Recent Historical Scholarship," in Crawford Gribben and Timothy C. F. Stunt (eds.), *Prisoners of Hope? Aspects of Evangelical Millennialism in Britain and Ireland, 1800–1880,* Studies in Evangelical History and Thought (Milton Keynes, UK: Paternoster, 2004), pp. 18–43.

101. Boyer, *When Time Shall Be No More,* p. ix.

102. O'Leary, *Arguing the Apocalypse,* p. 18.

103. Blodgett, *Protestant Evangelical Literary Culture and Contemporary Society,* p. ix. Paul Boyer's study of prophecy culture is a rare example of this kind of scholarship. Similarly, while several studies on American religious fiction have been published, little work has been published on evangelical fiction; Blodgett, *Protestant Evangelical Literary Culture and Contemporary Society,* p. 7. Hendershot's *Shaking the World for Jesus* is a model of sociocultural analysis.

104. The genre was of relatively minor significance before the publication of Stephen O'Leary's ground-breaking *Arguing the Apocalypse,* which attempted a full-scale theory for apocalyptic rhetoric, and O'Leary did not need to account for its existence. The success of Left Behind now calls for its consideration.

105. Tim LaHaye's new series alludes to *Left Behind,* for example: "if the believers in Christ got snatched up to heaven in midflight, like in that book Renee kept telling him to read, and the bad guys . . . were left to fend for themselves"; LaHaye and Philips, *The Secret on Ararat,* p. 46. An earlier rapture novel also began with "believers in Christ . . . snatched up to heaven in mid-flight," but it is most likely that LaHaye's reference is to his own work; Salem Kirban, *666* (Wheaton, IL: Tyndale House, 1970), p. 35.

106. Wade, *The Orion Conspiracy,* p. 161.

107. Lalonde, *Apocalypse,* pp. 179, 234.

108. "S. M. C.", *As the Clock Struck Twenty,* p. 69.

109. Ibid., pp. 92, 180; Lalonde, *Apocalypse,* pp. 254, 264; Wade, *The Orion Conspiracy,* p. 285. The same theme appears in *Prodigal Planet* (dir. Don Thompson, 1983). It is also interesting to note that tribulation saints in *The Prodigal Planet* and Pat Robertson, *The End of the Age* (Nashville, TN: Word, 1995) decide to hole up in Albuquerque, New Mexico. The protagonist of Don Thompson's *Image of the Beast* duplicates the mark of the beast with only the aid of a pocket calculator.

110. Jonathan R. Cash, *The Age of the Antichrist* (Hanover, MA: Christopher, 1999), p. 6.

111. Other journalist characters appear in Glenn Kleier, *The Last Day* (New York: Warner Vision, 1997).

112. Frykholm, *Rapture Culture,* pp. 205–7. Note that Frykholm has misdated the works of Sydney Watson.

113. P. Modersohn, "Die letzte Stunde auf der Weltenurh: Ein Blick in die Weltgeschichte nach Daniel 2," *Sabbathklänge* 43:17 (April 27, 1901), pp. 265–267, and 43:18 (May 4, 1901), pp. 275–79. I owe the reference to Danielson to Tordur Joannson. A full biography of Patterson's work is available at his Web site, www.georgepatterson.net/index.html, accessed August 1, 2007. Other biographical details were provided by George Patterson in an e-mail to the author.

114. On rapture movies, see Hendershot, *Shaking the World for Jesus,* pp. 176–209; John Wallis, "Celling the End Times: The Contours of Contemporary Rapture Films," *Journal of Religion and Popular Culture* (forthcoming).

115. BeauSeigneur, *In His Image,* p. 468.

CHAPTER 1

1. "The Author's Apology for His Book," in John Bunyan, *The Pilgrim's Progress,* ed. N. H. Keeble, The World's Classics (Oxford: Oxford University Press, 1984), p. 2. Bunyan's millennial interests are described in Gribben, *Puritan Millennium,* pp. 172–93.

2. On later seventeenth-century habits of reading and writing, see N. H. Keeble, *The Literary Culture of Nonconformity in Later Seventeenth-century England* (Leicester, UK: Leicester University Press, 1987).

3. Cotton Mather, *Manuductio Ad ministerium. Directions for a Candidate of the Ministry. Wherein, First, a Right Foundation Is Laid for His Future Improvement; and, Then, Rules Are Offered for Such a Management of His Academical and Preparatory Studies; and Thereupon, for Such a Conduct after His Appearance in the World; as May Render His a Skilful and Useful Minister of the Gospel* (Boston, 1726; repr. New York: Columbia University Press, 1938), pp. 42–43.

4. George Marsden, *Jonathan Edwards* (New Haven, CT: Yale University Press, 2003), p. 419. *Pamela* became more generally available in the colonies after 1744, when it was reprinted by Benjamin Franklin; Blodgett, *Protestant Evangelical Literary Culture and Contemporary Society,* p. 21.

5. J. C. Ryle, *Practical Religion: Plain Papers on Daily Duties, Experience, Dangers, Privileges of Professing Christians* (London: W. Hunt, 1878), chapter 3.

6. Edmund Gosse, *Father and Son: A Study of Two Temperaments* (1907; London: Penguin, 1989), p. 48.

7. The life of Edmund Gosse's father is described in Ann Thwaite, *Glimpses of the Wonderful: The Life of Philip Henry Gosse* (London: Faber and Faber, 2002).

8. Quoted in Blodgett, *Protestant Evangelical Literary Culture and Contemporary Society,* p. 1.

9. Bebbington, *Evangelicalism in Modern Britain,* pp. 60–63, 81–86; Bebbington, "The Place of the Brethren Movement in International Evangelicalism," pp. 241–60.

10. Bebbington, *Evangelicalism in Modern Britain*, p. 131.

11. Blodgett, *Protestant Evangelical Literary Culture and Contemporary Society*, p. 25.

12. Ibid., p. 13.

13. On the development of this civil religion, see Harry S. Stout, *Upon the Altar of the Nation: A Moral History of the Civil War* (New York: Viking, 2006), pp. xvi–xxii.

14. Theusen, *In Discordance with the Scriptures*, p. 36.

15. Ibid., p. 68.

16. M. W. Carpenter and George P. Landow, "Ambiguous Revelations: The Apocalypse and Victorian Literature," in C. A. Patrides and J. A. Wittreich (eds.), *The Apocalypse in English Renaissance Thought and Literature* (Manchester, UK: Manchester University Press, 1984), pp. 303–5.

17. Baumgartner, *Longing for the End*, p. 200.

18. Blodgett, *Protestant Evangelical Literary Culture and Contemporary Society*, p. 21; James H. Moorhead, "The Erosion of Postmillennialism in American Religious Thought, 1865–1925," *Church History* 53:1 (1984), p. 70.

19. P. Modersohn, "Die letzte Stunde auf der Weltenuhr," pp. 275–279.

20. I owe this point to Liam Harte.

21. Burroughs, *Titan*, p. 453.

22. Frykholm, *Rapture Culture*, passim.

23. Burroughs, *Titan*, title page.

24. Ibid., pp. 12–13.

25. Ibid., p. 5.

26. The *Scofield Reference Bible* would identify Antiochus only as a "type" of the Antichrist; p. 910.

27. Burroughs, *Titan*, p. 5.

28. Ibid., p. 453.

29. On the prophecy movements of the 1840s, see John de Patmos, *The Great Disappointment of 1844* (Brookline, MA: Miskatonic University Press, 2001).

30. Burroughs, *Titan*, pp. 25–26.

31. Ibid., p. 426.

32. Ibid., pp. 77, 375, 380. Each of these positions was to be elaborated in the *Scofield Reference Bible*: pp. 3–5, 914–15, 1296.

33. Ibid., p. 5.

34. Ibid., p. 73.

35. Ibid., pp. 75–76.

36. Ibid., p. 318.

37. On the seventeenth-century contexts of this idea, see Julie Hirst, *Jane Leade: Biography of a Seventeenth-century Mystic* (Aldershot, UK: Ashgate, 2005).

38. Burroughs, *Titan*, pp. 320, 330, 375, 424.

39. Ibid., pp. 39, 224, 279.

40. Ibid., pp. 41, 65.

41. Ibid., p. 67.

42. Ibid., p. 274.

43. Ibid., pp. 47–48.

44. Ibid., p. 47.

45. Ibid., p. 176.

46. Ibid., pp. 12, 35.

47. Ibid., p. 197.

48. Ibid., p. 197.

49. Ibid., p. 198.

50. Ibid., p. 198.

51. Ibid., p. 198.

52. Ibid., p. 65.

53. Ibid., p. 65.

54. Ibid., p. 62.

55. Ibid., p. 273.

56. Ibid., p. 199; cf. pp. 276–77.

57. Ibid., pp. 44–45.

58. Ibid., pp. 70–71.

59. Ibid., pp. 80, 84.

60. Nick Railton, "Gog and Magog: the History of a Symbol," *Evangelical Quarterly* 75:1 (2003), pp. 23–43, surveys this exegetical tradition.

61. Burroughs, *Titan*, pp. 90–91.

62. Ibid., p. 95.

63. Ibid., p. 97.

64. Ibid., pp. 153, 157, 229.

65. Ibid., pp. 158–59.

66. Ibid., p. 166.

67. Ibid., p. 167.

68. Ibid., p. 145.

69. Ibid., pp. 165–66.

70. Ibid., p. 200.

71. Ibid., p. 258.

72. Ibid., pp. 212, 340.

73. Ibid., p. 17.

74. Ibid., p. 179.

75. Ibid., p. 344; Cox, *Fire from Heaven*, p. 23.

76. Burroughs, *Titan*, p. 137.

77. Ibid., p. 363.

78. "Historical Review of Dauphin County," available at http://maley.net/transcription/sketches/stine_milton_h.thm, accessed November 18, 2006.

79. Mark A. Noll, *A History of Christianity in the United States and Canada* (Grand Rapids, MI: Eerdmans, 1992), pp. 214–15.

80. The cultural and religious impact of the Civil War has been surveyed in a series of recent publications: Edward J. Blum's *Reforging the White Republic: Race, Religion, and American Nationalism, 1865–1898* (Baton Rouge: Louisiana State University Press, 2005), Mark A. Noll's *The Civil War as a Theological Crisis* (Chapel Hill, NC: University of North Carolina Press, 2006) and Stout's *Upon the Altar of the Nation*.

81. Stout, *Upon the Altar of the Nation*, p. 93.

82. Milton H. Stine, *Studies on the Religious Problem of Our Country* (York, PA: Lutheran Printing House, 1888), p. 161.

83. Ibid., p. 5.

84. Ibid., p. 9.

85. Ibid., pp. 9, 16.

86. Ibid., pp. 167–69.

87. Ibid.

88. Ibid.

89. Ibid.

90. Ibid., pp. 51, 58.

91. Ibid., p. 35.

92. Ibid., p. 29.

93. Ibid., p. 81.

94. Ibid., p. 30.

95. Ibid,, p. 37.

96. Ibid., pp. 36–37.

97. Ibid., p. 83.

98. Ibid., p. 87.

99. Ibid., p. 142.

100. Ibid., p. 102.

101. Ibid., p. 102.

102. Ibid., p. 103–4.

103. Ibid., p. 127.

104. Ibid., pp. 67, 128.

105. Milton H. Stine, *The Niemans* (York, PA: P. Anstadt and Sons, 1897), n.p. [p. iii].

106. Stine, *Studies on the Religious Problem of Our Country*, p. 153.

107. Noll, *A History of Christianity in the United States and Canada*, pp. 214–15.

108. Milton H. Stine, *The Devil's Bride: A Present Day Arraignment of Formalism and Doubt in the Church and in Society, in the Light of the Holy Scriptures. Given in the Form of a Pleasing Story* (Harrisburg, PA: Minter, 1910), p. xi.

109. Ibid., pp. x–xi.

110. Ibid., p. xi.

111. Ibid., pp. 37–39.

112. Ibid., p. 39.

113. Ibid., p. 40.

114. Ibid., p. 42.

115. Ibid., pp. 43, 45.

116. Ibid., p. 47.

117. Ibid., p. 122.

118. Ibid., p. 46.

119. Ibid., pp. 48–49.

120. Ibid., p. 49.

121. Ibid., p. 50.

122. Ibid., p. 137.

123. Cox, *Fire from Heaven*, p. 23.

124. Stine, *The Devil's Bride*, pp. 116, 132.

125. Ibid., p. 57.

126. Ibid., pp. 58–59.

127. Ibid., p. 60.

128. See, for example, Thomas Hardy, *A Laodicean* (1881; London: Penguin, 1997).

129. Stine, *The Devil's Bride*, p. 50.

130. Ibid., p. 51.

131. Ibid., p. 56.

132. Ibid., p. 57.

133. Ibid., p. 61.

134. Ibid., p. 60. Stine's allusion is to Revelation 3:1.

135. Ibid., pp. 75–80.

136. Ibid., p. 81.

137. Ibid., p. 80.

138. Ibid., pp. 242–43.

139. Ibid., pp. 113, 246.

140. Ibid., pp. 83, 88.

141. Ibid., p. 86.

142. Ibid., pp. 85, 109–10.

143. Ibid., p. 165.

144. Ibid., pp. 155–61, 166–67.

145. Ibid., p. 171.

146. Ibid., p. 209.

147. Ibid., p. 303.

148. Ibid., p. 303.

149. Burroughs, *Titan*, p. 179. While the *Scofield Reference Bible* did not directly attack the keeping of the Sabbath, it clearly argued that the Ten Commandments, which included the Sabbath obligation, were "inseparable" from "the law of Moses," and that the Mosaic law, "as a method of the divine dealing with man, characterised the dispensation extending from the giving of the law to the death of Jesus Christ" (pp. 1244–45). The subject index of the *Scofield Reference Bible* explained that the Sabbath principle remained only as a "day of rest" (p. 1439). Later dispensational theologians extended this principle to further undermine the Sabbath ideal.

150. Stine, *Ancient Cities and Civilizations Modernized*, pp. 274–75.

151. Ibid., p. 278.

152. Ibid., p. 280.

CHAPTER 2

1. Stine, *Ancient Cities and Civilizations Modernized*, p. 280.

2. A. C. Dixon, Louis Meyer, and R. A. Torrey (eds.), *The Fundamentals: A Testimony to the Truth*, (Chicago: Testimony, 1910–15), vol. 1, foreword.

3. Ibid., vol. 4, foreword.

4. Ibid., vol. 5, p. 4.

5. Ibid., vol. 10, foreword, p. 128.

6. Ibid., vol. 11, pp. 100–12, 113–26.

7. "A Statement by the Two Laymen," in ibid., vol. 12, p. 4.

8. William G. Moorehead, "Millennial Dawn: A Counterfeit of Christianity," in ibid., vol. 7, pp. 106–27.

9. "Tributes to Christ and the Bible by Brainy Men Not Known as Active Christians," in ibid., vol. 2, pp. 120–26.

10. C. C. Martindale, "Benson, Robert Hugh (1871–1914)," rev. Robert Brown, *Oxford Dictionary of National Biography;* and Christopher Jackson, "Robert Hugh Benson (1871–1914): A Heart of Fire," in Nicholas Rogers (ed.), *Catholics in Cambridge* (Leominster, UK: Gracewing, 2003), pp. 153–60.

11. Brian Masters, *The Life of E. F. Benson* (London: Chatto and Windus, 1993), p. 206.

12. Robert Hugh Benson, *Lord of the World* (1907; repr. Cirencester, UK: Echo Library, 2007), p. 3.

13. Ibid., p. 33. Contemporary Catholic apocalyptic believers continue to point to the existence of a Masonic plot within the Vatican, which aims to supplant the true pope; Luebbers, "The Remnant Faithful," p. 230.

14. Benson, *Lord of the World,* p. 5.

15. Ibid., p. 6.

16. Ibid., pp. 25, 44.

17. Joshua Hill Foster senior was listed in the 1850 census as a thirty-one-year-old white male living on 7,000 acres; "1850 Federal Census Tuscaloosa County, Alabama," www.rootsweb.com/~cenfiles/al/tuscaloosa/1850/pg368.txt, accessed November 19, 2006. He was ordained in 1853, and his ordination sermon was published as *The Christian Preacher: A Sermon Delivered in the Baptist Church, Tuskaloosa, Ala., at the Ordination of the Pastor Elect, the Rev. Joshua H. Foster, on Sunday, March 13th, 1853.* His papers are archived as the Joshua H. Foster Papers, William Stanley Hoole Special Collections Library, University of Alabama, Tuscaloosa, AL; A. James Fuller, *Chaplain to the Confederacy: Basil Manly and Baptist Life in the Old South* (Baton Rouge: Louisiana State University Press, 2000), p. 277.

18. Joshua Hill Foster, *Sixty-four Years a Minister* (Wilmington, NC: First Baptist Church, 1948), p. 25.

19. W. B. Crumpton, *Our Baptist Centennials, 1808–1923* (Montgomery, AL: Paragon, 1923), p. 45; Wayne Flynt, "Dissent in Zion: Alabama Baptists and Social Issues, 1900–1914," *The Journal of Southern History* 35:4 (1969), pp. 526–27. Hill's address was published in Crumpton, *Our Baptist Centennials,* pp. 42–46.

20. Joshua H. Foster, *The Judgment Day: A Story of the Seven Years of the Great Tribulation* (Louisville, KY: Baptist World, 1910), p. 3.

21. Southern Presbyterian ministers occasionally held premillennial convictions; their number included Robert J. Breckinridge, a minister in Kentucky. A small number of Southern Presbyterian ministers moved from postmillennialism to premillennialism—for example, Benjamin M. Palmer and James H. Brookes; Jack P. Maddex,

"Proslavery Millennialism: Social Eschatology in Antebellum Southern Calvinism," *American Quarterly* 31:1 (1979), pp. 48, 60–61.

22. James H. Moorhead, "Between Progress and Apocalypse: A Reassessment of Millennialism in American Religious Thought, 1800–1880," *The Journal of American History* 71:3 (1984), p. 541.

23. Maddex, "Proslavery Millennialism," p. 58.

24. Ibid., p. 60.

25. This paragraph is indebted to James Spivey, "The Millennium," in Paul Basden (ed.), *Has Our Theology Changed? Southern Baptist Thought since 1845* (Nashville, TN: Broadman and Holden, 1994), pp. 230–62.

26. Foster, *The Judgment Day*, p. 3.

27. Spivey, "The Millennium," p. 238. See James P. Boyce's published lectures, *Abstract of Systematic Theology* (1887; Cape Coral, FL: Founder Press, 2006), chapter 40.

28. Spivey, "The Millennium," pp. 245, 261.

29. The *Abstract of Principles* repudiates premillennialism in anticipating only one day of resurrection: "God hath appointed a day, wherein he will judge the world by Jesus Christ, when every one shall receive according to his deeds; the wicked shall go into everlasting punishment; the righteous, into everlasting life." The *Abstract of Principles* is available at www.sbts.edu/pdf/abstract.pdf, accessed February 21, 2007.

30. On Gill's eschatology, see Crawford Gribben, "John Gill and Puritan Eschatology," *Evangelical Quarterly* 73:4 (2001), pp. 311–26, and Barry H. Howson, "The Eschatology of the Calvinistic Baptist John Gill (1697–1771) Examined and Compared," *Eusebeia* 5 (2005), pp. 33–66. On Gill's reception among Southern Baptists, see Gregory A. Wills, *Democratic Religion: Freedom, Authority, and Church Discipline in the Baptist South, 1785–1900* (Oxford: Oxford University Press, 1997), pp. 85–86. On Spurgeon's eschatology and views of slavery, see Lewis A. Drummond, *Spurgeon: Prince of Preachers* (Grand Rapids, MI: Kregel, 1993), pp. 533, 650.

31. Foster, *Sixty-four Years a Minister*, pp. 59–60, 76.

32. Foster, *The Judgment Day*, p. 3.

33. Ibid., p. 7.

34. Ibid., p. 29.

35. Ibid., p. 40.

36. Ibid., pp. 30, 32.

37. Ibid., p. 36.

38. Ibid., p. 30.

39. Ibid., p. 106.

40. Ibid., p. 130.

41. Ibid., pp. 33–34.

42. Ibid., p. 36.

43. Ibid., p. 53.

44. Scofield and Foster both describe the first dispensation as an "age of innocency [sic]"; ibid., pp. 54–55, 57; *Scofield Reference Bible*, p. 5.

45. Foster, *The Judgment Day*, pp. 112, 120.

46. Ibid., pp. 50, 86.

47. Ibid., p. 50.

48. Ibid., p. 51.

49. Ibid., pp. 67, 69, 87, 99.

50. Ibid., p. 79.

51. Ibid., p. 85.

52. Ibid., pp. 93–94. Foster roots these descriptions of immoral sentiments in a contemporary text, *Modern Spiritualism: The Judgment Day*, p. 81.

53. Ibid., pp. 75–76.

54. Ibid., p. 88.

55. On the early history of American philo-Semitism, see Robert K. Whalen, "'Christians Love the Jews!' The Development of American Philo-Semitism, 1790–1860," *Religion and American Culture* 6:2 (1996), pp. 225–59.

56. Foster, *The Judgment Day*, pp. 110, 118.

57. Ibid., p. 119.

58. Ibid., pp. 102, 135. Stine made the same mistake, describing the Christmas decorations in the Mosque of Mohammed Ali, Cairo, in *Ancient Cities and Civilizations Modernized*, p. 15.

59. Note the references to Protestant martyrs, such as Huss; Foster, *The Judgment Day*, p. 126.

60. Watson, *Brighter Years*, pp. 297, 301. Sydney Watson's prophetic trilogy was published as *Scarlet and Purple: A Story of Souls and "Signs"* (London: William Nicholson and Sons, [1913]; repr. Edinburgh: B. McCall Barbour, 1974); *The Mark of the Beast* (London: William Nicholson and Sons, [1915]; repr. Edinburgh: B. McCall Barbour, 1974); and *In the Twinkling of an Eye* (London: William Nicholson and Sons, [1916]).

61. Sydney Watson, *Life's Look-out: An Autobiography of Sydney Watson* (second edition, London: Hodder and Stoughton, 1899), p. 293.

62. Watson, *Brighter Years*, p. 200.

63. Ibid., p. 215.

64. Ibid., p. 203.

65. Ibid., p. 277; Watson, *Life's Look-out*, p. viii.

66. Watson, *Brighter Years*, p. 219.

67. Ibid., p. 219.

68. Ibid., pp. 219–20.

69. Watson, *Life's Look-out*, p. 260.

70. Ibid., pp. 17, 309.

71. Watson, *Brighter Years*, p. 219.

72. Lily Watson, *From Deck to Glory: Third Volume of the Late Sydney Watson's Life-story* (London: William Nicholson and Sons, 1920).

73. Watson, *Brighter Years*, pp. 216, 297.

74. Watson, *Life's Look-out*, p. vii.

75. Ibid., p. vii.

76. Ibid., pp. 352–53.

77. Ibid., p. 279.

78. Ibid., p. 271.

79. Ibid., p. 76. See also Watson, *Brighter Years,* pp. 266, 291.

80. Watson, *Life's Look-out,* p. 78.

81. For an account of Spurgeon's Romantic Calvinism, see Mark Hopkins, *Nonconformity's Romantic Generation: Evangelical and Liberal Theologies in Victorian England,* Studies in Evangelical History and Thought (Milton Keynes, UK: Paternoster, 2004).

82. Watson, *Life's Look-out,* p. 166; Watson, *Brighter Years,* pp. 20, 122, 137.

83. Watson, *Brighter Years,* p. 145.

84. Ibid., p. 55.

85. Ibid., p. 159.

86. Ibid., p. 64,

87. Ibid., pp. 150, 209.

88. Ibid., p. 183.

89. Watson, *Life's Look-out,* p. 262; Watson, *Brighter Years,* pp. 33, 182.

90. Watson, *Brighter Years,* p. 294.

91. Ibid., p. 294.

92. Ibid., p. 294.

93. Ibid., p. 295.

94. Ibid., p. 294.

95. Watson, *The New Europe,* p. 29.

96. Ibid., p. 202.

97. Watson, *Scarlet and Purple,* p. 160.

98. Watson, *In the Twinkling of an Eye,* p. vi.

99. Watson, *The Mark of the Beast,* p. 5.

100. Watson, *In the Twinkling of an Eye,* p. vi–vii.

101. Ibid., p. 12.

102. Ibid., p. 46.

103. Ibid., p. 43.

104. Ibid., p. 132.

105. Ibid., p. 136.

106. Ibid., p. 152.

107. Watson, *Life's Look-out,* pp. 65, 292.

108. Ibid., pp. 293–94.

109. Watson, *Brighter Years,* p. 89.

110. Watson, *In the Twinkling of an Eye,* pp. 32, 249–50.

111. Ibid., pp. 249–50.

112. Ibid., pp. 67–70.

113. Ibid., p. 242.

114. Watson, *Life's Look-out,* p. 31.

115. Watson, *The Mark of the Beast,* p. 95.

116. Ibid., p. 103.

117. Watson, *Scarlet and Purple,* p. 144; Watson, *The Mark of the Beast,* p. 41.

118. Watson, *In the Twinkling of an Eye,* p. 263; Watson, *Scarlet and Purple,* p. 54.

119. Watson, *The Mark of the Beast,* p. 110; Watson, *In the Twinkling of an Eye,* p. 226; Watson, *The New Europe,* p. 200.

120. Watson, *Brighter Years*, p. 257.

121. Watson, *The New Europe*, p. 173.

122. Watson, *In the Twinkling of an Eye*, p. 263; Watson, *Scarlet and Purple*, p. 147.

123. Watson, *The New Europe*, p. 221.

124. Watson, *Scarlet and Purple*, p. 160.

125. Ibid., p. 140; Watson, *In the Twinkling of an Eye*, pp. 125–26, 177.

126. Watson, *In the Twinkling of an Eye*, pp. 255, 258–59.

127. Watson, *The Mark of the Beast*, pp. 30–32.

128. Watson, *The New Europe*, p. 40.

129. Carpenter, *Revive Us Again*, pp. 101–5; Watson, *The New Europe*, pp. 108–10.

130. Watson, *The New Europe*, pp. 103–4, 107.

131. Foster, *The Judgment Day*, p. 119; Watson, *The Mark of the Beast*, pp. 15–17.

132. Watson, *The Mark of the Beast*, pp. 97, 58, 51.

133. Watson, *Scarlet and Purple*, pp. 162–63. Watson would again predict Irish independence in *The New Europe*, p. 113.

134. Watson, *The New Europe*, p. 69.

135. Watson, *The Mark of the Beast*, pp. 42–43, 104; Watson, *Scarlet and Purple*, p. 148.

136. Watson, *The Mark of the Beast*, p. 148.

137. Ibid., pp. 84, 170. Revelation 20:4 refers to "them that were beheaded for the witness of Jesus, and for the word of God," but the continuing references to the guillotine suggest that the interpretation of this passage has reflected a particular political tradition.

138. Sydney Watson, *The Lure of a Soul: Bewitched by Spiritualism* (London: William Nicholson and Sons, [1917]), p. vi.

139. Watson, *In the Twinkling of an Eye*, p. 139.

140. Watson, *The New Europe*, p. 124.

141. Ibid., p. 41.

142. Ibid., p. 134.

143. Watson followed *Scofield's* conventions in identifying the dispensations as "Innocency," Conscience, Human Government (Noah), Promises (Abraham), Law (Moses), Church; ibid., pp. 38–39. Watson also quoted from the *Scofield Reference Bible* in ibid., p. 204.

144. Watson, *The New Europe*, pp. 64, 102–3.

145. Ibid., p. 14.

146. Ibid., p. 42.

147. Ibid., p. 29.

148. Ibid., pp. 15, 32.

149. Ibid., pp. 117, 119–20, 121.

150. Shirley Jackson Case, *The Millennial Hope: A Phase of War-time Thinking* (Chicago: University of Chicago Press, 1918), p. 208.

151. Watson, *The New Europe*, p. 122.

152. This is evidenced from a general survey of the catalogues of British and American copyright deposit libraries.

153. Or perhaps the reason for Watson's enduring success was that his novels were published by a major London press with a solid network of distribution.

154. The expression is used by Noll in *A History of Christianity in the United States and Canada*, p. 286; Foster, *The Judgment Day*, p. 134.

155. Foster, *The Judgment Day*, p. 49.

CHAPTER 3

1. Sidney Fowler Wright, *Deluge*, ed. Brian Stableford, Early Classics of Science Fiction (1927; Middletown, CT: Wesleyan University Press, 2003).

2. Ibid., p. 127.

3. This regrouping is described in Carpenter, *Revive Us Again*. Susan Friend Harding errs in her argument that the term "evangelical" was invented in opposition to "fundamentalist" in the 1940s and 1950s; Harding, *The Book of Jerry Falwell*, p. 17.

4. Forrest Loman Oilar, *Be Thou Prepared for Jesus Is Coming* (Boston: Meador, 1937), p. 63. Mangum's *The Dispensational-Covenantal Rift* describes the competing varieties of conservative Presbyterianism in the late 1930s. I am grateful to Joe Walker, a Los Angeles historian, for information on the churchmanship of the Oilar family.

5. Oilar, *Be Thou Prepared*, p. 84.

6. Ibid., p. 97.

7. Ibid., p. 97.

8. Ibid., p. 18. "Mansion" appears in John 14:2 in the King James (Authorized) Version. Most modern translations prefer the term "room."

9. "The Publishers Announce Be Thou Prepared by Forrest Loman Oilar," n.p.

10. Oilar, *Be Thou Prepared*, pp. 87–88.

11. Ibid., pp. 128–29.

12. "The Publishers Announce Be Thou Prepared by Forrest Loman Oilar," n.p.

13. Oilar, *Be Thou Prepared*, pp. 7–8.

14. Ibid., p. 21.

15. "The Publishers Announce Be Thou Prepared by Forrest Loman Oilar," n.p.

16. Oilar, *Be Thou Prepared*, p. 8; "Pasadenan Slays Wife, Three Children with Hatchet," *Los Angeles Times*, December 20, 1954, p. 2; "Ax Slayer of Wife, Three Children Pleads Guilty," *Los Angeles Times*, February 3, 1955, p. 12. I am grateful to Joe Walker for information on the Highland College connection.

17. Oilar, *Be Thou Prepared*, p. 250.

18. See, for example, *The Companion Bible*, ed. E. W. Bullinger (London: Lamp Press, 1909), appendix 156, pp. 179–82. The idea was repeated in Beaucage, *Shiloh Project*, p. 317.

19. Oilar, *Be Thou Prepared*, p. 168.

20. Ibid., p. 167.

21. Ibid., p. 17.

22. Ibid., p. 19.

23. Ibid., p. 290.

24. Ibid., p. 31.

25. Ibid., pp. 146–47. Oilar did not specify which prophecy was fulfilled in contemporary unemployment.

26. Ibid., p. 146.

27. Ibid., p. 34.

28. Ibid., pp. 30–31.

29. Ibid., p. 74.

30. Ibid., p. 97.

31. Ibid., pp. 67, 144–45, 209.

32. Ibid., p. 320.

33. Ibid., p. 321.

34. Ibid., p. 50.

35. Ibid., p. 15.

36. Ibid., p. 39.

37. Ibid., pp. 13–14.

38. Ibid., p. 86.

39. Ibid., pp. 174, 298.

40. Ibid., p. 298.

41. Ibid., pp. 142, 270.

42. Ibid., pp. 303, 307.

43. Ibid., pp. 100, 102. *Left Behind,* by contrast, describes the rapture of babies in the womb; LaHaye and Jenkins, *Left Behind,* p. 33.

44. Oilar, *Be Thou Prepared,* p. 82.

45. Ibid., pp. 100, 136.

46. Ibid., p. 184.

47. Ibid., pp. 14–15, 101; see also pp. 107–8.

48. Ibid., p. 301.

49. Ibid., p. 315.

50. Ibid., p. 319.

51. Ibid., p. 173.

52. Ibid., p. 293.

53. Ibid., p. 293.

54. Ibid., p. 124.

55. Ibid., pp. 196–97.

56. Ibid., pp. 139, 193.

57. Ibid., p. 325.

58. Ibid., pp. 220, 223, 227–52.

59. Ibid., pp. 253–67.

60. Ibid., pp. 268–80.

61. Ibid., p. 340.

62. Ibid., p. 18.

63. Ibid., pp. 130, 148.

64. Ibid., p. 295; see also p. 299.

65. Ibid., p. 304.

66. Ibid., p. 304.

67. Ibid., p. 336; see also Burroughs, *Titan*, pp. 90–91.

68. Dayton A. Manker, *They That Remain: A Story of the End Times* (1941; repr. Cincinnati, OH: Sunshine Book and Bible House, 1946), title page.

69. Manker, *Youth's Dream Time*, p. 6.

70. Dayton A. Manker, *From the "Highways and Hedges": The Life of Rev. C. E. Myers* (Cadillac, MI: Dayton E. Manker, [1949]), p. 123.

71. Dayton A. Manker, *All Things DO Work Together for Our Good* (Marion, IN: Wesleyan, 1962), p. 17.

72. Manker, *From the Highways and Hedges*, pp. 123–24.

73. Ibid., p. 123.

74. Manker, *They That Remain*, p. 3.

75. James E. Ruark, *The House of Zondervan* (Grand Rapids, MI: Zondervan, 2006), pp. 1–20.

76. Manker, *From the Highways and Hedges*, pp. 60–61; Manker, *All Things DO Work Together for Our Good*, pp. 30, 32.

77. Michael G. Borgert, "Harry Bultema and the *Maranatha* Controversy in the Christian Reformed Church," *Calvin Theological Journal* 42:1 (2007), p. 91.

78. See Peter de Klerk and Richard R. DeRidder (eds.), *Perspectives on the Christian Reformed Church: Studies in its History, Theology, Ecumenicity* (Grand Rapids, MI: Baker, 1983). On the role of Zondervan in the debate, see Joseph H. Hall, "The Controversy over Fundamentalism in the Christian Reformed Church, 1915–1966" (Th.D. dissertation, Concordia Theological Seminary, 1974), pp. 140–55.

79. Blodgett, *Protestant Evangelical Literary Culture and Contemporary Society*, p. 49.

80. Manker, *They That Remain*, pp. 3, 5.

81. Perhaps, by the mid-1940s, premillennialism had become too contentious within the Christian Reformed Church for Zondervan to consider any further association with the text.

82. Manker, *They That Remain*, p. 40.

83. Ibid., p. 5.

84. Ibid., pp. 69, 71.

85. Ibid., pp. 69, 73, 74.

86. Ibid., p. 75; Oilar, *Be Thou Prepared*, p. 86.

87. Manker, *They That Remain*, p. 76.

88. Manker, *Youth's Dream Time*, p. 44.

89. Manker's death in 1994 was noted in a list of "our honored dead of the ministry" in the *Annual District Conference Journal of the North Michigan District of the Wesleyan Church* (2004), available at www.nmichwes.org/pdfs/Wesleyan%20Jour nal%202004.pdf, accessed May 28, 2007.

90. Manker, *They That Remain*, p. 36.

91. Ibid., pp. 48–49.

92. Ibid., p. 57. The conversion of a future evangelist, represented as a model for lay piety, was likewise characterized by Manker as involving "shouting and crying

196 NOTES TO PAGES 79–83

and praising God for victory"; Manker, *From the Highways and Hedges*, p. 21. Other penitents evidenced their faith in "such praying, crying, seeking, shouting and rejoicing you never heard!"; Manker, *From the Highways and Hedges*, p. 119.

93. Manker, *They That Remain*, p. 56; Watson, *Life's Look-out*, p. 166; Watson, *Brighter Years*, pp. 20, 122, 137.

94. Manker, *They That Remain*, pp. 91, 113.

95. Ibid., pp. 35, 179.

96. Ibid., p. 187.

97. Ibid., p. 206.

98. Ibid., p. 202.

99. Ibid., p. 3.

100. Manker elsewhere noted the debilitating moral impact of World War II; Manker, *From the Highways and Hedges*, p. 74.

101. Manker, *They That Remain*, p. 3.

102. Ibid., p. 61.

103. Ibid., p. 209.

104. Ibid., p. 6.

105. Ibid., p. 227.

106. Ibid., p. 4.

107. Manker, *Youth's Dream Time*, p. 6.

108. Manker, *They That Remain*, pp. 114, 116.

109. Manker, *Youth's Dream Time*, p. 6.

110. Manker, *They That Remain*, p. 116.

111. Ibid., p. 79.

112. Ibid., p. 30.

113. Ibid., p. 221.

114. Ibid., pp. 16, 34.

115. Ibid., p. 11.

116. Ibid., p. 227.

117. Ibid., p. 158.

118. Ibid., p. 12.

119. Ibid., p. 13.

120. Ibid., p. 158.

121. Manker, *From the Highways and Hedges*, p. 121.

122. Manker, *They That Remain*, p. 38.

123. Ibid., p. 38.

124. Ibid., p. 38.

125. Ibid., p. 61.

126. Ibid., pp. 86, 98.

127. Ibid., pp. 90–91.

128. Ibid., p. 112.

129. Ibid., p. 38.

130. Ibid., p. 18.

131. Ibid., p. 21.

132. Ibid., p. 21.

133. Ibid., p. 23.

134. Ibid., p. 27.

135. Ibid., p. 28.

136. Ibid., p. 28.

137. Ibid., p. 28.

138. Ibid., pp. 81, 119.

139. Ibid., p. 82.

140. Ibid., p. 35.

141. Ibid., p. 86.

142. Ibid., p. 84.

143. Ibid., p. 120.

144. Ibid., p. 85.

145. "S. M. C.," *As the Clock Struck Twenty*, p. 16.

146. Oilar, *Be Thou Prepared*, p. 321; Manker, *They That Remain*, pp. 230–31.

147. Manker, *All Things DO Work Together for Our Good*, p. 11.

CHAPTER 4

1. Baumgartner, *Longing for the End*, p. 215.

2. Walvoord, *The Return of the Lord*, p. 9.

3. Manker, *They That Remain*, p. 3.

4. See, for example, Cerullo, *The Omega Project*, p. 42.

5. From "The Rhymes of Gospel John," quoted in Myers, *The Trumpet Sounds*, p. 97.

6. Myers, *The Trumpet Sounds*, p. 97.

7. *Scofield Reference Bible*, pp. 25, 722.

8. Ibid., p. 1337.

9. Pentecost, *Things to Come*, p. 280.

10. Walvoord, *The Return of the Lord*, p. 35.

11. Sizer, *Christian Zionism*, p. 155.

12. Lindsey, *The Late Great Planet Earth*, pp. 43, 54.

13. Ibid., pp. 79–80.

14. Balizet, *The Seven Last Years*, p. 158.

15. This is the argument of Callum Brown, *The Death of Christian Britain* (London: Routledge, 2001).

16. Hendershot, *Shaking the World for Jesus*, p. 21; Blodgett, *Protestant Evangelical Literary Culture and Contemporary Society*, p. 42.

17. Nicholas Guyatt, *Have a Nice Doomsday: Why Millions of Americans Are Looking Forward to the End of the World* (London: Ebury, 2007), p. 150.

18. *New York Times Book Review*, April 6, 1980, p. 27.

19. Guyatt, *Have a Nice Doomsday*, p. 189.

20. Ernest W. Angley, *Raptured* (Wilmington, NC: Carolina Press, 1950), p. 16.

21. Tim LaHaye and Jerry B. Jenkins, *The Mark* (Wheaton, IL: Tyndale House, 2000), p. 284.

22. Walvoord, *The Return of the Lord*, p. 144.

23. "Angley, Ernest W.," in Randall Balmer, *Encyclopedia of Evangelicalism* (Louisville, KY: Westminster John Knox, 2002), p. 24.

24. Angley, *Raptured,* pp. 3, 40. While I was able to make contact with Angley, he did not respond to my questions about his novel.

25. Ibid., p. 40.

26. Ibid., p. 1.

27. Ibid., p. 131.

28. Ibid., pp. 12, 21, 28, 45, 73.

29. Ibid., p. 28.

30. Ibid., p. 42.

31. Ibid., p. 43.

32. Ibid., pp. 12, 19.

33. Ibid., pp. 12, 23, 36, 44.

34. Ibid., p. 74.

35. Ibid., p. 45.

36. Ibid,, p. 77.

37. Ibid., p. 77.

38. Ibid., pp. 100-1.

39. Ibid., pp. 1, 124.

40. Ibid., pp. 61-62, 117.

41. Ibid., p. 163.

42. Ibid., pp. 5-6.

43. Ibid., p. 1.

44. Ibid., p. 97.

45. Ibid., p. 106.

46. Ibid., p. 160.

47. Ibid., p. 138.

48. Ibid., pp. 164, 165, 189, 207-9.

49. Ibid., p. 162.

50. Ibid., p. 136.

51. I was unable to obtain any estimate of the novel's sales over the last six decades.

52. Myers, *The Trumpet Sounds,* p. 66.

53. Ibid., p. 60.

54. Ibid., p. 88.

55. Ibid., p. 118; see also Thuesen, *In Discordance with the Scriptures.*

56. Myers, *The Trumpet Sounds,* p. 92.

57. See Marsden, *Reforming Fundamentalism,* for a description of this painful and protracted process.

58. Myers, *The Trumpet Sounds,* p. 120.

59. Ibid., p. 116.

60. Ibid., pp. 11, 163.

61. Ibid., p. 10.

62. Ibid., p. 186.

63. Ibid., p. 24.

64. Ibid., p. 187.

65. Ibid., p. 199.

66. Ibid., "Author's Comment," n.p.

67. Ibid.

68. Ibid., pp. 34, 36.

69. Ibid., "Author's Comment," n.p.

70. Ibid., p. 184.

71. Ibid., pp. 203–4.

72. Ibid., p. 204.

73. Frederick Albert Tatford, *The Clock Strikes* (London: Lakeland, 1970).

74. Ibid., p. 7.

75. Ibid., p. 7.

76. Ibid., pp. 24–25.

77. Ibid., p. 24.

78. Ibid., p. 25.

79. Ibid., pp. 25, 78.

80. Ibid., p. 78.

81. Ibid., p. 26.

82. Ibid., pp. 26, 124.

83. The term is Didi Herman's; "Globalism's 'Siren Song': The United Nations and International Law in Christian Right Thought and Prophecy," *The Sociological Review* 49:1 (2001), pp. 56–77.

84. See Philip H. Melling, *Fundamentalism in America* (Edinburgh: Edinburgh University Press, 1999), pp. 95–102, for a recent discussion of Kirban's novel.

85. Melling, *Fundamentalism in America*, p. 99.

86. The sales figure is quoted on the front cover of my October 1973 edition of the novel.

87. Salem Kirban, *1000* (1973; Chattanooga, TN: Future Events Publications, n.d.), pp. 14, 89.

88. Ibid., pp. 88, 105.

89. Kirban, *666*, pp. 6–7.

90. Ibid., p. 7.

91. Ibid., p. 91.

92. Ibid., p. 183.

93. Ibid., p. 8.

94. Ibid., p. 8.

95. Ibid., pp. 284–85; Kirban, *1000*, p. 185.

96. Kirban, *1000*, p. 12.

97. Kirban, *666*, p. 4.

98. Cohen, *The Horsemen Are Coming*, p. 7.

99. Ibid., pp. 52, 56, 68, 140.

100. Ibid., p. 7.

101. Ibid., p. 8.

102. Ibid., p. 8.

103. Ibid., pp. 14, 20.

104. Ibid., p. 116.

105. Ibid., p. 12.

106. Ibid., p. 31.

107. Ibid., pp. 12–13.

108. Ibid., p. 195.

109. Ibid., p. 8.

110. Ibid., p. 9.

111. Ibid., p. 35.

112. Ibid., pp. 118–19.

113. Ibid., p. 15.

114. Ibid., p. 163.

115. Ibid., p. 42.

116. Ibid., p. 26.

117. Ibid., p. 66.

118. Ibid., p. 26.

119. Ibid., p. 27. Ironically, the pope quotes from the classically Protestant Authorized (King James) Version; ibid., p. 35.

120. Balizet, *The Seven Last Years,* p. 150.

121. Ibid., p. 160.

122. Ibid., p. 199.

123. Ibid., p. 216.

124. Ibid., p. 196.

125. Ibid., pp. 116, 230.

126. Ibid., p. 9.

127. Ibid., p. 140.

128. Ibid., p. 179.

129. Ibid., p. 179.

130. Ibid., p. 205.

131. Ibid., p. 223.

132. Ibid., p. 285.

133. Blodgett, *Protestant Evangelical Literary Culture and Contemporary Society,* p. 44.

134. Balizet, *The Seven Last Years,* p. 328.

135. Ibid., p. 165.

136. Ibid., p. 94.

137. Ibid., pp. 213–15.

138. Ibid., p. 261.

139. Robert L. Snow, *Deadly Cults: The Crimes of True Believers* (Westport, CT: Praeger, 2003), pp. 10–12; Pamela E. Klassen, *Blessed Events: Religion and Home Birth in America* (Princeton, NJ: Princeton University Press, 2001), pp. 105–6.

140. Dan Betzer, *Beast: A Novel of the Future World Dictator* (Lafayette, LA: Prescott, 1985), pp. 22, 29, 130.

141. Boyer, *When Time Shall Be No More,* p. 305.

142. *88 Reasons* was also published as *The Rosh Hash Ana 1988 and 88 Reasons Why.* See Boyer, *When Time Shall Be No More,* p. 130, and Gary North, "Publisher's Preface," in the 1991 edition of Wilson, *Armageddon Now!* pp. xi–xii.

143. Irene Martin, *Emerald Thorn* (Oklahoma City, OK: Hearthstone, 1991), p. 314.

CHAPTER 5

1. Michael Barkun, *A Culture of Conspiracy: Apocalyptic Visions in Contemporary America* (Berkeley: University of California Press, 2003), p. 64.

2. Ibid., p. 77.

3. Martin, *Emerald Thorn*, p. 314.

4. Tim LaHaye, *The Battle for the Mind: A Subtle Warfare* (Old Tappan, NJ: Revell, 1980), p. 217. See also Robert Clouse, "The New Christian Right, America, and the Kingdom of God," *Christian Scholars Review* 12 (1983), pp. 3–16; Steve Bruce, *The Rise and Fall of the New Christian Right: Conservative Protestant Politics in American, 1978–1988* (Oxford, UK: Clarendon, 1988).

5. Lindsey, *The Late Great Planet Earth*, p. 8.

6. Hendershot, *Shaking the World for Jesus*, p. 32.

7. Timothy P. Weber, *Living in the Shadow of the Second Coming: American Premillennialism, 1875–1982* (Grand Rapids, MI: Academie Books, 1983), has a chapter on Hal Lindsey's and Jerry Falwell's politics; pp. 204–26.

8. Kevin P. Phillips, *The Emerging Republican Majority* (New York: Arlington House, 1969).

9. Balizet, *The Seven Last Years*, pp. 110, 122.

10. For Reagan's dispensationalism, see Kurt Ritter, "Reagan's 1964 TV Speech for Goldwater: Millennial Themes in American Political Rhetoric," in Martin J. Medhurst and Thomas W. Benson (eds.), *Rhetorical Dimensions in Media: A Critical Casebook* (second edition, Dubuque, IA: Kendall/Hunt, 1991), pp. 58–72; Mills, "The Serious Implications of a 1971 Conversation with Ronald Reagan," p. 141; Reagan, "Address to the National Association of Evangelicals, March 8, 1983," pp. 165–69; Richard N. Ostling, "Armageddon and the End Times: Prophecies of the Last Days Surface as a Campaign Issue," *TIME*, November 5, 1984, p. 73; G. Thomas Goodnight, "Ronald Reagan's Re-formulation of the Rhetoric of War: Analysis of the 'Zero Option,' 'Evil Empire,' and 'Star Wars' Addresses," *Quarterly Journal of Speech* 72 (1986), pp. 390–414; Rebecca S. Bjork, "Reagan and the Nuclear Freeze: 'Star Wars' as a Rhetorical Strategy," *Journal of the American Forensic Association* 24 (1988), pp. 181–92; Janice Hocker Rushing, "Ronald Reagan's 'Star Wars' Address: Mythic Containment of Technical Reasoning," *Quarterly Journal of Speech* 72 (1986), pp. 415–33.

11. Irving Hexham, "The Evangelical Response to the New Age," in James R. Lewis and Gordon Melton (eds.), *Perspectives on the New Age* (New York: SUNY, 1992), pp. 152–63.

12. Blodgett, *Protestant Evangelical Literary Culture and Contemporary Society*, p. 47.

13. Balizet, *The Seven Last Years*, p. 116.

14. Betzer, *Beast*, p. 12; Grant, *The Revelation*, p. 146.

15. Martin, *Emerald Thorn*, p. 59.

16. Philip Jenkins and Daniel Maier-Katkin, "Satanism: Myth and Reality in a Contemporary Moral Panic," *Crime, Law and Social Change* 17 (1992), p. 54.

17. Ibid., p. 54.

18. Eileen Luhr, "Metal Missionaries to the Nation: Christian Heavy Metal Music, 'Family Values,' and Youth Culture, 1984–1994," *American Quarterly* 57:1 (2005), p. 124. The "paranoid style" was famously identified in Richard Hofstadter, *The Paranoid Style in American Politics* (Chicago: University of Chicago Press, 1979); see also George Johnson, *Architects of Fear* (Los Angeles: Jeremy P. Tarcher, 1983), and Seymour M. Lipset and Earl Raab, *The Politics of Unreason* (second edition, Chicago: University of Chicago Press, 1978).

19. Harding, *The Book of Jerry Falwell*, p. 10.

20. Jenkins and Maier-Katkin, "Satanism," p. 65.

21. Ibid., p. 54.

22. Ibid., p. 55.

23. Ibid., p. 64.

24. Biographical information is provided at http://frankperetti.com/1482.htm, accessed June 12, 2007.

25. Cox, *Fire from Heaven*, p. 28; Hendershot, *Shaking the World for Jesus*, p. 219 n. 35. Surprisingly, Randall Balmer's entry for Peretti in his *Encyclopedia of Evangelicalism* makes no reference to the spiritual warfare novels; "Peretti, Frank E.," in Balmer, *Encyclopedia of Evangelicalism*, pp. 446–47.

26. Blodgett, *Protestant Evangelical Literary Culture and Contemporary Society*, p. 98.

27. C. H. Kraft, "Spiritual Warfare," in Stanley M. Burgess (ed.), *The New International Dictionary of Pentecostal and Charismatic Movements* (revised and expanded edition, Grand Rapids, MI: Zondervan, 2002), pp. 1091–96.

28. Ironically, of course, earlier generations of fundamentalists would have regarded Peretti's use of the Revised Standard Version of the Bible as evidence that he himself was an agent of satanic influence.

29. Frank Peretti, *This Present Darkness* (1986; Eastbourne, UK: Minstrel, 1989), p. 426.

30. O'Leary, *Arguing the Apocalypse*, pp. 174–79.

31. Lindsey, *The Late Great Planet Earth*, p. 8; O'Leary, *Arguing the Apocalypse*, p. 172.

32. O'Leary, *Arguing the Apocalypse*, p. 174.

33. Ibid., p. 178.

34. Peretti, *This Present Darkness*, p. 16.

35. Ibid., p. 246.

36. Ibid., pp. 285, 442.

37. Ibid., p. 278.

38. Ibid., p. 281.

39. Frank Peretti, *Piercing the Darkness* (1989; Eastbourne, UK: Minstrel, 1990), p. 388.

40. Peretti, *This Present Darkness*, p. 426.

41. Robert A. Guelich, "Spiritual Warfare: Jesus, Paul, and Peretti," *Pneuma: The Journal of the Society for Pentecostal Studies*, 13:1 (1991), pp. 33–64.

42. P. G. A. Versteeg and A. F. Droogers, "A Typology of Domestication in Exorcism," *Culture and Religion* 8:1 (2007), p. 15.

43. David E. Stevens, "Daniel 10 and the Notion of Territorial Spirits," *Bibliotheca Sacra* 157:628 (2000), pp. 410–31.

44. Versteeg and Droogers, "A Typology of Domestication in Exorcism," p. 23. Peretti's influence was evident in Cash, *The Age of the Antichrist.*

45. "I've never read the Narnia books . . . I don't know the first thing about *Paradise Lost*"; www.frankperetti.com/gallery-119/franksbiganswerstoquestions bingemarch122007.htm, accessed June 12, 2007.

46. Paul A. Bramadat, *The Church on the World's Turf: An Evangelical Christian Group at a Secular University* (Oxford: Oxford University Press, 2000), p. 104.

47. Ibid., p. 104.

48. Ibid., p. 105.

49. Guelich, "Spiritual Warfare," p. 57.

50. Blodgett, *Protestant Evangelical Literary Culture and Contemporary Society,* p. 43.

51. Stevens, "Daniel 10 and the Notion of Territorial Spirits," p. 410.

52. See www.frankperetti.com/, accessed June 12, 2007.

53. Peretti, *This Present Darkness,* p. 11.

54. Peretti, *Piercing the Darkness,* p. 9.

55. Ibid., p. 9.

56. Peretti, *This Present Darkness,* pp. 59, 69.

57. Ibid., p. 34.

58. Ibid., p. 26.

59. Ibid., p. 97.

60. Ibid., p. 99.

61. Ibid., p. 126.

62. Ibid., p. 212.

63. Ibid., p. 382.

64. Ibid., p. 444.

65. Ibid., p. 430.

66. Ibid., p. 419.

67. Ibid., p. 137.

68. Peretti, *Piercing the Darkness,* p. 97.

69. Peretti, *This Present Darkness,* p. 241. The theme—to say the least—has very few parallels in the prayers recorded in the New Testament.

70. The New Age philosophy is explained in ibid., p. 159. The Christian gospel is explained in ibid., p. 423, and Peretti, *Piercing the Darkness,* pp. 155, 352–56.

71. Peretti, *This Present Darkness,* pp. 29, 61, 92.

72. Ibid., pp. 85, 93.

73. Ibid., pp. 471–92.

74. Ibid., p. 496.

75. Ibid., pp. 348, 424.

76. Ibid., pp. 431, 477, 482.

77. Ibid., p. 494.

78. Ibid., pp. 179, 199.

79. Ibid., pp. 236, 463.

80. Ibid., p. 439.

81. Blodgett, *Protestant Evangelical Literary Culture and Contemporary Society*, pp. 43, 94.

82. Robertson, *The End of the Age*, p. 127. For a discussion of Robertson's conspiratorial worldview, see Barkun, *A Culture of Conspiracy*, pp. 39–64.

83. Peretti, *This Present Darkness*, p. 508.

84. Ronald H. Nash, *Evangelicals in America: Who They Are, What They Believe* (Nashville, TN: Abingdon, 1987), pp. 92–93.

85. Robertson, *The Secret Kingdom*, p. 45. William Martin, *With God on Our Side: The Rise of the Religious Right in America* (New York: Broadway Books, 1996), pp. 258–59; John W. Robbins, *Pat Robertson: A Warning to America* (Jefferson, MD: Trinity Foundation, 1988), p. 16. Robertson's charismatic interests have been widely reported. Opposing U.S. representative Jack Kemp's call for more stringent sanctions against South Africa, Robertson stated that "I am a prophet of God. God himself will fight for me against you—and He will win"; Robert Walters, "Robertson's Holy Crusade," *The Frederick Post*, Frederick, MD, July 28, 1986. Similarly, John W. Robbins, writing from a Reformed perspective, has argued that "Pat Robertson's gospel is a gospel of experience. He has had experiences that he wants to share with everyone. He has been 'born again.' He has been 'baptized with the Spirit.' He has spoken in 'tongues.' He has performed 'miracles.' He has heard the 'voice of God' thousands of times. God has 'nudged' him. God has given him 'peace.' One looks in vain through his books and newsletters for a discussion of the attributes of God, the origin of the Bible, the person and work of Jesus Christ—the historical Christ, not the experiential Christ—the definition of faith, or the meaning of justification. All the major doctrines of Christianity are either totally missing from his writings or mentioned in passing with little or no discussion"; Robbins, *Pat Robertson*, p. 16.

86. Robertson, *The End of the Age*, p. 117; Martin, *With God on Our Side*, pp. 259–60.

87. Harding, *The Book of Jerry Falwell*, pp. 247–48.

88. The internal dynamics of the Robertson campaign are described in Balmer, *Mine Eyes Have Seen the Glory*, pp. 147–75.

89. Nevertheless, Robertson's conservatism should not be overstated: "Pat Robertson's political views, even though many of his supporters are conservatives, are not all conservative. He favors the repudiation of the national debt, the cancellation of all private debt, the periodic redistribution of 'all accumulated property,' the formation of an international police force, massive foreign aid, government control of education, and a military draft"; Robbins, *Pat Robertson*, p. 95.

90. Mark G. Toulouse, "Pat Robertson: Apocalyptic Theology and American Foreign Policy," *Journal of Church and State* 31:1 (1989), pp. 73–99, argued that Robertson had been expecting the end-time scenario to begin around 1982.

91. Baumgartner, *Longing for the End*, p. 240.

92. Robertson, *The Secret Kingdom*, pp. 15–16.

93. Baumgartner, *Longing for the End*, p. 240.

94. Gary North, *Is the World Running Down? Crisis in the Christian Worldview* (Tyler, TX: Institute for Christian Economics, 1988), p. 245; Stephen D. O'Leary and

Michael McFarland, "The Political use of Mythic Discourse: Prophetic Interpretation in Pat Robertson's Presidential Campaign," *Quarterly Journal of Speech* 75 (1989), pp. 433–52; O'Leary, *Arguing the Apocalypse*, pp. 184–89. Bruce Barron has described Robertson's relationship with the Reconstructionist movement; *Heaven on Earth? The Social and Political Agendas of Dominion Theology* (Grand Rapids, MI: Zondervan, 1992), pp. 53–66, 98–101. See also Baumgartner, *Longing for the End*, p. 240.

95. Balmer, *Mine Eyes Have Seen the Glory*, p. 173.

96. Michael Lienesch, *Redeeming America: Piety and Politics in the New Christian Right* (Chapel Hill: University of North Carolina Press, 1993), pp. 227–28.

97. O'Leary quotes their comments; *Arguing the Apocalypse*, p. 187.

98. Pat Robertson, *Answers to 200 of Life's Most Probing Questions* (Nashville, TN: Thomas Nelson, 1984), p. 158.

99. Robertson, *The Secret Kingdom*, p. 83.

100. The latter-rain doctrine is explained in Peter Althouse, "Left Behind—Fact or Fiction: Ecumenical Dilemmas of the Fundamentalist Millenarian Tensions within Pentecostalism," *Journal of Pentecostal Theology* 13 (2005), pp. 187–207.

101. Lienesch, *Redeeming America*, p. 244.

102. Justin Watson, "How Pat Finally Gets Even: Apocalyptic Asteroids and American Politics in Pat Robertson's *The End of the Age*," *Journal of Millennial Studies* (winter 2000), p. 4, available at www.mille.org.

103. Robertson, *The Secret Kingdom*, p. 30.

104. Pat Robertson, *The New World Order: It Will Change the Way You Live* (Dallas, TX: Word, 1991); Ephraim Radner, "New World Order, Old World Anti-Semitism—Pat Robertson of the Christian Coalition," *Christian Century*, September 13, 1995.

105. Barkun, *A Culture of Conspiracy*, p. 63.

106. Ibid., p. 53.

107. Ibid., p. 53.

108. The first reference to Israel in *The End of the Age* occurs on p. 313.

109. Robertson, *The End of the Age*, pp. 166, 170.

110. Ibid., pp. 37, 59, 252.

111. Ibid., p. 258. Spiritual warfare tropes are evidenced in the novel in that Beaulieu's New Age religion had actually been developed by "demons and demon princes"; ibid., p. 150.

112. Ibid., pp. 259, 261.

113. Ibid., p. 260.

114. Ibid., pp. 259–60.

115. Ibid., p. 117.

116. Ibid., p. 178.

117. Ibid., p. 295.

118. Ibid., p. 297.

119. Ibid., p. 298.

120. Ibid., p. 299.

121. Ibid., p. 300.

122. Ibid., pp. 285–86.

123. Ibid., p. 52.

124. Ibid., pp. 213–14, 221.

125. Ibid., pp. 308, 347.

126. Ibid., p. 347.

127. Ibid., p. 308.

128. Ibid., p. 139.

129. Ibid., p. 112. On the rally, see Harding, *The Book of Jerry Falwell*, pp. 20–21.

130. Robertson, *The End of the Age*, p. 339.

131. Jonathan Edwards's postmillennialism is outlined in Jonathan Edwards, *Apocalyptic Writings*, ed. Stephen J. Stein, The Works of Jonathan Edwards, vol. 5 (New Haven, CT: Yale University Press, 1977), pp. 15–53. Jonathan Edwards identified the collapse of Roman Catholicism as a significant end-time sign; Marsden, *Jonathan Edwards*, p. 88–90, 196–98, 337, 415–16

132. Robertson, *The End of the Age*, p. 140.

133. Ibid., p. 141.

134. Ibid., pp. 49–50, 147.

135. Ibid., p. 142.

136. Ibid., pp. 17, 55, 60, 210, 341.

137. Lindsey, *Blood Moon*, p. 95.

138. Robertson, *The End of the Age*, p. 343.

139. Ibid., p. 337.

140. Ibid., pp. 306–7, 337. Ernest Callenbach's *Ecotopia: The Notebooks and Reports of William Weston* (New York: Bantam Books, 1975) also involves its characters in nuclear blackmail in defense of the dissident regions in the Pacific Northwest.

141. Robertson, *The End of the Age*, pp. 327, 344.

142. Ibid., pp. 338, 361.

143. Ibid., pp. 46–52, 67–74.

144. Ibid., pp. 47–48, 178. The comment is made ironic by the fact that it comes from Pastor Jack Edwards, a descendent of Jonathan Edwards, perhaps the most famous postmillennialist in American religious history.

145. Ibid., pp. 121, 221.

146. Ibid., pp. 67–70, 138. Many of these signs of the times had been listed in Robertson, *Answers to 200 of Life's Most Probing Questions*, pp. 151–64.

147. Robertson, *The End of the Age*, pp. 180–91.

148. Ibid., p. 50.

149. Ibid., pp. 182–83.

150. Ibid., p. 183; Robertson, *The Secret Kingdom*, p. 13.

151. Robertson, *The New Millennium*, p. 313; Lienesch, *Redeeming America*, p. 243.

152. Robertson, *The New Millennium*, p. 312.

153. Ibid., p. 313.

154. Robertson, *The End of the Age*, p. 183.

155. Melling, *Fundamentalism in America*, pp. 77, 82–83.

156. Harding, *The Book of Jerry Falwell*, p. ix.

157. Ibid., p. 18.

158. Robertson, *The End of the Age*, p. 90.

159. Judith Gale, *A Promise of Forever* (Pittsburgh, PA: Dorrance, 1997), pp. 53, 59.

160. "Petra" is consistently misspelled in Gale, *A Promise of Forever*.

161. Martin, *Emerald Thorn*, p. 331.

162. Robertson, *The End of the Age*, p. 108.

163. The Antichrist also comes to control Robertson's rival network, the Trinity Broadcasting Network; Tim LaHaye and Jerry B. Jenkins, *Tribulation Force* (Wheaton, IL: Tyndale House, 1996), p. 338.

164. Robertson, *The End of the Age*, p. 362.

CHAPTER 6

1. Blodgett, *Protestant Evangelical Literary Culture and Contemporary Society*, pp. 157–59, contains an appendix listing the most significant genres in evangelical literary culture: biblical fiction, romance fiction, fantasy/science fiction, spiritual warfare, historical novels, westerns, action/adventure and mystery. Tim LaHaye is mentioned once in the text—and on that occasion his surname is misspelled (p. 116).

2. Jones, "The Liberal Antichrist," p. 98. This list of sales does not include data from Christian bookshops—which would have sold many more copies of the novels.

3. Bruce David Forbes, "How Popular Are the Left Behind Books," p. 8. See also Robert G. Clouse, Robert N. Hosack, and Richard V. Pierard, *The New Millennium Manual: A Once and Future Guide* (Grand Rapids, MI: Baker, 1999), p. 135; Paul S. Fiddes, "Facing the End: The Apocalyptic Experience in Some Modern Novels," in John Colwell (ed.), *Called to One Hope: Perspectives on the Life to Come* (Carlisle, UK: Paternoster, 2000), pp. 191–209; and Thomas M. Doyle, "Competing Fictions: The Uses of Christian Apocalyptic Imagery in Contemporary Popular Fictional Works," *Journal of Millennial Studies* 1:1 (2001), available at www.mille.org.

4. Guyatt, *Have a Nice Doomsday*, p. 217.

5. Ibid., p. 216.

6. *Left Behind* (dir. Vic Sarin, 2000); Michael Standaert, *Skipping towards Armageddon: The Politics and Propaganda of the Left Behind Novels and the LaHaye Empire* (Brooklyn, NY: Soft Skull Press, 2006), p. 22. The film was released to video in 2000 before being released into cinemas in 2001.

7. "*Left Behind* Fans Clamor for *The Remnant*," available at www.leftbehind.com, accessed August 7, 2002.

8. "Series Sells 50 Millionth Copy (January 14, 2002)," available at www.left behind.com, accessed August 7, 2002.

9. Nancy Gibbs, "The Bible and the Apocalypse," *Time*, July 1, 2002, repr. in the UK edition of *Time*, August 19, 2002, pp. 46–53. Gibbs suggests that the successful marketing of the series indicates that "interest in End Times is no fringe phenomenon" (p. 48).

10. Forbes, "How Popular Are the Left Behind Books," pp. 8–9.

11. On the video game controversy, see www.leftbehindgames.com/pages/controversy.htm, accessed November 18, 2006.

12. Blodgett, *Protestant Evangelical Literary Culture and Contemporary Society*, p. 45.

13. Sales figures quoted in Steve Rabey, "No Longer Left Behind," *Christianity Today*, April 22, 2002, p. 28.

14. Tim LaHaye, Jerry B. Jenkins, and Sandi L. Swanson, *The Authorized Left Behind Handbook* (Wheaton, IL: Tyndale House, 2005), p. 3.

15. Standaert, *Skipping towards Armageddon*, p. 19; David D. Kirkpatrick, "A Best-selling Formula in Religious Thrillers," *New York Times*, February 11, 2002. I owe this reference to Jennie Chapman. Hodder and Stoughton was established as a Christian publishing firm and published Sydney Watson's two volumes of autobiography. On trends in Christian publishing, see Richard Bartholomew, "Religious Mission and Business Reality: Trends in the Contemporary British Christian Book Industry," *Journal of Contemporary Religion* 20:1 (2005), pp. 41–42, and Gutjahr, "No Longer Left Behind," pp. 209–36.

16. Wojcik, "Embracing Doomsday," p. 305. See also Kirsch, "Hal Lindsey," pp. 30–32.

17. Tim LaHaye, "Preface," in Todd Strandberg and Terry James, *Are You Rapture Ready? Signs, Prophecies, Warnings, Threats, and Suspicions That the Endtime Is Now* (New York: Dutton, 2003), p. xii.

18. LaHaye, Jenkins, and Swanson, *The Authorized Left Behind Handbook*, p. 9.

19. Frykholm claims that this disparity can be traced even in the novels themselves; *Rapture Culture*, p. 30. This division is also evident in the interview with LaHaye and Jenkins in *The Authorized Left Behind Handbook*, pp. 14, 16, 18. On the diffusion of Left Behind products, see Malcolm Gold, "The *Left Behind* Series as Sacred Text," in Elizabeth Arweck and Peter Collins (eds.), *Reading Religion in Text and Context* (Aldershot, UK: Ashgate, 2006), pp. 34–49.

20. LaHaye, Jenkins, and Swanson, *The Authorized Left Behind Handbook*, pp. 14–18.

21. Ibid., p. 22. Jenkins appears to have expressed some embarrassment at LaHaye's controversial political outbursts; David Gates, "Religion: The Pop Prophets," *Newsweek*, May 24, 2004. I owe this point to Jennie Chapman.

22. I owe this information to Thomas Ice.

23. LaHaye, Jenkins, and Swanson, *The Authorized Left Behind Handbook*, p. 13.

24. Guyatt, *Have a Nice Doomsday*, p. 221. One of the movies' most remarkable innovations, for example, is an almost total failure to make any reference to Jesus Christ—a startling omission, when their dialogue is compared with that of the novels.

25. See www.boston.com/news/globe/living/articles/2006/12/13/groups_urge_chain_to_drop_christian_game/ and http://news.bbc.co.uk/1/hi/technology/6178055.stm, both accessed June 13, 2007.

26. The video game does, nevertheless, reinforce the gender politics of the series, in that female characters are much less useful than male characters in achieving goals; see Guyatt, *Have a Nice Doomsday*, pp. 223–28. Jennie Chapman claims that violence does become more explicit and central to the narrative in the later novels; see Chapman, "Selling Faith without Selling Out: Reading the Left Behind Novels in the Context of Popular Culture," in John Wallis and Kenneth G. C. Newport (eds.), *Apocalyptic Texts and Popular Culture* (London: Equinox, 2008).

27. Odom, *Apocalypse Dawn*, pp. 342, 363, 398.

28. Guyatt, *Have a Nice Doomsday*, pp. 230–43.

29. Ibid., pp. 237–38, 241.

30. See, respectively, McAlister, "Prophecy, Politics, and the Popular," pp. 773–98, and Jones, "The Liberal Antichrist," pp. 97–112; Ian S. Markham, "Engaging with the Theology That Really Sells," *Conversations in Religion and Theology* 1:2 (2003), pp. 115–18; Crawford Gribben, *Rapture Fiction and the Evangelical Crisis* (Webster, NY: Evangelical Press, 2006); Crawford Gribben, "After *Left Behind:* The Paradox of Evangelical Pessimism," in Kenneth G. C. Newport and Crawford Gribben (eds.), *Expecting the End: Millennialism in Social and Historical Context* (Baylor, TX: Baylor University Press, 2006), pp. 113–30; and Althouse, "'Left Behind'—Fact or Fiction," pp. 188–91.

31. Richard Morrison, "Armageddon Ahead, Please Fasten Your Bible Belt," *The Times* T2, September 20, 2002, pp. 2–3.

32. George Baxter Pfoertner, "The Profits of Doom," *The Independent on Sunday* magazine supplement, November 12, 2000, p. 10.

33. Christopher Tayler, "Rapt Attention," *Times Literary Supplement,* May 7, 2004, p. 36.

34. Tayler, "Rapt Attention," p. 36.

35. Nicholas D. Kristof, "Apocalypse (Almost) Now," *New York Times,* editorial, November 24, 2004, p. A23. I owe this reference to Jennie Chapman.

36. Gershom Gorenberg, *The End of Days: Fundamentalism and the Struggle for the Temple Mount* (New York: Oxford University Press, 2002), p. 32.

37. Frykholm, "What Social Messages Appear in the *Left Behind* Books?" pp. 167–95.

38. Shuck, *Marks of the Beast,* p. xiii.

39. Frykholm, *Rapture Culture,* pp. 89, 178; Anne Lamott, "Knocking on Heaven's Door," in *Travelling Mercies: Some Thoughts on Faith* (New York: Pantheon, 1999), p. 60. Frykholm warns against the paranoid reading style that finds the novels a confirmation of existing fears about Christian fundamentalists.

40. Jones, "The Liberal Antichrist," p. 104.

41. Flesher, *Left Behind? The Facts behind the Fiction,* p. 50.

42. David B. Currie, *Rapture: The End-times Error That Leaves the Bible Behind* (Manchester, NH: Sophia Institute Press, 2003), p. 378, 380–81.

43. Tim Kirk, *I Want to Be "Left Behind": An Examination of the Ideas behind the Popular Series and the End Times* (New York: Writers Club Press, 2002), pp. 29–82.

44. Daniel Hertzler, "Assessing the 'Left Behind' Phenomenon," in Loren L. Johns (ed.), *Apocalypticism and Millennialism: Shaping a Believers Church Eschatology for the Twenty-first Century* (Kitchener, ON: Pandora, 2000), p. 363. See also Gary DeMar, *End Times Fiction: A Biblical Consideration of the Left Behind Theology* (Nashville, TN: Thomas Nelson, 2001).

45. Quoted in Mark Reasoner, "What Does the Bible Say about the End Times? A Biblical Studies Discussion of Interpretive Methods," in Bruce David Forbes and Jeanne Halgren Kilde (eds.), *Rapture, Revelation and the End Times: Exploring the Left Behind Series* (New York: Palgrave Macmillan, 2004), p. 90. Mark Sweetnam

makes a similar point in his essay on "Tensions in Dispensational Eschatology," pp. 173–92. Other prophecy believers, writing on the Internet and with considerably less scholarly panache, have claimed that the novels reveal their authors' commitment to Satanism; see, for example, James Whisler, "Left Behind's and LaHaye's Masonic Connections," available at http://watch.pair.com/lahaye.html, accessed January 7, 2008.

46. Nathan D. Wilson, *Right Behind: A Parody of Last Days Goofiness* (Moscow, ID: Canon, 2001), p. 9.

47. Hank Hanegraaff and Sigmund Brouwer, *The Last Disciple* (Wheaton, IL: Tyndale House, 2004), pp. 393–94.

48. Ibid., p. 395.

49. Tim LaHaye, "Introduction," in Mark Hitchcock and Thomas Ice, *The Truth behind Left Behind: A Biblical View of the End Times* (Sisters, OR: Multnomah, 2004), p. 7.

50. LaHaye, "Introduction," in Hitchcock and Ice, *The Truth behind Left Behind*, p. 6.

51. Hitchcock and Ice, *The Truth behind Left Behind*, p. 17.

52. LaHaye, Jenkins, and Swanson, *The Authorized Left Behind Handbook*, p. 17.

53. Ibid., p. 8.

54. Ibid., p. 7.

55. William T. James, "When Millions Vanish!" in William T. James (ed.), *Raging into Apocalypse* (Green Forest, AR: New Leaf, 1995), p. 67. The same quotation is found in William T. James, "Suddenly Gone!" in William T. James (ed.), *Prophecy at Ground Zero: From Today's Mideast Madness to the Second Coming of Christ* (Lancaster, PA: Starburst, 2002), p. 202.

56. Tim LaHaye, "America's Perilous Times Have Come," in William T. James (ed.), *Forewarning: Approaching the Final Battle between Heaven and Hell* (Eugene, OR: Harvest House, 1998), p. 235.

57. "LaHaye, Tim," in Randall Balmer, *Encyclopedia of Evangelicalism* (Louisville, KY: Westminster John Knox, 2002), pp. 327–28. See also Guyatt, *Have a Nice Doomsday*, pp. 245–77.

58. LaHaye, Jenkins, and Swanson, *The Authorized Left Behind Handbook*, p. 8.

59. This older variant of dispensationalism is endorsed in contrast to the "progressive dispensationalism" expounded by Blaising and Bock, *Progressive Dispensationalism*. For a detailed study of the polemic see Heath Carter, "The Left Behind Series: An Evangelical Apocalypse" (theology honors thesis, Georgetown University, 2003).

60. Watson, *In the Twinkling of an Eye*, pp. 12, 46.

61. The extras on the *Thief in the Night* DVD explained this with reference to 1 Corinthians 7:14.

62. Tim LaHaye and Jerry B. Jenkins, *The Remnant* (Wheaton, IL: Tyndale House, 2002), p. 343.

63. LaHaye and Jenkins, *Tribulation Force*, p. 53.

64. Ibid., p. 273; J. N. D. Kelly, *The Oxford Dictionary of Popes* (Oxford: Oxford University Press, 1986), s.v.

65. LaHaye and Jenkins, *Tribulation Force*, p. 279.

66. Quoted in Forbes, "How Popular Are the Left Behind Books," p. 22.

67. LaHaye, Jenkins, and Swanson, *The Authorized Left Behind Handbook,* p. 13.

68. Forbes, "How Popular Are the Left Behind Books," p. 21.

69. LaHaye and Jenkins, *Tribulation Force,* p. 27.

70. Ibid., p. 251.

71. Tim LaHaye and Jerry B. Jenkins, *Assassins* (Wheaton, IL: Tyndale House, 1999), p. 50; Boyer, *When Time Shall Be No More,* pp. 282–83.

72. LaHaye and Jenkins, *The Mark,* pp. 17, 85.

73. Ibid., p. 156.

74. Tim LaHaye and Jerry B. Jenkins, *Apollyon* (Wheaton, IL: Tyndale House, 1999), pp. 104–5.

75. LaHaye and Jenkins, *Assassins,* p. 354.

76. LaHaye, Jenkins, and Swanson, *The Authorized Left Behind Handbook,* p. 29.

77. LaHaye and Jenkins, *The Mark,* p. 333.

78. LaHaye and Jenkins, *Tribulation Force,* pp. 150, 388, 360.

79. Tim LaHaye and Jerry B. Jenkins, *Nicolae* (Wheaton, IL: Tyndale House, 1997), p. 132, cf. p. 370.

80. LaHaye and Jenkins, *Apollyon,* p. 61.

81. LaHaye and Jenkins, *The Mark,* p. 334.

82. Tim LaHaye and Jerry B. Jenkins, *Soul Harvest* (Wheaton, IL: Tyndale House, 1998), p. 324.

83. LaHaye and Jenkins, *Tribulation Force,* p. 29.

84. Ibid., pp. 357, 370.

85. Ibid., p. 127.

86. Ibid., p. 424; LaHaye and Jenkins, *Nicolae,* p. 143.

87. LaHaye and Jenkins, *Tribulation Force,* p. 444.

88. Ibid., pp. 34, 45.

89. Ibid., pp. 65–66.

90. LaHaye and Jenkins, *Nicolae,* p. 359.

91. LaHaye and Jenkins, *Tribulation Force,* p. 366.

92. LaHaye and Jenkins, *Desecration,* p. 179.

93. Ibid., p. 179; LaHaye and Jenkins, *Assassins,* p. 334.

94. LaHaye and Jenkins, *The Remnant,* p. 328.

95. LaHaye and Jenkins, *Apollyon,* p. 258.

96. LaHaye and Jenkins, *Desecration,* p. 100.

97. LaHaye and Jenkins, *Apollyon,* p. 295; LaHaye and Jenkins, *The Remnant,* pp. 253–54; LaHaye and Jenkins, *Desecration,* p. 120.

98. Bartholomew, "Religious Mission and Business Reality," p. 50.

99. "Left Behind: Stronger than Fiction," *Today's Christian* 40:6 (November/December 2002), p. 14.

100. Gutjahr, "No Longer Left Behind," p. 226.

101. LaHaye, Jenkins, and Swanson, *The Authorized Left Behind Handbook,* p. 20.

102. Ibid., p. 4.

103. Ibid., p. 9.

104. McAlister, "Prophecy, Politics and the Popular," pp. 778, 792–93.

105. LaHaye and Jenkins, *Apollyon,* pp. 7, 192, 357; LaHaye and Jenkins, *Assassins,* p. 183; LaHaye and Jenkins, *The Mark,* p. 140; LaHaye and Jenkins, *The Remnant,* pp. 232, 323, 360.

106. LaHaye and Jenkins, *The Mark,* p. 147.

107. John J. Collins, "Introduction: Towards the Morphology of a Genre," *Semeia* 14 (1979), p. 7.

108. Watson, *The Mark of the Beast,* p. 56.

109. LaHaye and Jenkins, *Soul Harvest,* p. 176.

CHAPTER 7

1. For example, Warner Vision and Dell republished James BeauSeigneur's The Christ Clone Trilogy (1997–98; 2003–4) and Robert D. Van Kampen's *The Fourth Reich* (1997; 2000)—texts that challenged in fundamental ways traditional descriptions of the rapture.

2. Odom, *Apocalypse Dawn,* pp. 342, 363, 398.

3. Van Kampen, *The Fourth Reich,* p. 81.

4. Other aspects of Lindsey's interest in political Islam are addressed in Guyatt, *Have a Nice Doomsday,* pp. 187–88.

5. Michael Hyatt and George Grant, *Y2K: The Day the World Shut Down* (Nashville, TN: Word, 1998), p. 264.

6. Hanegraaff and Brouwer, *The Last Disciple,* p. 394.

7. Guyatt, *Have a Nice Doomsday,* pp. 279–305.

8. Ibid., p. 280.

9. Ibid., p. 290.

10. Barkun, *A Culture of Conspiracy,* describes a range of FEMA conspiracy theories.

11. LaHaye and Phillips, *The Secret on Ararat,* pp. 323–24. LaHaye and Phillips had previously coauthored the nonfictional psychological study, *Anger Is a Choice* (Grand Rapids, MI: Zondervan, 1983).

12. Lindsey, *The Late Great Planet Earth,* pp. 43, 45.

13. "End Times," *TIME,* June 23, 2002, available at www.time.com/time/covers/1101020701/story3.html, accessed January 8, 2008.

14. Paul Boyer makes a rare reference to *Blood Moon* in "The Middle East in Modern American Prophetic Belief," in Abbas Amanat and Magnus Bernhardsson (eds.), *Imagining the End: Visions of Apocalypse from the Ancient Middle East to Modern America* (London: I. B. Tauris, 2002), p. 331.

15. Lindsey, *Blood Moon,* p. 7.

16. Ibid., p. 67.

17. Ibid., p. 252.

18. Lindsey, *The Late Great Planet Earth,* p. 50.

19. Ibid., p. 7.

20. Lindsey, *Blood Moon,* pp. 6–7;

21. Lindsey, *The Late Great Planet Earth,* p. 54.

22. For "ascetic Jews," read "Hasidic Jews," and for "marshal law," read "martial law"; Young, *The Last Hour*, pp. 41, 61, 89.

23. Ibid., p. 9.

24. Ibid., pp. 9, 95.

25. Ibid., pp. 87, 110.

26. Ibid., p. 112.

27. The novel is set in the immediate aftermath of the death of Yitzhak Rabin (d. 1995); ibid., p. 165.

28. Ibid., p. 113.

29. Ibid., p. 113.

30. Ibid., p. 22.

31. Later this is blamed on "the Christian Right"; ibid., p. 110. It is significant in terms of the author's attempted self-fashioning of an evangelical identity that the novel implies the two groups can be plausibly conflated; ibid., pp. 64, 75. The First Lady also assumes presidential power in Robertson, *The End of the Age*.

32. Young, *The Last Hour*, p. 65.

33. Ibid., p. 169.

34. Ibid., pp. 117, 124, 134, 145, 151.

35. Ibid., p. 48.

36. Ibid., p. 34.

37. Ibid., p. 160.

38. Ibid., pp. 120–21.

39. Ibid., pp. 60, 137, 226, 247.

40. Ibid., p. 103.

41. Ibid., p. 139.

42. Ibid., pp. 27, 165.

43. Ibid., p. 88.

44. Ibid., pp. 131, 139.

45. Ibid., p. 127.

46. Hyatt and Grant, *Y2K*, p. 68.

47. Ibid., p. 159.

48. Ibid., p. 264.

49. Ibid., p. 41.

50. Ibid., pp. 63, 75; "How the Year 2000 Bug Will Hurt the Economy," *Business Week*, March 2, 1998, pp. 46–51.

51. Hyatt and Grant, *Y2K*, p. 49.

52. Ibid., p. 1.

53. Ibid., p. 84.

54. The prophetic culture that provided several of these myths has been described in Boyer, *When Time Shall Be No More*.

55. Hyatt and Grant, *Y2K*, p. 114.

56. Ibid., pp. 111–12.

57. Ibid., p. 165.

58. Ibid., p. 173.

59. Ibid., pp. 227–32.

60. Ibid., pp. 191, 203

61. Ibid., p. 207.

62. Ibid., p. 151.

63. Nancy A. Schaefer, "Y2K as an Endtime Sign: Apocalypticism in America at the *Fin-de-millennium*," *Journal of Popular Culture* 38:1 (2004), p. 88.

64. Hyatt and Grant, *Y2K,* p. 3.

65. James BeauSeigneur, *Acts of God,* The Christ Clone Trilogy (1998; reissued New York: Warner, 2004), p. 45.

66. James BeauSeigneur, *Military Avionics: Market Survey and Analysis* (Arlington, VA: Technology Trends Corporation, 1985) and *Strategic Defense* (Arlington, VA: Technology Trends Corporation, 1986).

67. See www.swcp.com/christian-fandom/oli-jbs.html, accessed January 21, 2007.

68. BeauSeigneur, *Acts of God,* p. 80; BeauSeigneur, *In His Image,* pp. 105, 132, 495.

69. See www.swcp.com/christian-fandom/oli-jbs.html, accessed January 21, 2007.

70. BeauSeigneur, *In His Image,* "Important Note from the Author," p. 217, n. 31; p. 462 n. 64; BeauSeigneur, *Birth of an Age,* p. 246.

71. BeauSeigneur has acknowledged wide research in scientific literature; see www.swcp.com/christian-fandom/oli-jbs.html, accessed January 21, 2007.

72. BeauSeigneur, *In His Image,* pp. 78–85.

73. BeauSeigneur, *Acts of God,* p. 141. The closest parallel is provided in Ken Abraham and Daniel Hart, *The Prodigal Project* (London: Hodder and Stoughton, 2003), in which the bodies of raptured believers are subject to instantaneous and "almost total decomposition" (p. 148).

74. BeauSeigneur, *Acts of God,* p. 142.

75. BeauSeigneur, *In His Image,* pp. 156, 163, 167, 168, 176.

76. BeauSeigneur, *Acts of God,* p. 300.

77. BeauSeigneur, *In His Image,* p. 314. Bush and Reagan, ironically, are pictured with BeauSeigneur on his Web site.

78. BeauSeigneur, *Acts of God,* pp. 149–64.

79. BeauSeigneur, *Birth of an Age,* p. 24.

80. BeauSeigneur, *Acts of God,* pp. 217, 354–59. On cognitive dissonance theory, see Leon Festinger, Henry W. Riecken, and Stanley Schachter, *When Prophecy Fails* (Minneapolis, MN: University of Minneapolis Press, 1956).

81. A structured argument from prophecy can be found on BeauSeigneur, *Acts of God,* p. 158.

82. BeauSeigneur, *In His Image,* p. 399.

83. BeauSeigneur, *Birth of an Age,* p. 271.

84. Ibid., p. 243.

85. BeauSeigneur, *In His Image,* p. 191.

86. See www.swcp.com/christian-fandom/oli-jbs.html, accessed January 21, 2007.

87. BeauSeigneur, *Acts of God,* pp. 51, 237.

88. Ibid., p. 46.

89. Ibid., pp. 57–58.

90. Ibid., p. 99.

91. Ibid., p. 100.

92. Ibid., p. 102.

93. Ibid., pp. 103, 105.

94. Ibid., pp. 209, 372.

95. Ibid., p. 195.

96. Ibid., p. 199.

97. Ibid., p. 209.

98. Jerry B. Jenkins, *Soon* (Wheaton, IL: Tyndale House, 2003), p. 4.

99. Ibid., pp. 10, 17.

100. Ibid., p. 9.

101. Ibid., pp. 4–5.

102. Ibid., p. 203.

103. Ibid., pp. 157, 199.

104. Ibid., p. 317.

105. Ibid., p. 318.

106. Ibid., p. 19.

107. Boyer, *When Time Shall Be No More*, pp. 225–53.

108. Marsden, *Jonathan Edwards*, pp. 197–98, 265–67.

109. Boyer, *When Time Shall Be No More*, pp. 225–53.

110. LaHaye and Jenkins, *Tribulation Force*, p. 29.

111. McAlister, "Prophecy, Politics and the Popular."

112. Boyer, *When Time Shall Be No More*, p. 177. The longevity of these prophetic polarities meant that this geopolitical analysis would have been familiar to such dispensational teachers as Donald Barnhouse in the 1950s, C. I. Scofield in the 1910s, and J. N. Darby in the 1840s.

113. Jenkins, *Soon*, pp. 34–35.

114. Ibid., p. 94. The expression is drawn from *The Economist*.

115. Shuck, *Marks of the Beast*, p. 24.

116. Boyer, *When Time Shall Be No More*, p. 258.

117. Kirban, *1000*, p. 67.

118. Jenkins, *Soon*, p. xv. The theories underlying these dispensational urban myths are represented in Boyer, *When Time Shall Be No More*, in the illustrations prior to p. 281.

119. Jenkins, *Soon*, p. 203.

120. Ibid., pp. 37–38.

121. Ibid., p. 262.

122. Ibid., pp. xiii, 38, 68.

123. Ibid., pp. 204, 295.

124. Richard Landes, "Millennialism," in James R. Lewis (ed.), *The Oxford Handbook of New Religious Movements* (Oxford: Oxford University Press, 2004), p. 340.

125. Jenkins, *Soon*, p. 105.

126. Ibid., pp. 35, 272. Indeed, the regime's strongly antireligious bias raises the question of where the predicted one-world religion will come from in a world where religion is illegal.

127. Steele's expression of thankfulness for being part of "the church" is a curious slip; LaHaye and Jenkins, *Assassins*, p. 70.

128. LaHaye and Jenkins, *Soul Harvest*, p. 364.

129. Ibid., p. 64, 84. Dispensational theologians teach that the Antichrist will be resurrected after an assassination to even great power.

130. Tim LaHaye and Jerry B. Jenkins, *The Indwelling* (Wheaton, IL: Tyndale House, 2000), p. 90.

131. Ibid., p. 166. Steele certainly has to undergo a rude awakening. Cameron "Buck" Williams was chagrined with his father-in-law's morality: "We don't play them, lie to them, cheat them, steal from them, blackmail them. We love them. We plead with them." Even in the tribulation, evangelicals had to love their enemies and try to win them to Christ; LaHaye and Jenkins, *Assassins*, p. 239.

132. The exodus/battle typology is explained in David G. Bromley, "Violence and New Religious Movements," in James R. Lewis (ed.), *The Oxford Handbook of New Religious Movements* (Oxford: Oxford University Press, 2004), p. 153.

133. Wilson, *Armageddon Now!* p. 186; Bromley, "Violence and New Religious Movements," p. 148.

134. Jenkins, *Soon*, p. 35.

135. Ibid., p. 199.

136. Ibid.

137. Ibid., p. 302.

138. Ibid., pp. 313, 317.

139. Ibid., p. 296.

140. Ibid., p. 347.

141. Bromley, "Violence and New Religious Movements," p. 151.

142. Ibid., pp. 156, 159.

143. Ibid., p. 145.

144. Landes, "Millennialism," p. 334.

145. Jenkins, *Soon*, p. 304.

146. Ibid., pp. 28, 201.

147. McAlister, "Prophecy, Politics and the Popular," p. 775.

148. Frykholm, *Rapture Culture*, p. 52.

149. Reader responses have been described by Frykholm.

150. Jenkins, *Soon*, p. 302.

CONCLUSION

1. On the deprivation thesis, see Sweet, "Millennialism in America: Recent Studies," pp. 512–13. "Born-again Christians in America today have roughly the same class, educational, and occupational profile as the population as a whole"; Harding, *The Book of Jerry Falwell*, p. 232.

2. Thorne, "The Revolutionary Energy of the Outmoded," p. 99; Milich, "Fundamentalism Hot and Cold: George W. Bush and the 'Return of the Sacred,'" pp. 92, 108.

3. Balmer, *Mine Eyes Have Seen the Glory,* pp. 290, 338.

4. Balmer makes the claim that evangelicalism has moved from being a counter-culture to a subculture; ibid., p. 299.

5. Brenneman, *Virtual Reality,* p. 86. Tim LaHaye has confirmed this calculation.

6. "People of colour are usually absent from Christian media, and when they do appear, it is not unusual for them to be marked as "the other" . . . for the most part, evangelical media are made by whites and for whites"; Hendershot, *Shaking the World for Jesus,* p. 10.

7. Marsden, *Fundamentalism and American Culture,* pp. 231–57.

8. Myers, *The Trumpet Sounds,* p. 17.

9. Bebbington, *Evangelicalism in Modern Britain,* pp. 17–18.

10. Ironically, for example, Wade's Seventh-day Adventist novel contains more encouragements to "evangelical" faith than do the ostensibly evangelical novels by Cerullo and Balizet.

11. I have explored this issue in *Rapture Fiction and the Evangelical Crisis.*

12. LaHaye, "America's Perilous Times Have Come," p. 269.

13. Pat Robertson, as quoted in Lienesch, *Redeeming America,* p. 245.

Bibliography

This bibliography distinguishes between primary and secondary publications. Nonfiction titles by authors of prophecy fiction are listed as primary sources. Some of these sources appear in the text and notes.

PRIMARY SOURCES

Abraham, Ken, and Daniel Hart. *Genesis* (New York: Plume, 2003).
———. *The Prodigal Project* (London: Hodder and Stoughton, 2003).
———. *Exodus* (New York: Plume, 2004).
———. *Kings* (New York: Plume, 2004).
———. *Numbers* (New York: Plume, 2004).
Andrews, C. W. *Religious Novels: An Argument against Their Use* (New York: Anson D. F. Randolph, 1856).
Angley, Ernest W. *Raptured* (Wilmington, NC: Carolina Press, 1950).
Balizet, Carol. *The Seven Last Years* (Lincoln, VA: Chosen Books, 1978).
———. *Born in Zion* (Grapevine, TX: ChristCenter Publications International, 1996).
Beaucage, David R. *The Shiloh Project* (Tulsa, OK: Virgil W. Hensley, 1993).
BeauSeigneur, James. *Military Avionics: Market Survey and Analysis* (Arlington, VA: Technology Trends Corporation, 1985).
———. *Strategic Defense* (Arlington, VA: Technology Trends Corporation, 1986).
———. *Birth of an Age,* The Christ Clone Trilogy (1997; reissued New York: Warner, 2003).
———. *In His Image,* The Christ Clone Trilogy (1997; reissued New York: Warner, 2003).
———. *Acts of God,* The Christ Clone Trilogy (1998; reissued New York: Warner, 2004).

Benson, R. H. *Lord of the World* (1907; repr. Cirencester, UK: Echo Library, 2007).

Betzer, Dan. *Beast: A Novel of the Future World Dictator* (Lafayette, LA: Prescott, 1985).

Blackstone, W. E. *Jesus Is Coming* (Chicago: Moody, 1898).

Brenneman, Jean D. *Virtual Reality (It's No Dream)* (Lima, OH: Allendale, 1997).

Brown, Charles Brockden. *Wieland* (New York: T. and J. Swords, for H. Caritat, 1798).

Brown, Dan. *The Da Vinci Code* (New York: Doubleday, 2003).

Bullinger, E. W., ed. *The Companion Bible* (London: Lamp Press, 1909).

Bunyan, John. *The Pilgrim's Progress,* ed. N. H. Keeble, The World's Classics (Oxford: Oxford University Press, 1984).

Burkett, Larry. *The Illuminati* (Nashville, TN: Thomas Nelson, 1991).

Burroughs, Joseph Birkbeck. *Titan, Son of Saturn: The Coming World Emperor: A Story of the Other Christ* (Oberlin, OH: Emeth, 1905, 1917).

Caldwell, Brian. *We All Fall Down* (Haverford, PA: Infinity, 2000).

Callenbach, Ernest. *Ecotopia: The Notebooks and Reports of William Weston* (New York: Bantam Books, 1975).

Cash, Jonathan R. *The Age of the Antichrist* (Hanover, MA: Christopher, 1999).

Cerullo, Morris. *The Omega Project* (San Diego, CA: World Evangelism, 1981).

Codrescu, Andrei. *Messiah: A Novel* (New York: Simon and Schuster, 1999).

Cohen, Gary G. *Understanding Revelation: A Chronology of the Apocalypse* (Chicago: Moody, 1968).

———. *Israel: Land of Prophecy, Land of Promise* (1974; repr. Eagan, MN: Abiding Word, 1988).

———. *The Horsemen Are Coming* (Chicago: Moody, 1979; first published as *Civilization's Last Hurrah: A Futuristic Novel about the End,* 1974).

Collier, John. *Choices: The Story of Three Young Men, Friends and Recent High School Graduates Whose Lives Are Changed by the Rapture and the Following Tribulation Period* (Columbus, GA: Brentwood Christian, 1996).

David, James F. *Judgment Day* (New York: Forge, 2005).

De Gruijter, Erik. *De Laatste Week* (Apeldoorn, Netherlands: Novapres, 1999).

A Distant Thunder (1978). Directed by Donald W. Thompson.

Dixon, A. C., Louis Meyer, and R. A. Torrey, eds. *The Fundamentals: A Testimony to the Truth,* 12 vols. (Chicago: Testimony, 1910–15).

Dolan, David. *The End of Days* (1995; repr. Springfield, MO: 21st Century Press, 2003).

Edwards, Jonathan. *Apocalyptic Writings,* ed. Stephen J. Stein (New Haven, CT: Yale University Press, 1977).

Everest, Mortimer. *What Will Have Happened* (Johnstown, NY: Mortimer Everest, 1936).

Folkee, Norman. *The Last Trumpet* (Monterey, CA: Nachman, 1978).

Foster, Joshua Hill. *The Christian Preacher: A Sermon Delivered in the Baptist Church, Tuscaloosa, Ala., at the Ordination of the Pastor Elect, the Rev. Joshua H. Foster, on Sunday, March 13th, 1853* (Tuscaloosa, AL, 1853).

———. *The Judgment Day: A Story of the Seven Years of Great Tribulation* (Louisville, KY: Baptist World, 1910).

———. *Sixty-four Years a Minister* (Wilmington, NC: First Baptist Church, 1948).

Fowler Wright, Sidney. *Deluge,* ed. Brian Stableford, Early Classics of Science Fiction (1927; Middletown, CT: Wesleyan University Press, 2003).

Gale, Judith. *A Promise of Forever* (Pittsburgh, PA: Dorrance, 1997).

Gardner, Jim. *Time, Times, and Half a Time* (New York: Vantage, 1997).

Gosse, Edmund. *Father and Son: A Study of Two Temperaments* (1907; London: Penguin, 1989).

Grant, Jean. *The Revelation: A Novel* (Nashville, TN: Word, 1992).

Hanegraaff, Hank, and Sigmund Brouwer. *The Last Disciple* (Wheaton, IL: Tyndale House, 2004).

———. *The Last Sacrifice* (Wheaton, IL: Tyndale House, 2005).

———. *Fuse of Armageddon* (Wheaton, IL: Tyndale House, 2007).

Hardy, Thomas. *A Laodicean* (1881; London: Penguin, 1997).

Harris, W. S. *Life in a Thousand Worlds* (Harrisburg, PA: Minter, 1905).

———. *Capital and Labor* (Harrisburg, PA: Minter, 1907).

Harriss, Nellie Scott. *Ruth's Rapture: The Book of Revelation in Story* (Los Angeles: privately printed, n.d.).

Hart, Neesa. *End of State* (Wheaton, IL: Tyndale House, 2004).

———. *Impeachable Offense* (Wheaton, IL: Tyndale House, 2004).

———. *Necessary Evils* (Wheaton, IL: Tyndale House, 2005).

Heinlein, Robert A. *Job: A Comedy of Justice* (New York: Ballantine, 1984).

Hill, Grace Livingston. *Dwelling* (Philadelphia, PA: J. B. Lippincott, 1938).

Hitchcock, Mark, and Thomas Ice. *The Truth behind Left Behind: A Biblical View of the End Times* (Sisters, OR: Multnomah, 2004).

Hunt, Dave. *The Archon Conspiracy* (Eugene, OR: Harvest House, 1989).

Hyatt, Michael. *The Millennium Bug: How to Survive the Coming Chaos* (Washington, DC: Regnery, 1998).

Hyatt, Michael, and George Grant. *Y2K: The Day the World Shut Down* (Nashville, TN: Word, 1998).

Ice, Thomas. "The Shout Heard around the World: Overview of the Rapture," in William T. James, ed., *Forewarning: Approaching the Final Battle between Heaven and Hell* (Eugene, OR: Harvest House, 1998), pp. 293–307.

———. "Rapture before Wrath," in William T. James, ed., *Foreshadows of Wrath and Redemption* (Eugene, OR: Harvest House, 1999), pp. 317–29.

———. *Tribulation Survival Guide* (Sisters, OR: Multnomah, 2002).

Ice, Thomas, and Kenneth L. Gentry, Jr. *The Great Tribulation: Past or Future? Two Evangelicals Debate the Question* (Grand Rapids, MI: Kregel, 1999).

Ice, Thomas, and Randall Price. *Ready to Rebuild: The Imminent Plan to Rebuild the Last Days Temple* (Eugene, OR: Harvest House, 1992).

Image of the Beast (1980). Directed by Donald W. Thompson.

Jeffrey, Grant R., and Angela Hunt. *Flee the Darkness* (Nashville, TN: Word, 1998).

———. *By Dawn's Early Light* (Nashville, TN: Word, 1999).

———. *The Spear of Tyranny* (Nashville, TN: Word, 2000).

Jenkins, Jerry B. *Soon,* Soon Series 1 (Wheaton, IL: Tyndale House, 2003).

———. *Silenced,* Soon Series 2 (Wheaton, IL: Tyndale House, 2004).

———. *Shadowed,* Soon Series 3 (Wheaton, IL: Tyndale House, 2006).

Kirban, Salem. *666* (Wheaton, IL: Tyndale House, 1970).

———. *1000* (1973; Chattanooga, TN: Future Events, n.d.).

Kleier, Glenn. *The Last Day* (New York: Warner Vision, 1997).

Koontz, Dean. *The Servants of Twilight* (London: Headline, 1991).

LaHaye, Tim. *The Battle for the Mind: A Subtle Warfare* (Old Tappan, NJ: Revell, 1980).

———. "America's Perilous Times Have Come," in William T. James, ed., *Forewarning: Approaching the Final Battle between Heaven and Hell* (Eugene, OR: Harvest House, 1998), pp. 235–69.

———. "Russia on Edge," in William T. James, ed., *Foreshadows of Wrath and Redemption* (Eugene, OR: Harvest House, 1999), pp. 147–74.

———. "Introduction," in Mark Hitchcock and Thomas Ice, *The Truth behind Left Behind: A Biblical View of the End Times* (Sisters, OR: Multnomah, 2004), pp. 5–9.

LaHaye, Tim, and Greg Dinallo. *Babylon Rising*, Babylon Rising 1 (New York: Bantam, 2003).

LaHaye, Tim, and Jerry B. Jenkins. *Left Behind*, Left Behind Series 1 (Wheaton, IL: Tyndale House, 1995).

———. *Tribulation Force*, Left Behind Series 2 (Wheaton, IL: Tyndale House, 1996).

———. *Nicolae*, Left Behind Series 3 (Wheaton, IL: Tyndale House, 1997).

———. *Soul Harvest*, Left Behind Series 4 (Wheaton, IL: Tyndale House, 1998).

———. *Apollyon*, Left Behind Series 5 (Wheaton, IL: Tyndale House, 1999).

———. *Assassins*, Left Behind Series 6 (Wheaton, IL: Tyndale House, 1999).

———. *The Indwelling*, Left Behind Series 7 (Wheaton, IL: Tyndale House, 2000).

———. *The Mark*, Left Behind Series 8 (Wheaton, IL: Tyndale House, 2000).

———. *Are We Living in the End Times?* (Wheaton, IL: Tyndale House, 2001).

———. *Desecration*, Left Behind Series 9 (Wheaton, IL: Tyndale House, 2001).

———. *The Remnant*, Left Behind Series 10 (Wheaton, IL: Tyndale House, 2002).

———. *Armageddon*, Left Behind Series 11 (Wheaton, IL: Tyndale House, 2003).

———. *The Glorious Appearing*, Left Behind Series 12 (Wheaton, IL: Tyndale House, 2004).

———. *The Rising*, Countdown to the Rapture 1 (Wheaton, IL: Tyndale House, 2005).

———. *The Regime*, Countdown to the Rapture 2 (Wheaton, IL: Tyndale House, 2005).

———. *John's Story: The Last Eyewitness*, Jesus Chronicles 1 (Wheaton, IL: Tyndale House, 2006).

———. *The Rapture*, Countdown to the Rapture 3 (Wheaton, IL: Tyndale House, 2007).

———. *Kingdom Come: The Final Victory*, Left Behind Series Sequel (Wheaton, IL: Tyndale House, 2007).

LaHaye, Tim, Jerry B. Jenkins, and Norman B. Rohrer. *These Will Not Be Left Behind* (Wheaton, IL: Tyndale House, 2003).

LaHaye, Tim, Jerry B. Jenkins, and Sandi L. Swanson. *The Authorized Left Behind Handbook* (Wheaton, IL: Tyndale House, 2005).

LaHaye, Tim, and Bob Phillips. *Anger Is a Choice* (Grand Rapids, MI: Zondervan, 1983).

———. *The Secret on Ararat*, Babylon Rising 2 (New York: Bantam, 2004).

———. *The Europa Conspiracy*, Babylon Rising 3 (New York: Bantam, 2005).

———. *The Edge of Darkness*, Babylon Rising 4 (New York: Bantam, 2006).

Lalonde, Peter, and Patti Lalonde. *Left Behind* (Eugene, OR: Harvest House, n.d.).

Lalonde, Peter, and Paul Lalonde. *Apocalypse* (Niagara Falls, NY: This Week in Bible Prophecy, 1998).

——. *Revelation* (Niagara Falls, NY: This Week in Bible Prophecy, 1999).

——. *Judgment* (Niagara Falls, NY: This Week in Bible Prophecy, 2001).

——. *Tribulation* (Niagara Falls, NY: This Week in Bible Prophecy, 2001).

Lee, Earl. *Kiss My Left Behind* (Chula Vista, CA: Aventine, 2003).

——. *Raptured: The Final Daze of the Late, Great Planet Earth* (Tucson, AZ: See Sharp Press, 2007).

Left Behind: The Movie (2000). Directed by Vic Sarin; produced by Ron Booth, Paul Lalonde, Peter Lalonde, and Bobby Neutz; based on the screenplay by Alan McElroy, Paul Lalonde, and Joe Goodman.

Lindsey, Hal. *The Late Great Planet Earth* (1970; repr. London: Marshall Pickering, 1971).

——. *The Terminal Generation* (Old Tappan, NJ: Spire Books, 1976).

——. *The 1980's: Countdown to Armageddon* (New York: Bantam, 1981).

——. *Blood Moon* (Palos Verdes, CA: Western Front, 1996).

Maddoux, Marlin. *Seal of Gaia* (Nashville, TN: Word, 1998).

Manker, Dayton A. *Youth's Dream Time* (Frankfort, MI: Victor, n.d.).

——. *They That Remain: A Story of the End Times* (1941; repr. Cincinnati, OH: Sunshine Book and Bible House, 1946).

——. *From the "Highways and Hedges": The Life of Rev. C. E. Myers* (Cadillac, MI: Dayton E. Manker, [1949]).

——. *All Things DO Work Together for Our Good* (Marion, IN: Wesley, 1962).

——. *Invasion from Heaven* (Salem, OH: Schmul, 1979).

——. *The Return to Majesty: Essays on Original and Ultimate Man* (1989).

Martin, Irene. *Emerald Thorn* (Oklahoma City, OK: Hearthstone, 1991).

Marzulli, L. A. *Nephilim* (Grand Rapids, MI: Zondervan, 1999).

——. *The Unholy Deception* (Grand Rapids, MI: Zondervan, 2003).

——. *The Revealing* (Grand Rapids, MI: Zondervan, 2004).

McCall, Tom, and Zola Levitt. *Raptured* (Irvine, CA: Harvest House, 1975).

Meier, Paul. *The Third Millennium* (Nashville, TN: Thomas Nelson, 1993).

——. *The Fourth Millennium* (Nashville, TN: Thomas Nelson, 1996).

——. *Beyond the Millennium* (Nashville, TN: Thomas Nelson, 1998).

Millett, Lydia. *Oh Pure and Radiant Heart* (London: William Heinemann, 2006).

Modersohn, P. "Die letzte Stunde auf der Weltenurh: Ein Blick in die Weltgeschichte nach Daniel 2," *Sabbathklänge* 43:17 (April 27, 1901), pp. 265–67, and 43:18 (May 4, 1901), pp. 275–79.

Moore, Philip N. *Nightmare of the Apocalypse: The Rabbi Conspiracy* (Atlanta, GA: Conspiracy, 1997).

Moorehead, William G. "Millennial Dawn: A Counterfeit of Christianity," in A. C. Dixon, Louis Meyer, and R. A. Torrey, eds., *The Fundamentals: A Testimony to the Truth*, 12 vols. (Chicago: Testimony, 1910–15), vol. 7, pp. 106–27.

Morris, Gilbert, Lynn Morris, and Alan Morris. *The Beginning of Sorrows* (Nashville, TN: Thomas Nelson, 1999).

——. *Fallen Stars, Bitter Waters* (Nashville, TN: Thomas Nelson, 2000).

——. "Seven Golden Vials" (unpublished ms.).

Myers, Bill. *Blood of Heaven* (Grand Rapids, MI: Zondervan, 1996).

———. *Threshold* (Grand Rapids, MI: Zondervan, 1997).

———. *Fire of Heaven* (Grand Rapids, MI: Zondervan, 1999).

Myers, John M. *The Trumpet Sounds* (New York: Pageant, 1965).

O'Brien, Michael D. *Father Elijah: An Apocalypse* (San Francisco, CA: Ignatius, 1996).

———. *Strangers and Sojourners* (San Francisco, CA: Ignatius, 1997).

———. *Eclipse of the Sun* (San Francisco, CA: Ignatius, 1998).

———. *Plague Journal* (San Francisco, CA: Ignatius, 1999).

———. *A Cry of Stone* (San Francisco, CA: Ignatius, 2003).

———. *Sophia House* (San Francisco, CA: Ignatius, 2005).

Odom, Mel. *Apocalypse Dawn* (Wheaton, IL: Tyndale House, 2003).

———. *Apocalypse Burning* (Wheaton, IL: Tyndale House, 2004).

———. *Apocalypse Crucible* (Wheaton, IL: Tyndale House, 2004).

Oilar, Forrest Loman. *How to Buy Furniture for the Home* (Indianapolis, IN: Oilar
  Brothers, 1913).

———. *Be Thou Prepared for Jesus Is Coming* (Boston: Meador, 1937).

Olson, Carl E. *Will Catholics Be "Left Behind"? A Catholic Critique of the Rapture and
  Today's Prophecy Preachers* (San Francisco, CA: Ignatius, 2003).

Pentecost, J. Dwight. *Things to Come: A Study in Biblical Eschatology* (Grand Rapids, MI:
  Zondervan, 1958).

Peretti, Frank. *This Present Darkness* (1986; Eastbourne, UK: Minstrel, 1989).

———. *Piercing the Darkness* (1989; Eastbourne, UK: Minstrel, 1990).

Phillips, Michael. *Rift in Time* (Wheaton, IL: Tyndale House, 1997).

———. *Hidden in Time* (Wheaton, IL: Tyndale House, 2000).

Prodigal Planet (1983). Directed by Donald W. Thompson.

Reagan, Ronald. *A Time for Choosing: The Speeches of Ronald Reagan, 1961–1982,* ed. Alfred
  Balitzer and Gerald M. Bonetto (Chicago: Regnery Gateway, 1983).

———. "Address to the National Association of Evangelicals, March 8, 1983," in Paul
  Boyer, ed., *Reagan as President: Contemporary Views of the Man, His Politics, and His
  Policies* (Chicago: Ivan R. Dee, 1990), pp. 165–69.

Redfield, James. *The Celestine Prophecy* (New York: Bantam, 1994).

Robertson, Pat. *Answers to 200 of Life's Most Probing Questions* (Nashville, TN: Thomas
  Nelson, 1984).

———. *The New Millennium: 10 Trends That Will Impact You and Your Family by the Year
  2000* (Dallas, TX: Word, 1990).

———. *The New World Order: It Will Change the Way You Live* (Dallas, TX: Word, 1991).

———. *The Secret Kingdom* (Dallas, TX: Word, 1992).

———. *The End of the Age* (Nashville, TN: Word, 1995).

Rogers, Mark E. *The Dead* (1990; repr. Six Star, 2000).

Roosevelt, Theodore. *The Winning of the West,* 4 vols. (New York: Putnam, 1889–96).

Rosenberg, Joel C. *The Last Jihad* (Wheaton, IL: Tyndale House, 2002).

———. *The Last Days* (Wheaton, IL: Tyndale House, 2003).

———. *The Ezekiel Option* (Wheaton, IL: Tyndale House, 2005).

———. *The Copper Scroll* (Wheaton, IL: Tyndale House, 2006).

Rossing, Barbara R. *The Rapture Exposed: The Message of Hope in the Book of Revelation*
  (Boulder, CO: Westview, 2004).

Ryle, J. C. *Practical Religion: Plain Papers on Daily Duties, Experience, Dangers, Privileges of Professing Christians* (London: W. Hunt, 1878).

Scofield, C. I., ed. *Scofield Reference Bible,* Authorized (King James) Version (Oxford: Oxford University Press, 1909; second edition, 1917).

Scofield, C. I., ed. *New Scofield Reference Bible* (Oxford: Oxford University Press, 1967).

"S. M. C." *As the Clock Struck Twenty* (Notre Dame, IN: Ave Maria, 1953).

Smith, Dodie. *The One Hundred and One Dalmatians* (London: Heinemann, 1956).

———. *It Ends with Revelations* (London: Heinemann, 1967).

———. *The Starlight Barking* (1967; repr. London: Puffin, 1970).

Solovyov, Vladimir. *The Antichrist,* trans. W. J. Barnes and H. H. Haynes (1900; Edinburgh: Floris Classics, 1982).

Stine, Milton H. *Studies on the Religious Problem of Our Country* (York, PA: Lutheran Printing House, 1888).

———. *The Niemans* (York, PA: P. Anstadt and Sons, 1897).

———. *The Devil's Bride: A Present Day Arraignment of Formalism and Doubt in the Church and in Society, in the Light of the Holy Scriptures. Given in the Form of a Pleasing Story* (Harrisburg, PA: Minter, 1910).

———. *Ancient Cities and Civilizations Modernized* (Harrisburg, PA: Evangelical Press, 1931).

Strandberg, Todd, and Terry James. *Are You Rapture Ready? Signs, Prophecies, Warnings, Threats, and Suspicions That the Endtime Is Now* (New York: Dutton, 2003).

Tatford, Frederick Albert. *Prophecy's Last Word* (London: Pickering and Inglis, 1947).

———. *The Rapture and the Tribulation* (Blackburn, UK: Durham and Sons, 1957).

———. *The Middle East: War Theatre of Prophecy* (London: Advent Testimony and Preparation Movement, 1959).

———. *Climax of the Ages: Studies in the Prophecy of Daniel* (London: Oliphants, 1964).

———. *God's Program of the Ages* (Grand Rapids, MI: Kregel, 1967).

———. *A One World Church and Prophecy* (Eastbourne, UK: Bible and Advent Testimony Movement, 1967).

———. *China and Prophecy* (Eastbourne, UK: Bible and Advent Testimony Movement, 1968).

———. *Egypt and Prophecy* (Eastbourne, UK: Bible and Advent Testimony Movement, 1968).

———. *Russia and Prophecy* (Eastbourne, UK: Bible and Advent Testimony Movement, 1968).

———. *The Jew and Prophecy* (Eastbourne, UK: Bible and Advent Testimony Movement, 1969).

———. *Will There Be a Millennium?* (Eastbourne, UK: Prophetic Witness, 1969).

———. *The Clock Strikes* (London: Lakeland, 1970).

———. *Daniel's Seventy Weeks* (Eastbourne, UK: Prophetic Witness, 1971).

———. *Five Minutes to Midnight* (London: Victory, 1971).

———. *Going into Europe: The Common Market and Prophecy* (Eastbourne, UK: Prophetic Witness, 1971).

———. *Israel and Her Future* (Eastbourne, UK: Prophetic Witness, 1971).

———. *Middle East Cauldron* (Eastbourne, UK: Prophetic Witness, 1971).

———. *Ten Nations: What Now? The European Community and Its Future* (Eastbourne, UK: Upperton, 1980).

A Thief in the Night (1972). Directed by Donald W. Thompson.

Thigpen, Paul. *The Rapture Trap: A Catholic Response to "End Times" Fever* (West Chester, PA: Ascension, 2001).

Tolkin, Michael. *The Player; the Rapture; the New Age; Three Screenplays* (New York: Grove, 2000).

"Tributes to Christ and the Bible by Brainy Men Not Known as Active Christians," in A. C. Dixon, Louis Meyer, and R. A. Torrey, eds., *The Fundamentals: A Testimony to the Truth,* 12 vols. (Chicago: Testimony, 1910–15), vol. 2, pp. 120–26.

Van Kampen, Robert D. *The Fourth Reich* (1997; New York: Dell, 2000).

Venning, Hugh. *The End: A Projection, Not a Prophecy* (Buffalo, NY: Desmond and Stapleton, 1948).

Wade, Ken. *The Orion Conspiracy: A Story of the End* (Boise, ID: Pacific Press, 1994).

Walker, Ken, and Val Walker. *Escape from Armageddon* (Glen Waverly, Australia: Good News Australia, 1997).

Walvoord, John F. *The Return of the Lord* (1955; Grand Rapids, MI: Zondervan, 1980).

———. *Armageddon, Oil, and the Middle East Crisis: What the Bible Says about the Future of the Middle East and the End of Western Civilization* (1974; revised edition, Grand Rapids, MI: Zondervan, 1991).

Watson, Lily. *From Deck to Glory: The Third Volume of the Late Sydney Watson's Life-story* (London: William Nicholson and Sons, 1920).

Watson, Sydney. *Brighter Years: The Second Part of the Autobiography of Sydney Watson* (London: Hodder and Stoughton, 1898).

———. *Life's Look-out: An Autobiography of Sydney Watson* (second edition, London: Hodder and Stoughton, 1899).

———. *Scarlet and Purple: A Story of Souls and "Signs"* (London: William Nicholson and Sons, 1913; repr. Edinburgh: B. McCall Barbour, 1974).

———. *The Mark of the Beast* (London: William Nicholson and Sons, 1915; repr. Edinburgh: B. McCall Barbour, 1974).

———. *In the Twinkling of an Eye* (London: William Nicholson and Sons, 1916).

———. *The Lure of a Soul: Bewitched by Spiritualism* (London: William Nicholson and Sons, 1917).

———. *The New Europe* (London: William Nicholson and Sons, 1918).

Wells, H. G. "The Story of the Last Trump," in *The Short Stories of H. G. Wells* (London: Ernest Benn, 1927).

Wilmington, H. L. *The King Is Coming* (Wheaton, IL: Tyndale House, 1973).

Wilson, Nathan D. *Right Behind: A Parody of Last Days Goofiness* (Moscow, ID: Canon, 2001).

———. *Supergeddon: A Really Big Geddon* (Moscow, ID: Canon, 2003).

Wise, Robert L. *Tagged* (New York: Warner, 2004).

———. *Wired* (New York: Warner, 2004).

Young, Kim. *The Last Hour* (Phoenix, AZ: ACW, 1997).

Zinn, Jay. *The Unveiling* (Mukilteo, WA: Wine Press, 1997).

"Zion Ben Judah," *Survivors* (Sydney, AU: Jesus Christians, 2002).

SECONDARY SOURCES

Abanes, Richard. *End-time Visions* (Nashville, TN: Broadman and Holman, 1998).

Abbott, Carl. "The Light on the Horizon: Imagining the Death of American Cities." *Journal of Urban History* 32:2 (2006), pp. 175–96.

Aberle, David F. "A Note on Relative Deprivation Theory as Applied to Millenarian and Other Cult Movements," in Sylvia Thrupp, ed., *Millennial Dreams in Action: Studies in Revolutionary Religious Movements* (New York: Schocken Books, 1970), pp. 209–14.

Abstract of Principles. Available at www.sbts.edu/pdf/abstract.pdf, accessed February 21, 2007.

Ahearn, Edward J. *Visionary Fictions: Apocalyptic Writing from Blake to the Modern Age* (New Haven, CT: Yale University Press, 1996).

Allan, Graham. "A Theory of Millennialism: The Irvingite Movement as an Illustration," *British Journal of Sociology* 25 (1974), pp. 296–311.

Almond, Gabriel Abraham, R. Scott Appleby, and Emmanuel Sivan. *Strong Religion: The Rise of Fundamentalisms around the World* (Chicago: University of Chicago Press, 2003).

Althouse, Peter. "Left Behind—Fact or Fiction: Ecumenical Dilemmas of the Fundamentalist Millenarian Tensions within Pentecostalism," *Journal of Pentecostal Theology* 13 (2005), pp. 187–207.

Amanat, Abbas, and Magnus Bernhardsson, eds. *Imagining the End: Visions of Apocalypse from the Ancient Middle East to Modern America* (London: I. B. Taurus, 2002).

Ammerman, Nancy. *Bible Believers: Fundamentalists in the Modern World* (New Brunswick, NJ: Rutgers University Press, 1987).

Anderson, Robert Mapes. *Visions of the Disinherited: The Making of American Pentecostalism* (Oxford: Oxford University Press, 1979).

Andraski, K. "The Evangelical Novel Comes of Age," *Christianity Today* 34 (September 1990), pp. 37–39.

Annual District Conference Journal of the North Michigan District of the Wesleyan Church (2004), available at www.nmichwes.org/pdfs/Wesleyan%20Journal%202004.pdf, accessed May 28, 2007.

Ansell, Nicholas John. "The Call of Wisdom/The Voice of the Serpent: A Canonical Approach to the Tree of Knowledge," *Christian Scholars Review* 31:1 (2001), pp. 31–57.

Ariel, Yaakov. "Doomsday in Jerusalem? Christian Messianic Groups and the Rebuilding of the Temple," *Terrorism and Political Violence* 13:1 (2001), pp. 1–14.

———. "How Are Jews and Israel Portrayed in the Left Behind Series?" in Bruce David Forbes and Jeanne Halgren Kilde, eds., *Rapture, Revelation, and the End Times: Exploring the Left Behind Series* (New York: Palgrave Macmillan, 2004), pp. 131–66.

"Ax Slayer of Wife, Three Children Pleads Guilty," *Los Angeles Times,* February 3, 1955, p. 12.

Backus, Irena. "The Church Fathers and the Canonicity of the Apocalypse in the Sixteenth Century: Erasmus, Frans Titelmans, and Theodore Beza," *Sixteenth Century Journal* 29 (1998), pp. 651–65.

———. *Reformation Readings of the Apocalypse: Geneva, Zurich, and Wittenberg* (Oxford: Oxford University Press, 2000).

Baigent, Michael, Richard Leigh, and Henry Lincoln. *Holy Blood, Holy Grail* (New York: Delacorte, 1982).

The Baker Book House Story, 1939–1989 (Grand Rapids, MI: Baker Book House, 1989).

Ball, B. W. *A Great Expectation: Eschatological Thought in English Protestantism to 1660* (Leiden, Netherlands: Brill, 1975).

Balmer, Randall. "Divided Apocalypse: Thinking about the End in Contemporary America," *Soundings* 66 (1983), pp. 257–80.

———. "Apocalypticism in America: The Argot of Premillennialism in Popular Culture," *Prospects* 13 (1988), pp. 417–33.

———. *Mine Eyes Have Seen the Glory: A Journey into the Evangelical Subculture in America* (1989; fourth edition, Oxford: Oxford University Press, 2006).

———. *Encyclopedia of Evangelicalism* (Louisville, KY: Westminster John Knox, 2002).

———. *Thy Kingdom Come: How the Religious Right Distorts the Faith and Threatens America: An Evangelical's Lament* (New York: Basic Books, 2006).

"Bank Boss Fears Global Crash in 2000," *Sunday Times: Money,* March 29, 1998, p. 1.

Barkun, Michael. *Crucible of the Millennium: The Burned-over District of New York in the 1840s* (Syracuse, NY: Syracuse University Press, 1986).

———. *Religion and the Racist Right: The Origins of the Christian Identity Movement* (Chapel Hill: University of North Carolina Press, 1994).

———. *A Culture of Conspiracy: Apocalyptic Visions in Contemporary America* (Berkeley: University of California Press, 2003).

Barowsky, Edward R. "The Popular Christian Novel in America, 1918–1953" (Ph.D. dissertation, Ball State University, 1975).

Barratt, David, Roger Pooley, and Leland Ryken., eds. *The Discerning Reader: Christian Perspectives on Literature and Theory* (Leicester, UK: Apollos, 1995).

Barron, Bruce. *Heaven on Earth? The Social and Political Agendas of Dominion Theology* (Grand Rapids, MI: Zondervan, 1992).

Bartholomew, Richard. "Religious Mission and Business Reality: Trends in the Contemporary British Christian Book Industry," *Journal of Contemporary Religion* 20:1 (2005), pp. 41–54.

Basden, Paul A., ed. *Has Our Theology Changed? Southern Baptist Thought since 1845* (Nashville, TN: Broadman and Holman, 1994).

Bauckham, Richard. *Tudor Apocalypse: Sixteenth Century Apocalypticism, Millenarianism, and the English Reformation: From John Bale to John Foxe and Thomas Brightman* (Appleford, UK: Sutton Courtenay, 1978).

Baumgartner, Frederic. *Longing for the End: A History of Millennialism in Western Civilization* (New York: Palgrave, 1999).

Bayley, Joe. "Biblical Novels: Popular Fiction for Today's Christians," *Bookstore Journal* 14 (November 1981), pp. 83–84.

Beals, Linda. "Quality Religious Fiction Is the Target at Crossway Books," *Publishers Weekly* 221 (February 12, 1982), pp. 65–67.

Bebbington, David W. "The Advent Hope in British Evangelicalism since 1800," *Scottish Journal of Religious Studies* 9 (1988), pp. 103–10.

———. *Evangelicalism in Modern Britain: A History from the 1730s to the 1980s* (London: Routledge, 1989).

———. "Evangelical Theology in the English-speaking World during the Nineteenth Century," *Scottish Bulletin of Evangelical Theology* 22:2 (2004), pp. 133–50.

———. *The Dominance of Evangelicalism: The Age of Spurgeon and Moody,* A History of Evangelicalism (Leicester, UK: IVP, 2005).

———. "The Place of the Brethren Movement in International Evangelicalism," in Neil T. R. Dickson and Tim Grass, eds., *The Growth of the Brethren Movement: National and International Experiences,* Studies in Evangelical History and Thought (Milton Keynes, UK: Paternoster, 2006), pp. 241–60.

Beechick, Allen. *The Pre-Tribulation Rapture* (Denver, CO: Accent, 1980).

Bell, Wendell. "On Becoming and Being a Futurist: An Interview with Wendell Bell," *Journal of Futures Studies* 10:2 (2005), pp. 113–24.

Bendle, Mervyn F. "The Apocalyptic Imagination and Popular Culture," *Journal of Religion and Popular Culture* 11 (2005), available at www.usask.ca/relst/jrpc/index.html, accessed June 26, 2008.

Bendroth, Margaret Lamberts. *Fundamentalism and Gender: 1875 to the Present* (New Haven, CT: Yale University Press, 1993).

Bercovitch, Sacvan, ed. *The American Puritan Imagination: Essays in Revaluation* (London: Cambridge University Press, 1974).

———. *The Puritan Origins of the American Self* (New Haven, CT: Yale University Press, 1975).

Berger, James. *After the End: Representations of Post-apocalypse* (Minneapolis: University of Minnesota, 1999).

"Between the Lines: Frank Peretti," *Bookstore Journal* 22 (January 1989), p. 163.

Bickersteth, Edward. *Practical Guide to the Prophecies* (fourth edition, London: R. B. Seeley and W. Burnside, 1835).

Bjork, Rebecca S. "Reagan and the Nuclear Freeze: 'Star Wars' as a Rhetorical Strategy," *Journal of the American Forensic Association* 24 (1988), pp. 181–92.

Blaising, Craig A., and Darrell L. Bock. *Progressive Dispensationalism* (Wheaton, IL: Victor, 1993).

Bloch, Ruth. *Visionary Republic: Millennial Themes in American Thought, 1756–1800* (Cambridge: Cambridge University Press, 1985).

Block, Robert. "Second Coming," in *The Eighth State of Fandom* (Chicago: Advent, 1962).

Blodgett, Jan. *Protestant Evangelical Literary Culture and Contemporary Society* (Westport, CT: Greenwood, 1997).

Blum, Edward J. *Reforging the White Republic: Race, Religion, and American Nationalism, 1865–1898* (Baton Rouge: Louisiana State University Press, 2005).

Blumenthal, Sidney. "The Religious Right and Republicans," in Richard John Neuhaus and Michael Cromartie, eds., *Piety and Politics: Evangelicals and Fundamentalists Confront the World* (Washington, DC: Ethics and Public Policy Center, 1987), pp. 269–86.

Boesky, Amy. *Founding Fictions: Utopias in Early Modern England* (Athens: University of Georgia Press, 1996).

Borgert, Michael G. "Harry Bultema and the *Maranatha* Controversy in the Christian Reformed Church," *Calvin Theological Journal* 42:1 (2007), pp. 90–109.

Boyce, James P. *Abstract of Systematic Theology* (1887; Cape Coral, FL: Founders Press, 2006).

Boyer, Paul. *By the Bomb's Early Light: American Thought and Culture at the Dawn of the Atomic Age* (New York: Pantheon Books, 1985).

———, ed. *Reagan as President: Contemporary Views of the Man, His Politics, and His Policies* (Chicago: Ivan R. Dee, 1990).

———. *When Time Shall Be No More: Prophecy Belief in Modern American Culture* (Cambridge, MA: Belknap Press of Harvard University Press, 1992).

———. "The Middle East in Modern American Prophetic Belief," in Abbas Amanat and Magnus Bernhardsson, eds., *Imagining the End: Visions of Apocalypse from the Ancient Middle East to Modern America* (London: I. B. Tauris, 2002), pp. 312–35.

Bozeman, John. "Technological Millenarianism in the United States," in Thomas Robbins and Susan Palmer, eds., *Millennium, Messiahs and Mayhem* (New York: Routledge, 1997), pp. 139–58.

Bozeman, Theodore Dwight. *To Live Ancient Lives: The Primitivist Dimension in Puritanism* (Chapel Hill: University of North Carolina Press, 1988).

Brady, David. "The Number of the Beast in Seventeenth- and Eighteenth-century England," *Evangelical Quarterly* 45 (1973), pp. 219–40.

———. *The Contribution of British Writers between 1560 and 1830 to the Interpretation of Revelation 13.16–18* (Tübingen, Germany: J. C. B. Mohr, 1983).

Bramadat, Paul A. *The Church on the World's Turf: An Evangelical Christian Group at a Secular University* (Oxford: Oxford University Press, 2000).

Brasher, Brenda E. and Lee Quinby. *Gender and Apocalyptic Desire*, Millennialism and Society (London: Equinox, 2006).

Brereton, Virginia Lieson. *Training God's Army: The American Bible School, 1880–1940* (Bloomington: Indiana University Press, 1990).

Bromley, David G. "Violence and New Religious Movements," in James R. Lewis, ed., *The Oxford Handbook of New Religious Movements* (Oxford: Oxford University Press, 2004), pp. 143–62.

Brophy, Susan J. "The Fiction Explosion," *Christian Retailing* 38 (November 15, 1989), p. 15.

Brouwer, Steve, Paul Gifford, and Susan D. Rose. *Exporting the American Gospel: Global Christian Fundamentalism* (New York: Routledge, 1996).

Brown, Callum. *The Death of Christian Britain* (London: Routledge, 2001).

Brown, Ralph. "Victorian Anglican Evangelicalism: The Radical Legacy of Edward Irving," *Journal of Ecclesiastical History* 58:4 (2007), pp. 675–704.

Brown, William Hill. *The Power of Sympathy* (1789; repr. London: Penguin, 1996).

Browne, Renni. "The Power of Fiction," *Christian Retailing* 38 (November 15, 1989), pp. 16–17.

Bruce, Steve. *The Rise and Fall of the New Christian Right: Conservative Protestant Politics in American, 1978–1988* (Oxford, UK: Clarendon Press, 1988).

Bruce, Steve, Peter Kivisto, and William H. Swatos, eds. *The Rapture of Politics: The Christian Right as the United States Approaches the Year 2000* (London: Transaction, 1995).

Brummett, Barry. "Premillennial Apocalypse as a Rhetorical Genre," *Central States Speech Journal* 35 (1984), pp. 84–93.

Buell, Lawrence. *New England Literary Culture: From Revolution to Renaissance* (Cambridge: Cambridge University Press, 1986).

Bull, Malcolm, ed. *Apocalypse Theory and the Ends of the World* (Oxford, UK: Blackwell, 1995).

Burdon, Christopher. *The Apocalypse in England: Revelation Unravelling, 1700–1834* (London: Macmillan, 1997).

Bussard, Dave. *Who Will Be Left Behind and When?* (Lancaster, PA: Strong Tower, 2002).

Butler, Jon. *Awash in a Sea of Faith: Christianizing the American People* (Cambridge, MA: Harvard University Press, 1990).

Butler, Jonathan M. *Softly and Tenderly Jesus Is Calling: Heaven and Hell in American Revivalism, 1870–1920* (Brooklyn, NY: Carlson, 1991).

Carpenter, Joel A. *Revive Us Again: The Reawakening of American Fundamentalism* (Oxford: Oxford University Press, 1997).

Carpenter, M. W., and George P. Landow. "Ambiguous Revelations: The Apocalypse and Victorian Literature," in C. A. Patrides and J. A. Wittreich, eds., *The Apocalypse in English Renaissance Thought and Literature* (Manchester, UK: Manchester University Press, 1984), pp. 299–322.

Carter, Heath. "The Left Behind Series: An Evangelical Apocalypse" (theology honors thesis, Georgetown University, 2003).

Carwardine, Richard. *Transatlantic Revivalism: Popular Evangelicalism in Britain and America* (Westport, CT: Greenwood, 1978).

Case, Shirley Jackson. *The Millennial Hope: A Phase of War-time Thinking* (Chicago: University of Chicago Press, 1918).

Castelli, James. "The Environmental Gospel according to James Watt," *Chicago Tribune*, October 25, 1981, p. B2.

Cawelti, John. *Adventure, Mystery, and Romance: Formula Stories as Art and Popular Culture* (Chicago: University of Chicago Press, 1976).

Chafer, Lewis Sperry. *Systematic Theology* (1948; repr. Dallas, TX: Dallas Theological Seminary, 1975).

Chandler, Ralph Clark. "The Wicked Shall Not Bear Rule: The Fundamentalist Heritage of the New Christian Right," in David G. Bromley and Anson Shupe, eds., *New Christian Politics* (Macon, GA: Mercer University Press, 1984), pp. 41–58.

Chapman, Jennie. "Selling Faith without Selling Out: Reading the Left Behind Novels in the Context of Popular Culture," in John Wallis and Kenneth G. C. Newport, eds., *Apocalyptic Texts and Popular Culture* (London: Equinox, 2008).

———. "Paradoxes of Power: Apocalyptic Agency in the Left Behind Series" (Ph.D. dissertation, University of Manchester, forthcoming).

Chatham, Doug. *The Rapture Book: Exciting Teaching about the Next Event on the Prophetic Calendar* (New Kensington, PA: Whitaker House, 1974).

Chilton, David. *The Great Tribulation* (Fort Worth, TX: Dominion, 1987).

Christianson, Paul. *Reformers and Babylon: English Apocalyptic Visions from the Reformation to the Eve of the Civil War* (Toronto: University of Toronto Press, 1978).

Cioffi, Frank. *Formula Fiction? An Anatomy of American Science Fiction, 1930–1940* (Westport, CT: Greenwood, 1982).

Clareson, Thomas D. *Some Kind of Paradise: The Emergence of American Science Fiction* (Westport, CT: Greenwood, 1985).

Clark, Stephen R. "An Interview with Jerry Jenkins," *Christian Bookseller and Librarian* 29 (March 1983), pp. 10–11.

Clouse, Robert G. "The New Christian Right, America, and the Kingdom of God," *Christian Scholars Review* 12 (1983), pp. 3–16.

Clouse, Robert G., Robert N. Hosack, and Richard V. Pierard. *The New Millennium Manual: A Once and Future Guide* (Grand Rapids, MI: Baker, 1999).

Coad, F. Roy. *A History of the Brethren Movement* (Exeter, UK: Paternoster, 1968).

Cogley, Richard. "The Fall of the Ottoman Empire and the Restoration of Israel in the 'Judeo-centric' Strand of Puritan Millenarianism," *Church History* 72 (2003), pp. 303–32.

Cohen, Paul A. "Time, Culture, and Christian Eschatology: The Year 2000 in the West and the World," *American Historical Review* 104:5 (1999), pp. 1615–28.

Cohn, Norman. *The Pursuit of the Millennium* (1957; repr. London: Mercury Books, 1962).

———. *Cosmos, Chaos and the World to Come: The Ancient Roots of Apocalyptic Faith* (London: Yale University Press, 1993).

Collins, John J. "Introduction: Towards the Morphology of a Genre," *Semeia* 14 (1979), pp. 1–20.

Connors, Richard, and Andrew Colin Gow, eds. *Anglo-American Millennialism, from Milton to the Millerites* (Leiden, Netherlands: Brill, 2004).

Cox, Harvey. *Fire from Heaven: The Rise of Pentecostal Spirituality and the Re-shaping of Religion in the Twenty-first Century* (Reading, MA: Addison-Wesley, 1995).

Croft, Stuart. *Culture, Crisis, and America's War on Terror* (Cambridge: Cambridge University Press, 2006).

Crumpton, W. B. *Our Baptist Centennials, 1808–1923* (Montgomery, AL: Paragon, 1923).

Cumbey, Constance E. *The Hidden Dangers of the Rainbow: The New Age Movement and Our Coming Age of Barbarism* (Lafayette, LA: Huntington House, 1985).

Cuneo, M. "The Vengeful Virgin: Case Studies in Contemporary American Catholic Apocalypticism," in T. Robbins and S. J. Palmer, eds., *Millennium, Messiahs, and Mayhem: Contemporary Apocalyptic Movements* (New York: Routledge, 1997), pp. 175–94.

Currie, David B. *Rapture: The End-times Error That Leaves the Bible Behind* (Manchester, NH: Sophia Institute Press, 2003).

Daley, Brian E. *The Hope of the Early Church: Eschatology in the Patristic Age* (Cambridge: Cambridge University Press, 1991).

Davidson, James West. *The Logic of Millennial Thought: Eighteenth-century New England* (New Haven, CT: Yale University Press, 1977).

Davis, Kenneth C. *Two-bit Culture: The Paperbacking of America* (Boston: Houghton-Mifflin, 1984).

Dayton, Donald W. "Some Doubts about the Usefulness of the Category 'Evangelical,'" in Donald W. Dayton and Robert K. Johnston, eds., *The Variety of American Evangelicalism* (Downers Grove, IL: InterVarsity, 1991), pp. 245–51.

———. "'The Search for the Historical Evangelicalism': George Marsden's History of Fuller Seminary as a Case Study," *Christian Scholar's Review* 33 (1993), pp. 12–33.

Dayton, Donald W., and Robert K. Johnston, eds. *The Variety of American Evangelicalism* (Downers Grove, IL: InterVarsity, 1991).

De Jong, James A. *As the Waters Cover the Sea: Millennial Expectations in the Rise of Anglo-American Missions 1640–1810* (Kampen, Netherlands: J. H. Kok, 1970).

De Klerk, Peter, and Richard R. DeRidder, eds. *Perspectives on the Christian Reformed Church: Studies in Its History, Theology, Ecumenicity* (Grand Rapids, MI: Baker, 1983).

DeMar, Gary. *End Times Fiction: A Biblical Consideration of the Left Behind Theology* (Nashville, TN: Thomas Nelson, 2001).

——. "The Fiction behind Left Behind," *Biblical Worldview* (July 2004), pp. 3, 12–17.

De Patmos, John. *The Great Disappointment of 1844* (Brookline, MA: Miskatonic University Press, 2001).

Derrida, Jacques. "Of an Apocalyptic Tone Recently Adopted in Philosophy," *Semeia* 23 (1982), pp. 63–97.

——. *A Derrida Reader: Between the Blinds,* ed. Peggy Kamuf (New York: Harvester Wheatsheaf, 1991).

Dessauer, John P., Hendrik Edelman, University of Scranton, and Paul D. Doebler. *Christian Book Publishing and Distribution in the United States and Canada* (Scranton, PA: Center for Book Research, University of Scranton, 1989).

Detweiler, Robert. "Christ in American Religious Fiction," *Journal of the Bible and Religion* 32 (1964), pp. 8–14.

Dickerson, Matthew. "A Case for Fiction," *Christian Retailing* 36 (October 15, 1990), p. 39.

Doan, Ruth Alden. *The Miller Heresy, Millennialism, and American Culture* (Philadelphia, PA: Temple University Press, 1987).

Dobson, Ed, and Ed Hindson. "Apocalypse Now? What Fundamentalists Believe about the End of the World," *Policy Review* 38 (1986), pp. 16–23.

Doyle, Thomas M. "Competing Fictions: The Uses of Christian Apocalyptic Imagery in Contemporary Popular Fictional Works," *Journal of Millennial Studies* 1:1 (2001), available at www.mille.org, accessed January 19, 2008.

——. "Christian Apocalyptic Fiction," *Strange Horizons,* April 8, 2002, available at www.strangehorizons.com/2002/20020408/apocalyptic.shtml, accessed June 26, 2008.

——. "Anti-apocalyptic Fiction," *Strange Horizons,* May 27, 2002, available at www.strangehorizons.com/2002/20020527/anti-apocalyptic.shtml, accessed June 26, 2008.

——. "Christian Apocalyptic Fiction, Science Fiction, and Technology," in Cathy Gutierrez and Hillel Schwartz, eds., *The End That Does: Art, Science, and Millennial Accomplishment,* Millennialism and Society (London: Equinox, 2006), pp. 195–210.

Drummond, Lewis A. *Spurgeon: Prince of Preachers* (Grand Rapids, MI: Kregel, 1993).

Durham, Martin. *The Christian Right, the Far Right, and the Boundaries of American Conservatism* (Manchester, UK: Manchester University Press, 2000).

Eagleton, Terry. *Holy Terror* (Oxford: Oxford University Press, 2005).

Edgoose, Julian. "Where Creeds Meet Incredulity: Educational Research in a Post-utopianAge," *Studies in Philosophy and Education* 25 (2006), pp. 289–302.

Edwards, Michael. *Towards a Christian Poetics* (London: Macmillan, 1984).

Eichler, Margrit. "Charismatic and Ideological Leadership in Secular and Religious Millenarian Movements: A Sociological Study" (Ph.D. dissertation, Duke University, 1971).

"1850 Federal Census Tuscaloosa County, Alabama," available at www.rootsweb.com/~cenfiles/al/tuscaloosa/1850/pg368.txt, accessed November 19, 2006.

Elson, Ruth Miller. *Myths and Mores in American Best Sellers, 1865–1965* (New York: Garland, 1985).

Elzey, Wayne. "Popular Culture," in Charles H. Lippy and Peter W. Williams, eds., *Encyclopedia of the American Religious Experience* (New York: Scribners, 1988), pp. 1727–41.

"End Times," *TIME*, June 23, 2002, available at www.time.com/time/covers/1101020701/story3.html, accessed January 8, 2008.

Erwin, John Stuart. "Like a Thief in the Night: Cotton Mather's Millennialism" (Ph.D. dissertation, Indiana University, 1987).

Etulain, Richard, and Noel Riley Fitch. *Faith and Imagination: Essays on Evangelicals and Literature Honoring Marian B. Washburn* (Albuquerque, NM: Far West Books, 1985).

Faubion, James D. *The Shadows and Lights of Waco: Millennialism Today* (Princeton, NJ: Princeton University Press, 2001).

Ferre, John P. *Channels of Belief: Religion and American Commercial Television* (Ames: Iowa State University Press, 1990).

———. "Searching for the Great Commission: Evangelical Book Publishing since the 1970s," in Quentin Schultze, ed., *American Evangelicals and the Mass Media* (Grand Rapids, MI: Academie Books, 1990), pp. 99–117.

Festinger, Leon, Henry W. Riecken, and Stanley Schachter. *When Prophecy Fails* (Minneapolis, MN: University of Minneapolis Press, 1956).

Fickett, Harold. "Christian Fiction: The Coming Renaissance," *Christian Bookseller and Librarian* 29 (March 1983), pp. 28–29.

Fiddes, Paul S. "Facing the End: The Apocalyptic Experience in Some Modern Novels," in John Colwell, ed., *Called to One Hope: Perspectives on the Life to Come* (Carlisle, UK: Paternoster, 2000), pp. 191–209.

———. *The Promised End: Eschatology in Theology and Literature* (Oxford, UK: Blackwell, 2000).

Firth, Katherine. *The Apocalyptic Tradition in Reformation Britain, 1530–1645* (Oxford: Oxford University Press, 1979).

Flake, Carol. *Redemptorama: Culture, Politics, and the New Evangelicalism* (Garden City, NY: Anchor, 1984).

Flesher, LeAnn Snow. *Left Behind? The Facts behind the Fiction* (Valley Forge, PA: Judson, 2006).

Flynt, Wayne. "Dissent in Zion: Alabama Baptists and Social Issues, 1900–1914," *The Journal of Southern History* 35:4 (1969), pp. 523–42.

Forbes, Bruce David. "How Popular Are the Left Behind Books . . . and Why? A Discussion of Popular Culture," in Bruce David Forbes and Jeanne Halgren Kilde, eds., *Rapture, Revelation, and the End Times: Exploring the Left Behind Series* (New York: Palgrave Macmillan, 2004), pp. 5–32.

Forbes, Bruce David, and Jeanne Halgren Kilde, eds. *Rapture, Revelation, and the End Times: Exploring the Left Behind Series* (New York: Palgrave Macmillan, 2004).

Forbes, Bruce David, and Jeffrey H. Mahan, eds. *Religion and Popular Culture in America* (Berkeley: University of California Press, 2000).

Force, James E. and Richard H. Popkin, eds. *The Millenarian Turn: Millenarian Contexts of Science, Politics, and Everyday Anglo-American Life in the Seventeenth and Eighteenth Centuries* (Dordrecht, Netherlands: Kluwer, 2001).

25

Forster, A. Diana. "The Paradox of Paradise Regained in the *Left Behind* Series," *Chrestomathy: Annual Review of Undergraduate Research, School of Humanities and Social Sciences, College of Charleston* 4 (2005), pp. 65–79.

Fosdick, Harry Emerson. "Shall the Fundamentalists Win?" (1922), in Paul H. Sherry, ed., *The Riverside Preachers* (New York: Pilgrim, 1978), pp. 27–38.

Fowler, Robert Booth. *A New Engagement: Evangelical Political Thought, 1966–1976* (Grand Rapids, MI: Eerdmans, 1982).

Fox, Richard Wrightman. "The Culture of Liberal Protestant Progressivism, 1875–1925," *The Journal of Interdisciplinary History* 23 (1993), pp. 639–60.

Frank, Douglas W. *Less than Conquerors: How Evangelicals Entered the Twentieth Century* (Grand Rapids, MI: Eerdmans, 1986).

Frankl, Razelle. *Televangelism: The Marketing of Popular Religion* (Carbondale, IL: Southern Illinois University Press, 1987).

Freedman, Carl. *Critical Theory and Science Fiction* (London: University Press of New England, 2000).

Froese, Brian. "A Pacific Ending: Situating California in Late Twentieth-century Popular Evangelical Endtime Literature," *Didiskalia* 15:2 (2004), pp. 49–62.

Froom, L. E. *The Prophetic Faith of Our Fathers: The Historical Development of Prophetic Interpretation,* 4 vols. (Washington, DC: Review and Herald, 1948).

Fruchtman, Jack. *The Apocalyptic Politics of Richard Price and Joseph Priestly: A Study in Late Eighteenth-century English Republican Millennialism* (Philadelphia, PA: American Philosophical Society, 1983).

Frykholm, Amy Johnson. *Rapture Culture: Left Behind in Evangelical America* (New York: Oxford University Press, 2004).

———. "What Social Messages Appear in the *Left Behind* Books? A Literary Discussion of Millenarian Fiction," in Bruce David Forbes and Jeanne Halgren Kilde, eds., *Rapture, Revelation, and the End Times: Exploring the Left Behind Series* (New York: Palgrave Macmillan, 2004), pp. 167–95.

Fukuyama, Francis. *The End of History and the Last Man* (New York: Free Press, 1992).

Fuller, A. James. *Chaplain to the Confederacy: Basil Manly and Baptist Life in the Old South* (Baton Rouge: Louisiana State University Press, 2000).

Fuller, Daniel P. *Gospel and Law: Contrast or Continuum? The Hermeneutics of Dispensationalism and Covenant Theology* (Grand Rapids, MI: Eerdmans, 1980).

Fuller, Robert. *Naming the Antichrist: The History of an American Obsession* (New York: Oxford University Press, 1995).

Fulop, Timothy E. "'The Future Golden Day of the Race': Millennialism and Black Americans in the Nadir, 1877–1901," *The Harvard Theological Review* 84:1 (1991), pp. 75–99.

Gallagher, Sally K. *Evangelical Identity and Gendered Family Life* (New Brunswick, NJ: Rutgers University Press, 2003).

Gates, David. "Religion: The Pop Prophets," *Newsweek* (May 24, 2004), available at http://findarticles.com/p/articles/mi_kmnew/is_200405/ai_kepm470011?tag=artBody;col1, accessed June 26, 2008.

Gaustad, Edwin Scott, ed. *The Rise of Adventism: A Commentary on the Social and Religious Ferment of Mid-nineteenth Century America* (New York: Harper and Row, 1974).

Gibbs, Nancy. "The Bible and the Apocalypse," *TIME*, July 1, 2002, repr. UK edition of *TIME*, August 19, 2002, pp. 46–53.

Gloege, T. "Gray, James Martin," in Timothy Larsen, ed., *Biographical Dictionary of Evangelicals* (Leicester, UK: IVP, 2003), pp. 266–67.

Goen, C. C. "Jonathan Edwards: A New Departure in Eschatology," *Church History* 28 (1959), pp. 25–40.

Gold, Malcolm. "The *Left Behind* Series as Sacred Text," in Elizabeth Arweck and Peter Collins, eds., *Reading Religion in Text and Context* (Aldershot, UK: Ashgate, 2006), pp. 34–49.

Goodnight, G. Thomas. "Ronald Reagan's Re-formulation of the Rhetoric of War: Analysis of the 'Zero Option,' 'Evil Empire,' and 'Star Wars' Addresses," *Quarterly Journal of Speech* 72 (1986), pp. 390–414.

Gorenberg, Gershom. *The End of Days: Fundamentalism and the Struggle for the Temple Mount* (New York: Oxford University Press, 2002).

Goss, Leonard G., and Dan M. Aycock. *Inside Religious Publishing: A Look behind the Scenes* (Grand Rapids, MI: Zondervan, 1991).

Greene, Suzanne Ellery. *Books for Pleasure: Popular Fiction, 1914–1945* (Bowling Green, OH: Bowling Green University Popular Press, 1974).

Gribben, Crawford. *The Puritan Millennium: Literature and Theology, 1550–1682* (Dublin: Four Courts, 2000).

———. "John Gill and Puritan Eschatology," *Evangelical Quarterly* 73:4 (2001), pp. 311–26.

———. "'The Worst Sect That a Christian Man Can Meet': Opposition to the Plymouth Brethren in Ireland and Scotland, 1859–1900," *Scottish Studies Review* 3:2 (2002), pp. 34–53.

———. "Before Left Behind," *Books and Culture* (July/August 2003), p. 11.

———. "Rapture Fictions and the Changing Evangelical Condition," *Literature and Theology* 18:1 (2004), pp. 77–94.

———. "After *Left Behind*: The Paradox of Evangelical Pessimism," in Kenneth G. C. Newport and Crawford Gribben, eds., *Expecting the End: Contemporary Millennialism in Social and Historical Context* (Baylor, TX: Baylor University Press, 2006), pp. 113–30.

———. "The Future of Millennial Expectation," in Kenneth G. C. Newport and Crawford Gribben, eds., *Expecting the End: Contemporary Millennialism in Social and Historical Context* (Baylor, TX: Baylor University Press, 2006), pp. 237–40.

———. *Rapture Fiction and the Evangelical Crisis* (Webster, NY: Evangelical Press, 2006).

———. "Protestant Millennialism, Political Violence, and the Ulster Conflict," *Irish Studies Review* 15:1 (2007), pp. 51–63.

———. "Evangelical Eschatology and 'the Puritan Hope,'" in Michael Haykin and Kenneth Stewart, eds., *The Emergence of Evangelicalism: Exploring Historical Continuities* (Leicester, UK: Apollos, 2008), pp. 375–93.

———. "Evangelical Spirituality in Recent Prophecy Fiction," in Mark Sweetnam, ed., *Each Waking Band: Aspects of Dispensational Spirituality* (Milton Keynes, UK: Paternoster, forthcoming).

———. "Novel Doctrines and Doctrinal Novels: Brethren and Dispensational Fiction," in Neil Dickson, ed., *Brethren and Popular Culture* (Milton Keynes, UK: Paternoster, forthcoming).